Tom Cruise

BY THE SAME AUTHOR

The Arnhem Report: A Bridge Too Far
Dustin Hoffman: Little Big Man
Clint Eastwood: The Man With No Name
The Bond Companion: The World is Not Enough
Fierce Creatures (novelization)
Cannes: The Novel
Wimbledon 2000
Richard by Kathryn (with Kathy Apanowicz)

Tom Cruise

All the World's a Stage

HODDER &
STOUGHTON

For Oliver

Copyright © 2006 by Iain Johnstone

First published in Great Britain in 2006 by Hodder & Stoughton
A division of Hodder Headline

The right of Iain Johnstone to be identified as the Author
of the Work has been asserted by him in accordance
with the Copyright, Designs and Patents Act 1988.

A Hodder & Stoughton Book

1

A CIP catalogue record for this title is available from the British Library

ISBN 978 0 340 89920 4
ISBN 0 340 89920 4

Typeset in Sabon by Hewer Text UK Ltd, Edinburgh
Printed and bound by Clays Ltd, St Ives plc

Hodder Headline's policy is to use papers that are natural, renewable
and recyclable products and made from wood grown in sustainable forests.
The logging and manufacturing processes are expected to conform
to the environmental regulations of the country of origin.

Hodder & Stoughton Ltd
A division of Hodder Headline
338 Euston Road
London NW1 3BH

CONTENTS

PROLOGUE

All the world's a stage,
And all the men and women merely players.
They have their exits and their entrances;
And one man in his time plays many parts.
William Shakespeare,
As You Like It, Act II Scene 7

By coincidence, I was appointed film critic of the London *Sunday Times* in 1983, the same year that Tom Cruise came to prominence in *Risky Business*. His memorable, improvised Fruit of the Loom dance solo in the film (so known because he was clad in that brand of underpants), playing an invisible guitar to the strains of Bob Seger's 'Old Time Rock and Roll' and posturing round his living room like a wrinkle-free Mick Jagger, made a lasting impression, all the more so because it was featured in television commercials for the movie. I was not alone in thinking that here was a youthful actor (he was only nineteen when he shot it) with a film star's baton in his knapsack. And so it proved. Today Tom Cruise is, by some measure, the most popular film star in the world.

During my dozen years as a critic, I observed and analysed this arrestingly handsome young man with his perfectly symmetrical features, searchlight blue eyes and killer smile. When he cropped up in 1986 as Maverick, the all-American hero of *Top Gun*, I anticipated he was going to assume the mantle of Harrison Ford (some twenty years his senior) and rely on his undoubted charisma to play variations of himself, largely in major action movies. But I didn't have long to wait to discover this was not to be the case; the actor was far more ambitious than that. Later the same year Cruise surfaced as a far from clean-cut pool hustler, Vince Lauria, in *The Color of Money*. The film was a sequel to *The Hustler* and Paul Newman played an ageing Eddie Felsen, no longer as fast as he had been thirty years ago. In fact it had been Newman who had suggested to the director, Martin Scorsese, that Tom was the man for the part, and they didn't see any other candidate. A great actor can smell out talent, and although he had turned Cruise down for his directing debut, *Harry and Son*, Newman filed his name away, knowing he could tackle a role not dissimilar to his own in the original. He was right: Cruise cleverly tainted his good looks with a less than attractive vanity; he managed to subtract fifty points from his IQ and embellished Vince with an uncomfortable nerviness, never still, like a fugitive on the run.

Cruise seemed almost hell-bent on demonstrating his powerful screen presence by playing opposite Hollywood legends from previous generations. He certainly matched Newman in *The Color of Money* and more than matched Dustin Hoffman, the master character actor, whom he sought out to co-star with him in *Rain Man* (1988). Once Hoffman had found the blank physiognomy and the right vocal note for his autistic savant, Raymond Babbitt, his task was to keep them up throughout the film. Cruise, on the other hand, as Raymond's brother, Charlie, had more than a road journey to tackle. He has the character arc to follow: from an unfeeling, uncaring car salesman to someone who confronts his emotions for the first time in his life. I have considerable admiration for Cruise as an actor and feel he is too frequently under-rated, especially by the Academy. Inevitably, it was Hoffman who got the Oscar.

Anxious to prove that he could carry a film without the adornment of his gleaming good looks, Cruise was determined to get the part of the crippled Vietnam vet Ron Kovic in *Born on the Fourth of July* (1989). This character was a man with straggly, thinning, hippy hair, an angry, unkempt moustache and an attitude powered by bitterness; Kovic, who had been peddling his own screenplay, didn't see how the smooth young actor could come anywhere near the real him. But Cruise, fully prepared, drove himself round to his house to win him over. Kovic watched from a window as Cruise struggled alone out of his car into a wheelchair. The veteran needed no further persuasion.

But the actor, still young at twenty-nine, got a reminder that he had some way to go to match the old masters when he confronted the reigning king of the jungle, fifty-five-year-old Jack Nicholson, in the 1992 court martial movie *A Few Good Men*, set in Guantanamo Bay, a location which has since become less of a landmark as a citadel of military justice. Jack's bark left an indelible bite.

Anne Rice, author of *Interview with the Vampire*, followed in the footsteps of Ron Kovic by pronouncing that Tom Cruise was wholly unsuitable to play the lead in the film of her novel. Was this going to become a national epidemic among authors, warning Hollywood that its brightest ascending star would spoil their book? Admittedly Cruise did not look like Rutger Hauer, on whom Rice had based her main character, Lestat de Lioncourt – a tall, blond, European vampire. Cruise circumvented her criticism using a technique vouchsafed by Laurence Olivier to Dustin Hoffman during the filming of *Marathon Man*: 'It is called acting.' The author's criticism might better have been addressed to the curiously horror-free screenplay (by Anne Rice herself) or to the loose direction of Neil Jordan.

That year, 1994, I stopped being a movie critic, not because of *Interview with the Vampire* – starring Tom and Brad Pitt, it inevitably did reasonable business – but because John Cleese, the former Python and subsequent proprietor of Fawlty Towers, invited me to write a film with him that would use the same cast as his popular comedy *A Fish Called Wanda*. This 1998 movie *Fierce Creatures* was based on two obsessions of John's: his love of small furry creatures in zoos, and his distaste for Rupert Murdoch of whom he pronounced: 'If he could double the profit of a paper or television station by halving its quality, he would.' Unfortunately for those of us who were profit participants in the film, we were to discover that few people in the main cinema-going age group (fifteen to twenty-four) had any interest in zoos or the iniquities of Rupert Murdoch – indeed, it was found that not many had even heard of him. But hey, we all make mistakes – and the film still gets a few chuckles when it has its annual outing on the telly. We shot it at Pinewood Studios, the nearest structure England has to Hollywood, in usually rain-washed Buckinghamshire forty miles northwest of London. And it was there that I met Tom Cruise for the first time.

Since Cleese was star-co-director-writer-producer-guru-shrink of the film, it was agreed that I would be remunerated (out of profits!) as a producer to help him. Thus on an airless July day in 1996, when the temperature ascended into the nineties Fahrenheit and the sun beat down without pity on the zoo set in the back lot, I huddled with the zoo-keepers in the only available shade – an artificial stairwell leading to the awnings of the dolphin pool. The keepers were no humble extras – their number included Ronnie Corbett, Robert Lindsay, Carey Lowell (a Bond girl who was later to marry Richard Gere), Derek Griffiths, and John's daughter, Cynthia. Morale was decidedly low. The cast seemed to feel that our director, who had acquitted himself with credit in television drama, was all at sea when it came to directing a Hollywood comedy. This was not a proposition I felt able to argue against and so, in cowardice, I invented an appointment with Pat, our animal trainer, who lived with her small mammals in the attractively named Shed 13.

It was a happy temple to enter in times of trouble, with the meerkats and lemurs and kinkajous and tamarins and mongooses and aardvarks and even the tapirs seemingly pleased to see you. And so, unfailingly, was Pat – a loving, rounded Mrs Doolittle who controlled her charges in a language unknown to man. But today I was not alone. There were a couple, and some children and babies, with her.

Pat greeted me warmly and introduced me. 'This is Iain, John Cleese's partner . . . Do you know Sarah and Tom?'

Indeed I did – though not personally. But I had seen Sarah's wedding to Prince Andrew on TV, and Tom Cruise in the movies.

We exchanged pleasantries.

'How's *Fierce Creatures* going?' Tom asked me.

'Pretty disastrously,' I replied with total candour. 'What about *Mission Impossible*?'

'An absolute nightmare,' he laughed. (It is possible he may not have been completely joking; he, as producer, and his director, Brian De Palma, did have healthy creative 'discussions' as befits two top professionals. But their film did go on to earn half a billion dollars.)

'Want to come and see our zoo?' I enquired, inwardly congratulating myself on spotting a morale-raising opportunity. It had been a closed set, always an object of intrigue in the film world.

'You bet,' said Fergie.

Tom drove her, Pat, assorted children and me in one of those electric carts that scuttle around film studios down to the area where I pointed out our assorted keepers. They recognised the Duchess of York, her red mane not being the best disguise in the world; but not our chauffeur in his baseball cap and dark shades. All eyes turned to Fergie, who attracts a slightly mixed reaction amongst the British public – and so it was that suffocating summer's morning. Little attention was paid to the man in black. Until he smiled – that smile. Cynthia Cleese, normally the coolest of customers, permitted her mouth to fall open when she realised who was addressing her. I cannot claim that morale soared as high as the temperature, but at least his arrival broke the ennui.

Fergie has a natural gift with people and Tom, knowing he was with fellow actors, immediately became one of the boys – and girls. I warmed to him immensely. We moved on to the main unit where John was rehearsing with Michael Palin. People were pleased to take a break and chat and John, on discovering that Tom and Nicole had rented a house near his in Holland Park in west London, made plans for a barbecue in his back garden. Sadly, *Fierce Creatures* spiralled downwards into such an abyss of chaos that we never managed it. But, later that afternoon, Sarah sent a van with iced tea for the entire cast and crew from St George's Hotel in Windsor.

Tom, it transpired, was quite friendly with the younger royals. On another, much colder, day we got a call from Paula Wagner, Tom's co-producer, saying they had just had lunch with Princess Diana at Pinewood and suggested she come over and visit us. She arrived, the epitome of cool, with short golden hair, tight designer jeans and an immaculately cut blue blazer. Certainly she was the most glamorous star in Pinewood that day. Prince William was with her, very much the schoolboy in mufti – neat parting, sports jacket and tie.

Steven Spielberg too was acquainted with Diana. She suggested he give her a miniature E.T. at the film's London premiere, and the photograph girdled the globe. He had to cough loudly in her ear to cover two 'shits' at the premiere of *Indiana Jones and the Temple of Doom*. When she died, he telephoned Tony Blair and asked for tickets to her funeral for himself, Tom Hanks and the Cruises. Spielberg knew the Blairs; their children used to play soccer together at Chequers. Although the television commentators said that the famous four Americans had flown in for the funeral they were, in fact, all working in London: Tom and Nicole on the interminable shoot of Stanley Kubrick's *Eyes Wide Shut*, and the other Tom and Steven on *Saving Private Ryan*. After the assorted mourners had said goodbye to the coffin outside Westminster Abbey as it began its unforgettable flower-strewn journey to Diana's childhood home, Althorp, Sarah Ferguson invited the Americans to dinner that night at her and Prince Andrew's home. Tom Hanks told me it was a surreal evening that ended with Chris De Burgh singing his songs at the piano and Fergie dancing alone in the giant, empty fireplace at Sunningdale with a drink in her hand.

Eyes Wide Shut (1999) may well have had a more detrimental effect on Cruise's marriage to Kidman than it did to his career, which was gushing cash like an oil well with the success of his *Mission Impossible* films, which he both produced and starred in. The first two made more than a billion dollars. Plus he was receiving critical acclaim portraying some repellent characters in *Jerry Maguire* (1996) and *Magnolia* (1999).

I didn't meet Cruise again until I was reintroduced to him by Steven Spielberg in the summer of 2001. Spielberg had always had his eye on the young actor – indeed, eighteen years previously he had sent him a letter to say how much he liked his performance in *Risky Business*. Now they were working together for the first time in *Minority Report*. My own first encounter with Steven had come when Tom was only twelve years old and I shot an interview-profile of Spielberg on the Martha's Vineyard location of *Jaws* in 1974. Since then I have made ten television programmes to accompany his films, including the two Tom ones: a study of future policing for *Minority Report* and the interpretation of H. G. Wells's book for *War of the Worlds*.

In *Minority Report* (2002) Tom played Chief John Anderton. The film is set fifty years in the future, and through accurate mediums called 'precogs' crime can be predicted before it is committed; more of that later. I went to stay with the film unit on location in a wonderfully olde worlde resort hotel in Virginia – a state that seems still to regard itself as part of the British Empire. Spielberg had been invited to go to Japan to the premiere of *A.I.* but, as he was filming, Japan had to come to Spielberg. A vast satellite dish, the sort that track space-shots, was put in place by our nineteenth-century clapboard abode. I watched in the colonial living room as hundreds of journalists filled a theatre in central Tokyo. A couple of television cameras were set up to cover Steven. He came down after dinner, took his place to great applause (Japanese journalists would appear to be less reserved than their American and British counterparts) and conducted a press conference.

About twenty minutes in, the doors of our living room were thrown open and Tom Cruise and Colin Farrell, an Irish actor appearing in *Minority Report*, burst in. It was not planned. They were pretty high: Colin, I suspect, on the local brew and Tom, I suspect, on his own adrenalin. They leaned over Steven's shoulders and, well before Tom spoke, a gasp went through the Tokyo theatre. Before he even said 'Hello, Japan' the reporters were on their feet, applauding. It was evident that he was popular in that country. Tom promised that he would come over and visit them when *Minority Report* opened, and the applause grew to a crescendo. Many, I suspect, knew he was soon to film *The Last Samurai*.

The boys left and Spielberg, who was amused by the episode, concluded the press conference. He then embarked on a one-on-one interview with Japan's leading television interviewer, who was in a separate studio. Five minutes into that, the living room doors flew open again and Tom rushed in and repeated his performance. Steven retained his sang-froid but after the interview, which was being recorded, he asked his interviewer to cut that bit out.

In retrospect, *aprés Oprah*, I could see that Tom was capable of an adrenalin rush like few other humans – who wouldn't, if you were worshipped like a Roman emperor? – but also was not always aware when enough is enough. What is not in doubt is the fact that Cruise has guts. It is as if he believes an invisible cloak protects him from physical harm. Indeed, Cruise had once been white-water rafting with some studio executives, and three helicopters were lined up to take them all back to Los Angeles. One junior executive climbed into the helicopter containing Cruise and, once airborne, a vice-president asked him why he had ended up there and not in the helicopter with the rest of the junior staff. 'Because helicopters with Tom Cruise in them don't crash,' the nervous young man replied. And here he put his finger on a question that is central to this book. Is there a line of demarcation between Cruise's films and his life? Could it be that all the world really is his stage?

Cruise does his own stunts when the film insurance permits, and sometimes when it doesn't. He rides horses hard and motorcycles harder. He skydives. He can drive a racing car up to professional standards. And he pilots jet planes and helicopters. In Virginia, this last was a bone of contention between him and his director. The location was a stately family home on its own island, connected to the mainland by a bridge. The travel time from the hotel by car was an hour, by helicopter ten minutes. Tom knew which form of transport he preferred, but Spielberg is less sure of his own immortality and preferred four wheels. Using statistical evidence, Tom eventually persuaded him that the skies were safer – the crowning argument being that the helicopter gave Spielberg more time in which to work.

Steven has never made any secret of his physical fears to me, not least because I share them. He required Kate Capshaw, later to be his wife, to cross a perilous rope bridge several hundred feet above a gorge in *Indiana Jones and the Temple of Doom*, but felt disinclined to follow the Steadicam that was tracking her and Harrison Ford across the slight structure. And although he designed the Jurassic Ride in the Universal Theme Park, he told me he always got out of the boat before the final scream-inducing drop into a lake.

In fact, Kiwa Island in that soft September of 2001 had many of the aspects of a theme park. There were stalls selling – no, giving away – coffee and ice cream and doughnuts and sweetmeats. And children running around playing football, or listening to the assistant directors on their headphones. It wasn't normal for a film set – but this was no normal film set. It was Spielberg and Cruise safely hidden from the crowds that normally flock to their locations. Kate Spielberg sat beneath an almond tree concentrating on her embroidery, with the occasional glance at her brood – she and Steven have seven children between them. Tom's mother was there and so were his three sisters. When he was shooting, they kept an eye on Isabella (eight) and Connor (six), the children he had adopted with Nicole Kidman whom he had divorced at the beginning of the year. The world's most popular film star seemed sublimely content with his family – and his work. I suspect that that day was one of the most calm and contented of his life – with no hint of the frenzied headlines and controversy that lay ahead.

I

JUMPING THE COUCH

The year 2005 was, without doubt, the most astonishing in Tom Cruise's life – possibly in any film star's life. On Wednesday, 25 May the star bounced up and down on the couch of the television celebrity Oprah Winfrey, and announced he was in love with Katie Holmes, a young actress from television's *Dawson's Creek*.

'You've never had this kind of feeling before?' the experienced hostess prompted him.

Shaking his head he cried: 'I honestly haven't – and I'm not gonna pretend.'

It is most unusual for a major Hollywood star to talk with such candour in public about his private life, but the hitherto rather reclusive Cruise threw the stable doors wide open to the world on that show. A columnist on the *Los Angeles Times* suggested that this was 'probably one of the biggest stories in the history of Hollywood.' A little hyperbolic, perhaps, but whoever saw it is hardly likely to forget it – and many saw it. In fact it won a subsequent poll of Wildest Celebrity Meltdown Moments beating Michael Jackson dangling his baby from a Berlin hotel balcony into second place.

It had been agreed by the Paramount Marketing Department that Oprah would have first bite at the publicity cherry for Spielberg's *War of the Worlds*, with Tom baring clips and behind-the-scenes anecdotes to her. But she got more than she bargained for. The previous month Cruise had flown to Rome to be given a Lifetime Achievement Award at the David di Donatella ceremony – very much Italy's equivalent of the Oscars. They needed to attract big overseas names to get decent television exposure – the previous year Steven Spielberg had collected exactly the same honour, although the breaking news that Iraqis had murdered their Italian hostage marred the light-hearted atmosphere. Spielberg presented the Best Actress Award to Penelope Cruz for *Don't Move* only a few days after it had been announced that the Spanish actress had broken up with Tom Cruise. It was Paramount's intention that Cruise would tantalise the prime-time Italian television audience with a taste of *War of the Worlds*, but unfortunately the ceremony was recorded and transmitted at an off-peak hour. There was only one Cruise story which made headlines that week. It was the fact that he had a new girlfriend, Katie Holmes, a twenty-six-year-old actress best known as Joey Potter in the hit young people's television series *Dawson's Creek*.

The couple gave the paparazzi ample opportunity to

photograph them as, hand-in-hand, they strolled back to the Hassler Hotel by Rome's Spanish Steps. Normally, when rumours of a film star romance are the subject of press speculation, the couple get their publicity people to deny them. But in this instance precisely the reverse was to take place. Cruise's press agent (and sister), Lee Anne DeVette, said that they had been dating for a few weeks. Simultaneously Holmes's public relations firm, Baker Winokur Ryder, confirmed that this was the case. Few Hollywood watchers had ever experienced such candid press releases about the private lives of two stars. But soon they had it from the horses' mouths, so to speak. Associated Press quoted Tom as saying it was 'like a dream' to have her with him for the awards ceremony.

He went on: 'She's such an extraordinary woman. It's beautiful. I feel really happy. I'm more than enamoured.'

Katie's body language, as they strolled round Rome over the next days, left onlookers and photographers in little doubt that she reciprocated these feelings.

They were both free. Penelope Cruz, Tom's previous innamorata, was a fling of the past, and a few weeks previously Holmes had broken off her engagement to the *American Pie* star Chris Klein. They had been together for nearly five years but it was unlikely that the relationship had benefited from an interview she gave to *Seventeen* magazine in which she revealed: 'I think every little girl dreams about her wedding. I used to think I was going to marry Tom Cruise.'

Oprah Winfrey, through courtesy or design, had invited Tom and Katie to her 'Legends' ball shortly before she taped her show with the star. She had planned the glittering evening to pay tribute to African-American artists who had 'paved the way for their fellow men and women to follow in their footsteps'. And when Oprah invites you, you turn up. Angela Bassett, Ruby Dee, Sidney Poitier, Maya Angelou, Gladys Knight, Diahann Carroll, Toni Morrison, Aretha Franklin, Mariah Carey, Halle Berry, Diana Ross, Jesse Jackson and Corretta King were a mere sampling of the names, along with Barbra Streisand, Barbara Walters, John Travolta and Stedman Graham, Oprah's husband.

A waiter came across to Tom's table and handed him a single rose, saying it was from Tina Turner. Since she was being honoured as a legend that night, she couldn't leave the top table to meet him so would he come and meet her? Not unnaturally, he did. Later that night, Tina, who was staying with Oprah, was in seventh heaven.

'I met Tom Cruise! I met Tom Cruise! My God, he's so good-looking.'

Someone else who shared these sentiments was Katie Holmes. They danced and kissed and hugged the whole night long. However, not everyone there knew who Katie Holmes was, since *Dawson's Creek* attracted a largely teenage audience. Indeed, it revolved round the lives and problems of six teenagers who lived in the fictional community of Capeside, Massachusetts. The eponymous Dawson Leery (James Van Der Beek) was an aspiring film-maker and Katie played his good buddy, something of a tomboy. Others in their gang had problems ranging from homosexuality to mental illness. It proved hugely popular nationally and internationally over its six seasons on television.

It had not been the intention of Katherine Noelle Holmes's father that she should end up in show business – rather, that she should pursue a career in medicine. He was an affluent lawyer in Toledo, Ohio where she was born on 18 December 1976, the youngest of his five children. She was sent to a good all-girl Catholic school, Notre Dame Academy. 'In hindsight I think we missed out socially,' she recalls. 'We came out of school and it was suddenly: "Oh, my God! Boys!"' But while there she exhibited a predilection for all things musical – the piano, singing and dancing – as well as acting, and her mother, Kathleen, acknowledged that her daughter should have the opportunity to make use of her looks and talent. She attended a local modelling academy which sent its brightest and best to an international competition in New York. There she was spotted by a talent scout and, ultimately, this yielded her a part in Ang Lee's *The Ice Storm* when she was only seventeen.

The film was too cerebral to be widely popular – it dealt with the disintegration of Kevin Kline's marriage to Joan Allen and his affair with Sigourney Weaver. A sub-plot was the quest of the married couple's son, Tobey Maguire, for a relationship with the rich and pure Manhattanite Katie Holmes. The role didn't lead to cinema stardom, but Kathleen Holmes knew that there was a demand for her daughter's clean-cut type in television. They made an audition tape together and, although it failed to open the door to daytime soaps or even *Buffy, the Vampire*

Slayer, it did land on the desk of Kevin Williamson, the current god of teen movies such as *Scream* and *I Know What You Did Last Summer*. When he came up with a television series inspired by his own teenage years, Katie looked a possible candidate for the female lead.

But, amazingly, she didn't fly out to Los Angeles for the auditions. Why? Because she was playing Lola in the Notre Dame production of *Damn Yankees* and didn't want to let down the school. Such splendidly decent behaviour paradoxically made her a perfect Joey. Rearranged auditions took place, and Joey she was for 128 episodes.

Settling into the image of a bit of a goody-goody, Katie was anxious to disabuse people of this perception in order to extend her range of parts. So, between series, she played a school slut in the film *Disturbing Behavior*, a drug dealer's girlfriend in *Go* and a tattooed rebel in *Pieces of April*, and went topless as something of a tart without much of a heart in *The Gift* – which, despite a cast that included Hilary Swank, Keanu Reeves and Cate Blanchett, a script by Billy Bob Thornton and Sam Raimi as director – did badly at the box-office. But not as appallingly as *The Singing Detective* of 2003, in which Katie did a suggestive song and dance that caused the bedridden Robert Downey Jr to . . . well . . . ejaculate. Katie herself demurely denies that she was trying to downgrade her image with these unruly roles: 'I just want to run the gamut of parts. There are an awful lot of stories to tell.'

Her ambition remained undimmed. She may have failed to play opposite Leo DiCaprio in *The Beach*, but she became better known on the big screen as Colin Farrell's girlfriend in *Phone Booth* (2002). Then she really hit the big time opposite Christian Bale as New York assistant DA and childhood friend of mild-mannered Bruce Wayne in *Batman Begins*, which opened in June 2005. More insinuatingly, she became familiar on television as the face of Garnier Lumia hair colour.

So how did Tom meet her? It was a question that Oprah was not slow to ask. 'Is it true you called her for a meeting for something?'

Tom demurred. 'Do we have to go into details of everything?'

'Yes, yes,' his hostess insisted.

'I admired her and I thought that I wanted to meet her, so I called her. You see someone's work and you hear from people what a special person she is. I met her. She's extraordinary . . . I can't be cool . . . I can't be laid back . . . I want to celebrate her.'

He certainly wasn't cool or laid back. He went down on one knee, making a fist with his right hand as if he had just won a major tennis tournament, he persistently clasped Oprah's hands in the way a child might play with a parent and, most notoriously, he bounced up and down on her sofa. It has to be said that Tom had walked into a cauldron of female hysteria, adroitly whipped up by Oprah at the very start of the show. He fed off the audience and they encouraged him.

'You're gone, you're gone,' his hostess chanted at him, and certainly his behaviour was that of someone who had taken some amazing magic potion or, almost certainly in

Tom's case, generated such a tidal wave of adrenalin in himself that it drowned all inhibition.

In fact, recent research by Dr Fisher at Rutgers University reveals that the state of being in love is characterised by feelings of exhilaration and intrusive, obsessive thoughts about the object of one's affection. Some researchers suggest this mental state might share neurochemical characteristics with the manic phase of manic depression. Dr Fisher's work, however, suggests that the actual behavioural patterns of those in love – such as attempting to evoke reciprocal responses in one's loved one – resemble obsessive compulsive disorder (OCD). Moreover, the brain areas active in love are different from the areas activated in other emotional states such as fear and anger. Parts of the brain that are love-bitten include the one responsible for gut feelings, and the ones which generate the euphoria induced by drugs such as cocaine. So the brains of people deeply in love do not look like those of people experiencing strong emotions, but instead like those of people snorting coke. Love, in other words, uses the neural mechanisms that are activated during the process of taking the drug. And since Tom Cruise is the man most *un*likely to be snorting cocaine, the Rutgers research may go some way to explaining his behaviour.

When Oprah made so bold as to ask him if he had covered their hotel room in Rome with rose petals Tom leaned back, laughed – and then nodded. On a roll, she pushed him on the question of marriage even though it seemed the couple had only known each other for a few weeks.

'I don't want to disappoint her,' Tom confessed, adding, 'I've got to discuss it with her first.'

The audience was joyous.

'I like seeing people happy,' Tom responded, 'and I want to share it with people because it's something very special. She is an extraordinary woman. She really is a very, very special person. She has spirit, generosity, elan, she cares about other people and she has a real joy about life. I've spoken to her parents and she's met my mother and my family.'

He had also told Steven Spielberg about Katie, and Spielberg had observed: 'You look so happy,' as had his sister and publicist, Lee Anne DeVette. In a prerecorded tape venerable, wise Spielberg seemed to have anticipated what might – and did – happen. 'What your audience sees of Tom is the Tom I know. There are no secrets. There is no hidden agenda. This is why you have so many millions of fans all over the world,' he said, before adding, 'I just hope that Tom will say a little bit about *War of the Worlds* and you don't just obsess about Tom and Katie, Katie and Tom.' Spielberg avowed that working with Tom was 'one of the greatest gifts I've ever been given by this business', and Tom in turned opined that Steven was the 'greatest storyteller the cinema has ever known'.

In truth, Tom had little need to plug the movie. Reminding her vast television audience that *Premiere* magazine had recently named Tom Cruise the greatest movie star of all time, Oprah commanded them to mark the 29 June opening date on their calendars and to buy their seats ahead of time. And she hadn't even seen the film. Recalling a time when she had been at the same hotel as Tom in Oslo, she told the audience how people stood outside it screaming and enquired if he liked that.

Tom was dutifully modest. 'I feel really honoured to be where I am. No joke.'

Having got Tom to open up to such an unusual extent, Oprah put to him a question that no journalist had dared mention before. 'You have a bi-racial son . . . you have never mentioned it.'

'He's from the human race' – Tom had calmed down. 'He's from mankind.'

The screen showed a picture of Tom and his adopted ten-year-old, Connor, kicking a ball around. Unusually, the child's face was not blurred out as it is in magazines. Oprah boldly asked him if the boy's ethnicity was ever discussed in the family.

Tom seemed surprised. 'What's there to talk about? I love him. I've never thought about colour. We're all here together and we've got to work it out together, okay?'

And there the matter rested. But Oprah did not acquire her reputation through failing to ask bold, even intrusive, questions. Producing the June cover of *Details* magazine, she quoted her guest as saying that he had the best sex when he was in a serious relationship.

'That's the only time it works,' he confirmed. 'It's that intimacy, that relationship, that communication. That's what it's all about.'

'You can tell you're not a one-night stand kind of guy.'

'No.'

'Too intense for that.'

'Too intense. I like intimacy. I want to know about my woman.'

And now it was the audience's turn to know about his woman – or, at least, look at her. 'I know Katie's here,' Oprah revealed. 'Tell her to come out.'

'She's gonna run,' Tom warned.

But it was he who did the running, followed by a camera as he went into the office bowels of the *Oprah* show. Katie did indeed seem a little shy – but not too shy to spoil the show. She permitted Tom to take her by the hand and lead her on to the set. The audience went wild, and Oprah asked her how it felt growing up wanting to marry Tom Cruise and now standing hand-in-hand in front of millions.

'I'm glad I was a big dreamer,' she smiled, and then Tom kissed her.

The audience, applauding and screaming, were in raptures. On the other hand, what kind of reaction must Penelope Cruz or Nicole Kidman have had to this telecast? Certainly Nicole could hardly be filled with delight that Tom's avowal that he had never felt like this before would, sooner or later, reach the ears of their children.

One might think that, since Hollywood likes nothing more than lovers and the cult of celebrity has reached epidemic proportions, America would welcome this demonstration of affection from its most popular star and the unequivocal enthusiasm of the *Oprah* audience. But this proved not to be universally the case. Most probably any negative reaction had been fuelled by the way the press were fed the fact of Tom's relationship with Katie as if it were a wedding announcement in the local paper. Sceptical writers wondered whether the pairing was just a publicity stunt – not only did Tom have a film to promote but so did Katie, with the imminent release of *Batman Begins*.

Even Oprah Winfrey herself later observed: 'I was trying to think what to do. I didn't know how to react. I couldn't figure it out. I was thinking "Is this real?" And then I realized it was. I'd interviewed him before and he'd been so intensely private, so this was beyond anything I'd expected. I wonder if he regrets it?'

Spielberg himself was 'a little upset' by the press's reaction. 'Tom lost his cool because he was deliriously happy and now he is being punished for his public display of honesty. What Tom did on *Oprah* was exactly what Tom did with me when he first told me about Katie Holmes – he bared his soul.'

They certainly got plenty of publicity on covers of *Big Three*, *US Weekly*, *Star* and *People* plus the ubiquitous *Hola/Hello* celebrity magazines and their clones throughout the globe. But a certain cynicism was fanned in their readers, and when *People* magazine conducted a small opinion poll asking them if they thought it was a publicity stunt 62 per cent replied that it was, a figure mirrored by the 100 people stopped at Rockefeller Center in New York, of whom 65 said they believed it was just a stunt. (It should, of course, be pointed out that these samples are comparatively small in the light of the millions of people who subsequently went to see *War of the Worlds*.)

Tom's attitude was sanguine. 'It's amusing at first. It's funny. But then you sit back and realise how sad it is that there are people who can't even imagine feeling like this. But my friends are happy for me. The people who know me are happy. My mom is happy. My family is happy.'

Satirical websites popped up such as TomCruiseIs-Nuts.com and Freekatie.net, the latter selling T-shirts with 'Free Katie' or 'Save the Couch' splashed on them. The online Urban Dictionary, which provides new slang definitions, added 'jumping the couch', which now means, apparently, '1. The defining moment when you know someone has gone off the deep end, or 2. Acting wildly foolish.'

Tom was aware of the fact that people were sending him up. So when he went on the Jay Leno show and the host made a point of alluding to his 'silly' behaviour, Tom replied: 'When I start to think about her, things happen. So cease talking.' The audience whooped with delight as he climbed up on the couch, victoriously raising both hands in the air. Katie, too, was delighted: when she announced Tom as winner of the Lifetime Achievement Award at the 2005 MTV Awards she entertained the audience with a visual parody of her new boyfriend's gesture on *Oprah*, going down on her knee and pumping her fist in the air. Then, to good-natured laughter, she went back-stage to drag him out.

Nicole Kidman was in the audience. Subsequently she told David Letterman: 'Honestly, if Tom's in love I'm so happy for him and that's a very good thing.'

Perhaps Tom's greatest problem was that with one bound (literally) his attitude towards his private life had gone from famine to feast, from obsessive secrecy to over-communication. Writing in *The New York Times*, Mireya Navarro was of the opinion: 'Cruise and Holmes may very well be head over heels, but they should not be surprised that even their most star-struck fan seems to be having trouble embracing their romance.'

Had the Cruise Controversy of the summer of 2005 merely been about his antics on *Oprah* it would most probably have faded away like the grin on the Cheshire Cat. But it wasn't. Tom gave other interviews. The actor's views on psychology, psychiatry and prescription drugs are well known. He believes that such things are wrong – evil, even. Two years previously, on the *Larry King Show* to promote *The Last Samurai*, he confirmed that this was the case, based on knowledge acquired through his adherence to the Church of Scientology (of which more later). Interviewed on *Access Hollywood* on 26 May he reiterated and expanded on these views, citing an example of how he and fellow Scientologists had weaned a child off prescription drugs for Attention Deficit Hyperactivity Disorder and on to vitamins and healthy food, which caused her to grow seven inches in four months. 'I have an easier time stepping people off heroin than these psychotropic drugs. Any drug is a poison.'

It so happened that the actress Brooke Shields had recently published a well-received book entitled *Down Came the Rain: My Journey Through Postpartum Depression*. It chronicled in detail the difficulty she had had in conceiving and giving birth to her first baby, Rowan. But worse was to follow: after the birth she descended into a depression so deep that she couldn't even communicate with her daughter, let alone the world. But she slowly fought her way back to mental health thanks to psychiatry and the drug Paxil.

Asked about Paxil and postpartum depression, Tom did not hold back his views. 'It is not a cure; it is actually lethal. I care about Brooke Shields because she is incredibly talented but look at where her career has gone. Is she happy? Is she really happy? She doesn't know what these drugs are and for her to promote them is irresponsible. I wish her well in life but it is irresponsible to do that.'

This *ad hominem* – or *ad feminam* – attack on a fellow star shattered every rule in the Hollywood public relations book. Commentators were not slow to point out that Cruise's first movie part was a few lines as Billy, a chum of Martin Hewitt who starred with Brooke Shields in the 1981 Franco Zeffirelli film *Endless Love*. In the movie Martin and Brooke visit the Planetarium and he says, 'I'm going to name a star after you', whereupon, at the New York Press Show, some wit yelled out, 'Brooke Shields already is a star.' Indeed she had been one since the age of twelve, when she played a child prostitute in a 1917 New Orleans brothel in Louis Malle's controversial *Pretty Baby* of 1978. Her face was already famous; urged on by her fiercely ambitious mother, Teri, Brooke had been the face of Ivory Snow soap when she was only eleven. Brooke became the dream girl of teenage boys as she frolicked barely clad through *Blue Lagoon* the year before *Endless Love*. Although Tom was two years older he was, at the time, unknown.

His implication that her career had slipped somewhat is valid. Brooke continued to act in movies and television, but none became blockbusters. Possibly she was more interested in her academic life at Princeton university or her romances, evidently ranging from Michael Jackson to Prince Albert of Monaco, with a quick marriage to tennis star André Agassi before she settled with the writer and producer Chris Henchy. However, with her depression beaten she flew to London to star in the West End as Roxie Hart in *Chicago*. It was during this run that Tom's remarks came to her ears, and she didn't take them lying down.

'As far as I know Tom Cruise has never given birth to a baby,' came her dry riposte. 'He should stick to saving the world from aliens and let women who are experiencing postpartum depression decide what treatment options are best for them.'

Show business journalists booted up their laptops with glee. They were tired of being the supplicant scribes of Hollywood junkets, which meant that if they wrote ill of a movie or star their flow of free flights, meals and hotel rooms would be quickly terminated. They had had enough of manipulative PRs (or 'flacks' as they called them behind their backs) who manoeuvred them from room to room in overheated hotels for five-minute interviews with stars who gushed about how absolutely wonderful everyone else in their current movie was. Here, at last, was a story with some seltzer in it! And they were determined to make it run and run.

Of course, it should have been cut off at the pass with a

diplomatically arranged rapprochement between the two stars – even if it was not a genuine one. Indeed, it should never have happened in the first place.

So why did it?

2

KISS ME KATE

The explanation goes back to 5 April 2004. On that day it was announced that Tom had split up with Penelope Cruz, the siren from Spain whom he had cast in *Vanilla Sky* (2001) and who had been his partner on the red carpet since his divorce from Nicole Kidman. But as Adam Sternbergh of National Public Radio concluded: 'Strangely this wasn't the most momentous split Cruise experienced that week.'

Tom had dispensed with the services of his long-time personal publicist, Pat Kingsley. The announcement of his break with Penelope was made by his new publicist, his sister, Lee Anne DeVette (who later spread the emphatic news that Tom and Katie were an item). Lee Anne had worked for Cruise-Wagner Productions for many years and is obsessively protective of her brother's image. She is also a committed Scientologist and that may well have paved her path to the job.

It had fallen to Pat Kingsley to inform him that he had begun to promote Scientology rather than movies on his publicity tours. The news did not fall on receptive ears. The people at Warners said that Tom did the honourable thing when he decided to part company with Pat: he went to the headquarters of PMK, the company she had founded, and explained face-to-face. She in turn took him round the offices to meet the people who had been working for him for the past fourteen years. Tom had engaged her when he was making *Far and Away* (1992) with Nicole, and she had been by his side, when needed, on every press occasion since then.

Kingsley, now seventy four, grew up in a Hollywood where big-name columnists such as Hedda Hopper and Louella Parsons ruled the roost. The studios deferred to them, believing, as Kingsley recalls, that 'they could make or break a star'. She learnt the business in the sixties as a 'planter' – someone who places items in celebrity columns – and was further schooled at Rogers and Cowan, the original pre-eminent international movie publicists (Paul Newman, Warren Beatty and Ronald Reagan were among their clients). But when she sensed the time was right to leave and start her own firm, Pat Kingsley slowly and boldly rewrote the rules. The power should no longer repose with the press; it lay with the stars – and her staff. She was happy to turn away much publicity; and if a major magazine wanted to talk to one of her top clients (Tom Hanks, Al Pacino, Jodie Foster) she would usually require approval of the copy and the photos and, quite often, obtain an agreement that it would be the cover story.

When Cruise became king, he had an unimpeachable press. Would Kingsley have counselled him to temper his exuberance on the Oprah Winfrey show? The answer can be best given in the form of the old Irish joke about the motorist who stopped and asked a farmer ploughing a field how to get to Killarney Castle. The answer came: 'If I was you, I wouldn't start out from here.' Pat Kingsley would never have announced in Rome that Tom and Katie were a couple. Apart from anything else, it took away from the mystique of the star. At much the same time Cindy Guagenti, Brad Pitt's publicist, was telling the press it was 'absolutely untrue' that he and Angelina Jolie were romantically involved while there was incontrovertible photographic evidence to the contrary. In Tom and Katie's case, the Rome picture-call even had captions supplied by the respective PRs. With no announcement about his private life, Tom's subsequent appearance on *Oprah* would have been less open to ridicule.

Kingsley has said: 'I believe in the freedom of the press. Most people agree there is a line between a person's private life and public lives. It's just that I could never find a member of the press who could tell me where that line was.'

Tom's acquiescence in questions about his private life, even to the extent of parading his girlfriend on a TV show, thus went completely against the philosophy of his erstwhile publicity guru. As for the attack on Brooke Shields, Kingsley would have had that cut out of the tape before you could have said Edward Scissorhands. But Kingsley insisted to the *New York Daily News* that she and Cruise had had an 'amicable parting,' but she would, wouldn't she?

'I adore the guy,' she went on. 'I have the greatest respect for him professionally and personally. We've had a great ride.'

Although, as Adam Sternbergh observed on National Public Radio: 'Their break-up isn't just the end of the most successful partnership of its kind. It may well mark the demise of the very tactics this tandem perfected. There may never be another flack quite as powerful as Kingsley or a star quite as inscrutable as Cruise. In an age of scandal and non-stop scrutiny, Cruise is a curious celebrity conundrum: the world's most famous movie star and the one about whom the least is known or understood.'

Cruise's sister, Lee Anne DeVette, agreed in public with Kingsley. 'It was an amicable separation and the two remain friends. He still cares a great deal for Pat. Clearly, it was time for a change. It was a decision he came to.' As for Cruise's role in Scientology, she said: 'In earlier years, he didn't talk about Scientology, and everybody said he was keeping it a big mystery. Now, he talks about it and it's wrong. It's damned if you do, damned if you don't.'

Under his new PR management he didn't just talk about it, it was made an almost absolute requirement for anybody coming to interview him that they should spend the best part of a day at the Church of Scientology in Los Angeles learning about the religion. Lee Anne said she thought it would help people to understand him better. But it was not without controversy. One of the first journalists to talk to Tom on *War of the Worlds* was from *Der Spiegel* – the leading magazine in Germany, a huge market in terms of non-domestic box-office. The reporter had been 'amazed' to see the Scientology tents on the set.

'What were you amazed about?' Cruise countered.

'Why do you go so extremely public about your personal convictions?'

'I believe in freedom of speech,' Cruise replied. 'I felt honored to have volunteer Scientology ministers on the set. They were helping the crew. When I'm working on a movie, I do anything I can to help the people I'm spending time with. I believe in communication.

'The tent of a sect at someone's working place still seems somewhat strange to us,' the reporter persisted, and asked Spielberg if he hadn't thought it unusual.

Most people in the Paramount marketing department certainly thought it was unusual. It had fallen to Spielberg to put Tom's request not only to Paramount but also to Universal, where they shot the film's interiors. Few people in Hollywood say no to Steven Spielberg, so the tent was duly erected. He hardly wanted to alienate his star, but he remained guarded about how personally enthusiastic he was.

'I saw it as an information tent. No one was compelled to frequent it, but it was available for anybody who had an open mind and was curious about someone else's belief system.'

But the post-Kingsley Tom was determined to stick up for his decision. 'The volunteer Scientology ministers were there to help the sick and injured. People on the set appreciated that. I have absolutely nothing against talking about my beliefs. But I do so much more. We live in a world where people are on drugs for ever. Where even children get drugged. Where crimes against humanity are so extreme that most people turn away in horror and dismay. Those are the things that I care about. I don't care what someone believes. I don't care what nationality they are. But if someone wants to get off drugs, I can help them. If someone wants to learn how to read, I can help them. If someone doesn't want to be a criminal any more, I can give them tools that can better their life. You have no idea how many people want to know what Scientology is. I'm a helper. For instance, I myself have helped hundreds of people get off drugs. In Scientology, we have the only successful drug rehabilitation program in the world. It's called Narconon.'

The German stood his ground. 'That's not correct. Yours is never mentioned among the recognised detox programs. Independent experts warn against it because it is rooted in pseudo science.'

But Cruise was not prepared to concede this. 'You don't understand what I am saying. It's a statistically proven fact that there is only one successful drug rehabilitation program in the world. Period.'

Even the reminder that Scientology had been under federal surveillance in Germany did not concern him. It was not considered a religion there, but rather an exploitative cult with totalitarian tendencies.

Tom struck back at this. 'The surveillance is nothing like as strict any more. And you know why? Because the intelligence authorities never found anything. Because there was nothing to find. We've won over fifty court cases in Germany. And it's not true that everyone in Germany supports that line against us. Whenever I go to Germany, I have incredible experiences. I always meet very generous and extraordinary people. A minority wants to hate – okay.'

Reminding the star that, when *Mission: Impossible* came out in 1996, German politicians called for a boycott of his movies, Cruise's interlocutor boldly enquired: 'Are you worried that your support for Scientology could hurt your career?'

At that moment, Tom was in the business not of selling cinema tickets but of standing up for his beliefs: 'Not at all. I've always been very outspoken. I've been a Scientologist for twenty years. If someone is so intolerant that he doesn't want to see a Scientologist in a movie, then he shouldn't go to the movie theatre. I don't care. Here in the United States, Scientology is a religion. If some of the politicians in your country don't agree with that, I couldn't care less.'

'I couldn't care less' – rarely heard words for a star selling a movie although, in truth, Cruise did promote the merits of *War of the Worlds*. However, a new asperity had entered his style, never more so than in his encounter with Australia's leading television interviewer, Peter Overton of *60 Minutes*. It had been recorded before joyous Tom had bared his emotions to the world on Oprah.

The Australian programme made a virtue of promised controversy and pursued high ratings in trailers of what was in store for the viewers. Overton obliged the Cruise camp by attending the Scientology session, but it hardly converted him. In his introduction to the interview, taped after the event, he warned his audience: 'I discovered there's another side to Tom Cruise — that when he's angry, the cool man of Hollywood can become downright icy.'

Their chat started out chummily enough, with both men giving the impression that they were good buddies.

Cruise: How are you? Hey, how you been?

Overton: Nice to see you.

Cruise: Good to see you.

Overton: Long time.

Cruise: I know.

But it would not be long before the bonhomie turned slightly rancid as Overton complained about his four and a half hours at the Scientology Celebrity Centre in Los Angeles. He asked the star if he agreed there was perception out there that it gets a bad press — cult-like secrecy, controlling — and Tom almost had to defend it.

Overton: Do you feel discriminated against when people say this is what Scientology is, that you're a bunch of lunatic fringe or whatever?

Cruise: Peter.

Overton: Tom?

Cruise: No one's ever said that to me.

Overton: No, I mean that perception out there.

Cruise: But that's not the perception out there. That is absolutely — maybe from your perspective.

Overton: This isn't my personal opinion, I'm just saying, how do you feel about that when people . . . .

Cruise: Well, how would you feel?

Overton: If it was my faith, I'd feel really . . . .

Cruise: Not even your own faith — I find that appalling when people who don't know what they're talking about say things like that.

Journalists don't come any tougher than they do in Australia so after Peter Overton had steered the interview into the less intimidating topic of *War of the Worlds* he stepped into the ring again with another controversial subject, namely one of Australia's favourite daughters. Pat Kingsley had abruptly announced on 5 February 2001 that Tom and Nicole were separating. The news evidently came as something as a surprise to Mrs Cruise, and her husband's only explanation to the world had been: 'She knows why.' As a topic it was, if anything, more incendiary than Scientology.

Overton: When you were married, it was like you were an adopted part of Australia. Do you still have a connection to Australia?

Cruise: Yeah. My children are Australian. Absolutely. Absolutely. I have a lot of friends in Australia. I love Australia.

Overton: Was Nicole the love of your life?

Cruise: What do you mean, Peter?

Overton: You were married for ten years.

Cruise: Listen, we raised children, I . . . you know . . . . I mean, how do you answer that question? She's someone that I . . . . I plan on getting married again.

Overton: You do?

Cruise: Absolutely, yeah.

Overton: And having kids?

Cruise: Absolutely.

39

Overton: But Nicole was a major part of your life and a love of your life at the time?

Cruise: I loved Nic very much, there's no question.

Overton: Would you like Nicole to remarry?

Cruise: Yes. I want Nicole to be happy. That's what I want.

Overton: And do you have a relationship where you talk — a parenting relationship — and talk professionally about each other's . . .

Cruise: Listen, here's the thing, Peter. You're stepping over a line now. You're stepping over a line, you know you are.

Overton: I suppose they're questions that people want to know.

Cruise: Peter, *you* want to know. Take responsibility for what you want to know. Don't say what other people . . . . This is a conversation that I'm having with you right now. So I'm just telling you right now, okay, just put your manners back in.

To tell Australia's leading interviewer to 'put his manners back in' was less than likely to endear the film star to the watching audience. However, one of the aims of a 'clear' Scientologist is to control not just yourself but your environment as well, and this line of questioning was not an environment where Cruise wanted to be. Besides, a certain recklessness was beginning to attend his public utterances. He no longer had to pander to the press; he was the number one star in the world with the millions to match.

These interviews were taped pre-Katie and certainly the brittle, slightly crusty Cruise was a creature of the past from the moment he announced his new-found love. Ten days after the Australian interview aired, Tom took off for Paris to promote *War of the Worlds*. Spielberg needed to finesse the film further but was unable to go; however eleven-year-old Dakota Fanning, the precocious actress who plays Tom's daughter in the film, was well up to handling the press. The press conference in a gilded ballroom in Paris, a place more suited to signing international treaties than to movie junkets, was well attended by national papers and radio and television stations. And, like Oprah, they got more than they had bargained for.

Katie Holmes was spotted in the audience, sitting beside Lee Anne DeVette. Somebody – prompted or unprompted – asked Tom if he was going to marry Katie.

'Yes,' was the answer. He had proposed to her in the early hours of that morning at the end of a candlelit dinner at the Michelin-starred Jules Verne Restaurant on the second floor of the Eiffel Tower. 'I haven't slept at all.' No, he did not get down on one knee but he would like to return to the Eiffel Tower, a place neither he nor Katie had ever visited before, to get married, surrounded by his and Katie's families.

Katie said nothing. But her beaming smile said it all – that and the substantial gleaming diamond on her finger.

The actual French premiere of *War of the Worlds* was not in Paris but in Marseilles, two hundred miles to the south on the Riviera coast. Cruise, whose appetite for speed by car, bike or plane was well chronicled, was allowed to take the controls of France's pride and joy, the super-fast TGV (*Train à Grande Vitesse*) which could travel at speeds of up to 225 miles per hour. The photographs of him in a peaked train driver's hat gave maximum publicity to both the man and the machine.

Attention now focused on the next wife of the world's favourite film star. She certainly reciprocated the outgoing ardour of her fiancé. 'I'm so happy. Tom is fuss-worthy, for sure. He's the most artistic man I've met. He's a joy. He makes me laugh like I've never laughed. It's good to be me right now. Everything is just amazing. It's lovely to meet people, because this is the best I have ever been. You just burst and glow all the time. I strongly recommend it. He's an amazing man and I'm a very lucky woman.'

The relationship had her parents' approval. 'They're thrilled. They're just happy for me. For us. It's really lovely.'

Some people had questioned the sixteen-year age gap between her and Tom and the fact that he was twice divorced. But not her father, Martin, sixty. 'From all we have read about Tom,' he is reported to have said, 'he's a humanitarian and a real class act. I've seen a lot of unconventional relationships flourish. From my perspective as an attorney the age gap is not a factor.'

Nor was it a problem for her mother, Kathleen, fifty-eight, nor her siblings, Tamara, thirty-seven, Holly, thirty-five, Martin Jr, thirty-four or Nancy, thirty. This strong Catholic family grew up in a spacious house with a swimming pool in a fashionable part of Toledo which, it must be said, is a deeply unfashionable town. From their white picket fence to collecting Barbie dolls to cheer-leading, Katie was brought up as an all-American girl. She even gained a place at Columbia University to study medicine, but all that was swept away by *Dawson's Creek*.

That was shot in Wilmington, North Carolina where Katie acquired a house and a boyfriend, Joshua Jackson, another member of the close-knit cast. When she moved to an apartment in New York and took up with the phone-sex star of *American Pie*, Chris Klein, Joshua observed ruefully of her: 'She's very clean-cut. The only thing that's changed over the years is that maybe she's been to a bar now.' Indeed she had, her favourite being in the Hotel Gansevoort on 9th Avenue. Other favoured haunts, she revealed, were Billy's Bakery, Left Bank Books, Chanel, DKNY and Prada.

Katie is always at pains to point out what an unstarry life she leads, well away from the red carpets of Los Angeles. Half a dozen times a year she returns to Toledo, where her family and friends keep her grounded. 'My mom says I have to keep my apartment and car clean. I'm not dirty but I can be a little messy, a little disorganized.' She will sleep on the sofa of her childhood chum, Meghann Birie. 'She makes me get out of the car to scrape ice from the windshield. The "Do you know who I am?" stuff doesn't fly with her. I've tried it,' she recalls with a laugh. But, as she cut through France on the speeding TGV, Katie Holmes was fully aware that her life was about to undergo a seismic change.

The caravan moved on to London where set decorators had artfully turned Leicester Square into a dystopian wasteland devastated by aliens. Upturned cars lay burning, smoke and water poured from the remains of buildings and even ragged, injured actors dragged themselves along the ruined street. Dakota Fanning told us she had never been to London before and was looking forward to seeing the sights. Did anyone inform her that Leicester Square didn't usually look like this?

Tom, always a star who enjoyed being a star, had taken to working the crowds at London premieres, a favourite trick being to borrow the mobile phone of some fan and talk to her mother at home. 'Yes, you really are speaking to Tom Cruise.' Unfortunately this used to hold him up for more than an hour and those inside waiting for the film to start became restless, if not tetchy. So someone in UIP had come up with a cunning plan: Tom would nip into the cinema, introduce the movie and then go to meet and greet the thousands.

Those who were privileged to be inside and had walked through the remains of Leicester Square had first been searched most rigorously and had to show their passports, something that was no longer an absolute when crossing borders in the European Union. However, the fans had not been similarly vetted, and when Tom moved along the barriers dispensing signatures and goodwill he encountered a reporter and his television crew. They were fakes: an outfit who were making a 'comedy' programme for Channel Four. The reporter had rigged his microphone to squirt water into Cruise's face.

The soaking star struggled to maintain his composure and rounded on the man, saying: 'Why would you do that . . . why would you do that . . . why would you do that?'

As the prankster offered a barely audible excuse, Cruise

said: 'What's so funny about that? It's ridiculous. Do you like making less of people, is that it?'

After an uncomfortable silence the man started to walk away, but Cruise detained him: 'Don't run away.' He told his assailant: 'That's incredibly rude. I'm here giving you an interview, answering your questions and you do that . . . it's incredibly rude.'

The star then said forcefully: 'You're a jerk . . . jerk . . . you're a jerk.'

The TV crew were arrested by the police, who were prepared to press charges. An aide brought a towel and, despite his soaked shirt, the star continued his progress along the crowd.

Curiously, the incident repaired a lot of damage in the British media. When clips had been shown of him jumping the couch on *Oprah* there had been widespread ridicule; this now gave way to widespread respect because of the way he had comported himself. Even more so when he decided not to press charges against someone who had humiliated himself in the cowardly assault.

Last stop in Tom and Katie's grand European tour was Madrid, for the Spanish premiere. There Tom was reunited with his quondam partner, Penelope Cruz. The meeting was arranged at the headquarters of the Church of Scientology. Penelope gave Katie a warm hug – they already knew each other – and informed attendant reporters: 'I really like her.' But the Spanish actress did not choose to dine with her ex. Instead she went out on the town with Ralph Fiennes, who was over with a touring production of *Julius Caesar*. Penelope had played opposite Ralph in his sister's film *Chromophobia*, which had had an outing at the Cannes film festival but then disappeared.

However Penelope's family were happy to have supper at Madrid's leading restaurant, Casa Lucio, with the newly engaged couple. It is doubtful if the disparity in their ages caused any concern since the Cruzes consisted of Eduardo Jnr (brother), Monica (sister), Encarnacion (mother), Eduardo (father) – and father's girlfriend, Carmen, who, to judge from her photo, looks younger than thirty-one-year-old Penelope.

Madrid's sweltering Gran Via was packed with cheering fans – more male than female, surprisingly – who yelled '*torero*', literally 'bullfighter' but slang for 'macho man', and waved placards with sentiments such as '*España te Quiere*' (Spain loves you) as Tom and Katie emerged from the premiere. He was dressed, as usual, in black but she wore a full-length vivid red ball gown. They looked almost regal. They cuddled, they kissed and Tom swept Katie off her feet in a deliberately flamenco gesture. The crowd went wild. Tom's grand European tour had been an undiluted success, and he was left in no doubt of the astonishing reaction he provoked abroad and also his fans' ecstatic approval of his bride-to-be.

Matters did not run as smoothly on his return to New York. It is questionable whether, if Pat Kingsley had still been his agent, he would have appeared on NBC's *Today* show. In 1999 Pat had informed the producer that her client Calista Flockhart was not to be questioned about her weight, and the producer responded that nobody told the *Today* show what to ask or not to ask. So Pat cancelled

Calista's long-standing booking on the show and *Today* didn't cover her film, *A Midsummer Night's Dream* (which desperately needed the publicity). When *Today* subsequently wanted to talk to Cruise and Kidman about Kubrick's *Eyes Wide Shut*, Kingsley told them they couldn't. In retaliation the show's executive producer, Jeff Zucker, sent out an edict to his staff that no Kingsley clients would be allowed on the show.

And so it stayed until two years later when Zucker had departed and Tom was invited on the programme to promote *Vanilla Sky* in an interview with Katie Couric. In the case of *War of the Worlds* his interviewer was the handsome but subtly obdurate host, Matt Lauer. The interview began gently enough with questions about the movie and congratulations on Tom's worldwide publicity, but then Matt put to him what he said the cynics were saying. 'This is Tom Cruise in his forties trying to stay relevant for a younger audience and that's why he's out there talking about this relationship with this lovely young lady.'

Cruise seemed wholly unfazed. 'You know what? There will always be cynics. I have never worried, Matt, about what other people think and what other people say.'

The temperature was raised, however, when Lauer started to deal with Cruise's criticism of Brooke Shields, psychiatry and drugs such as Ritalin, avowing that he had friends who had been helped by it. (More than three million young Americans were taking Ritalin, a controversial stimulant that had proved effective in lessening Attention Deficit Disorder.)

It was hardly surprising that Cruise would beg to differ with Lauer – his views were well known, after all – but the manner in which he did so was pretty aggressive. 'To talk about it in a way of saying "Well, isn't it okay?" and being reasonable about it when you don't know and I do – I think you should be a bit more responsible in knowing what it is.'

The star was even more vehement on the subject of shrinks. 'I've never agreed with psychiatry, ever. Before I was a Scientologist I never agreed with psychiatry. And when I started studying the history of psychiatry, I understood more and more why I didn't believe in psychology.' He went on to admonish the TV star: 'Here's the problem. You don't know the history of psychiatry. I do.'

Curiously, Matt chose to turn the other cheek to this – but the rest of the media didn't.

The following week, Princeton-educated Brooke Shields published a piece on the Op-Ed page of *The New York Times*. 'I was hoping it wouldn't come to this,' she wrote, 'but after Tom Cruise's interview with Matt Lauer, I feel compelled to speak not just for myself but for the hundreds of thousands of women who had suffered from postpartum depression. I'm going to take a wild guess and say that Mr Cruise has never suffered from it. The drugs (mainly Praxil), along with weekly therapy sessions, are what saved me – and my family . . . comments like those made by Mr Cruise are a disservice to mothers everywhere . . . if any good can come of Mr Cruise's ridiculous rant, let's hope that it gives much needed attention to a serious disease.'

Battle lines were drawn, with star Scientologists such as John Travolta, Kelly Preston, Kirstie Alley and Tom

Arnold coming out for Tom and most psychiatrists, not unnaturally, dismissing him. Cruise's suggestion that vitamins and exercise alone can cure postpartum depression were denounced as 'destructive' by Michael M. Faenza, president of the National Mental Health Association. 'Each year, 54 million Americans experience a mental illness, such as depression or an anxiety disorder. Yet, only one-third receive any treatment at all despite very high treatment success rates,' Faenza said in a published statement, adding, 'Cruise's comments could have very damaging consequences for Americans with mental health needs by increasing stigma and shame, discouraging treatment and forcing people to go without needed care.' Scientologists point out, however, that the National Mental Health Association is heavily funded by pharmaceutical companies.

It was just as well, as Tom confessed to Matt, that he didn't care what other people thought of him. His outspoken words and behaviour began to attract an adverse press. *Vanity Fair* ran a red stripe in the corner of its cover with the rhetorical question: 'DOMINICK DUNNE: HAS TOM CRUISE LOST HIS MARBLES?' The veteran columnist noted: 'For Cruise, it was a mistake. I think it's wonderful that his belief in Scientology is so strong, but I resented being preached at by him. Through Scientology, he claimed, he has helped hundreds of people get off drugs with the use of vitamins, and that is very commendable. But when he told Billy Bush that he gets calls at 2 o'clock in the morning from drug addicts who need his counsel, he lost me. Would the Church of Scientology really make the number of the telephone on Tom Cruise's bedside table in his gated and guarded mansion available to a street druggie with a needle in his arm? I don't think so.'

'If vitamins and exercise alone explain why Tom Cruise is so, um, knowledgeable and well-grounded, pass the Prozac,' was the editorial in the *Chicago Tribune*. 'I'll never quite be able to see Cruise the same way. It will take more than Cruise's power of positive thinking to bring back the nice guy with the megawatt smile. Now, he's the zealot who jumps on Oprah's couch like a love-crazed monkey and lectures America about our nasty pharmaceutical habits,' said Paige Newman of MSNBC, the US cable news channel. Even cities joined in. In a debate on 12 July the socialist-controlled municipal assembly of Paris approved a resolution 'never to welcome the actor Tom Cruise, spokesman for Scientology and self-declared militant for this organisation'.

If Katie hoped her whirlwind romance would generate universal approbation, she must have been disappointed. Nicole Kidman cryptically told *Vanity Fair*: 'In terms of your life, if you start to exploit it, then what's real, and what's not? What's yours, and what isn't?' Did she think her former husband failed to draw a clear line between acting and being? Eighty-one-year old Lauren Bacall was more blunt in an interview with *Time* magazine. 'His whole behaviour is so shocking. It's inappropriate and vulgar and absolutely unacceptable to use your private life to sell anything commercially. I think it's a kind of sickness.'

But it wasn't all adverse news. 'It's Tom Cruise that inspired me to come to the US from a small village of China to pursue my own American dream,' said Niki Yan, the young Chinese writer/actress who had just completed a book called *My Love for You, Tom Cruise – a Desperate Chinese Girl's Confession*. 'This insightful and inspirational fun book', ran the publicity, 'is devoted to the person who changed her life forever – Tom Cruise, the Hollywood movie star who has been her hero and role model since she was 11 years old.'

Meanwhile Katie had some good news to impart – or rather Lee Anne DeVette did – on 5 October 2005: Tom and Katie were going to have a baby.

3

ESCAPE TO LOUISVILLE

There is a scene near the beginning of Steven Spielberg's *War of the Worlds*, before the aliens appear, in which Tom Cruise as Ray Farrier and his son Robbie, played by Justin Chatwin, throw a baseball to one another in the front yard. It is something nearly every American father and son must have done since the game became popular. But in this instance there is a vicious undertone, with Ray chucking the ball harder and harder, indicating to us the bitter rift between the two of them.

There was no need for any scriptwriter to invent this scene: Tom Cruise had experienced it himself at the age of nine when confronting his own father. 'Every kid's a little afraid of that hardball when you go from T-ball to hardball. He'd take me out there – and this guy's six foot two – and he'd just start lightly with the ball, then just start hammering this baseball into my glove. Sometimes, if it hit my head, my nose would bleed and some tears would come up. He wasn't very comforting.' His father, Thomas Cruise Mapother III, was clearly something of a sadist. 'He was a bully and a coward. He was the person where, if something goes wrong, they kick you. It was a great lesson in my life – how he'd lull you in, make you feel safe and then, bang! For me it was like, "There's something wrong with this guy. Don't trust him. Be careful around him." There's that anxiety.'

No wonder that,when the family was finally rid of him, Tom also got rid of the Mapother and the IV. Once they went skiing together in Canada. It was a two-hour drive and Tom complained that he was starving. But his father was not prepared to stop. Instead, he suggested they create imaginary sandwiches. 'It was like "What do you want on this sandwich?" "Oh, I want ham on the sandwich." "What else?" "Lettuce." We took a long time to create this sandwich and then we took a lot of time eating it, with chips and soda. But we had nothing.'

To his credit, Tom has subsequently tried to rationalise why Mapother III, an electrical engineer with a degree from Louisville University, Kentucky, had this cruel streak. In other respects he was a sensitive man, happy to write and participate in amateur theatricals. 'He was a very complex individual and created a lot of chaos for the family before we left him. If I came home from a fight and I had lost, then I had to go back out there. "You do it again and you don't lose. Period." And I certainly wasn't the biggest guy on campus. It had to do with his own way of loving me. He was the kind of guy who really got picked on at school a lot when he was growing up. He also had been small, though he ended up being six foot two. People had been quite brutal to him. Inside, I believe he was a really sensitive individual. He just didn't want me to have to go through the kind of pain he had felt in his life. I think that all this was a solution to solving that problem. He was very tough on me in many ways. As a kid I had a lot of hidden anger about that. I'd get hit and I didn't understand it.'

The Jesuits say that if they can have a child for his first seven years, he will be theirs for life. Although Cruise was without his father in his teenage years, his character had already been shaped by what, today, could be considered child abuse. It was a cruel formative experience but a key to understanding what makes Tom tick today. You don't mess with Tom Cruise. Behind that beguiling smile, he is as tough as titanium. Apart from his school yard fights – for which he got suspended – he was a member of the school wrestling team. Many of the activities he enjoys in his adult life – racing cars, flying planes and helicopters, sky diving, scuba diving – are an assertion of this toughness. It appears almost as if he is without fear. And this has spilled over into his dealings with people. Actors, tempered by auditions, rejections and the need to please, tend to be gentle, accommodating people. Cruise is prepared to counter any personal criticism and, as we have seen with Peter Overton and Matt Lauer, can be abrasive to the point of belligerency if crossed.

His father's brutish behaviour did not extend to Tom's three sisters. Thomas Mapother III had married Mary Lee Pfeiffer from Louisiana. Their first daughter, Lee Anne –

who has worked diligently and devotedly for her younger brother for nearly twenty years – was born in Louisville, but Thomas was then posted by General Electric to Syracuse in New York State where Mary Lee gave birth to Marian, Tom (on 3 July 1962) and Cass. Tom's father was something of a dreamer and, later, something of a drinker. He came from a family of Irish immigrants who established themselves as eminent Louisville lawyers. Indeed, his brother, William, was a judge by the age of twenty-nine. But Thomas wanted to do better than that. He wanted to make millions and he felt certain that, with the right breakthrough, he could quit GE and achieve that.

But it never came. Accordingly his frustration increased – and his temper. He dragged the family across America – Cruise estimates he attended fifteen high schools – to pursue his ambition. So the family rarely settled, and this hit his son the hardest. Tom looks back at a time of bullying at different schools because he was the new guy on the block and he was regarded as hick for not being up to fashion with the latest Nikes. He stood up for himself. 'It was either sink or swim and I decided to swim.' Moreover he had severe dyslexia (as did his mother and sisters), which he was reluctant to reveal to each new school – and thus it was some time before he got the necessary Special Needs help. And then it would soon be time to move on again. Schooldays were definitely not the happiest days of his life. 'I can't wait to grow up; it's got to be better than this,' he told his sisters as they walked to school, advising them, 'let's just get through today.'

There were compensations in his life, as he told Barbara

Walters on American TV. His three sisters used to bring girlfriends home and sit eight-year-old Tom on the refrigerator where he would be instructed in the art of French kissing. 'The first time I almost suffocated,' he revealed. The ramifications of this sort of early exposure to women would need a psychiatrist to analyse.

One move, in the early seventies, took the family to Canada, where they lived in a small town on the outskirts of Ottawa. Although Tom was more than proficient at soccer, baseball, wrestling and football, he didn't even know how to skate – and ice hockey was Canada's national game. Then as now, the rules were not always adhered to, and every so often the players would break off for an unruly brawl. Fearing for the features of her small son, Mary Lee told Tom not to play the game. But with the tenacity that was to become his trademark he learnt to skate – forwards and backwards – on a rink before and after school, and made the team. He also escaped injury, but somehow managed to chip a tooth while playing tennis. This, it is said, caused him to be shy with girls in his teenage years, despite the training he had obtained in osculation in his youth.

His mother had acting aspirations and might have prefigured her son's presence in Hollywood were it not for strong Catholic convictions that kept her out of that city of sin. So Mary Lee taught creative drama locally and was able to indulge in amateur dramatics, even founding an amdram society in Canada. Young Tom has memories of attending a rehearsal of a play which she had written and both she and her husband were acting in. He recalled that his father was rather stiff but that his mother was good and 'held herself well' – an art in which he was later to excel. For the time being he contented himself with imitations in the kitchen: Mickey Rooney, John Wayne, W. C. Fields and Daffy Duck.

It was all the more remarkable that his father was prepared to join in the play since the marriage had seriously deteriorated. In the summer of 1974 both parents called their four children into the living room and told them they had decided to get a divorce. It was a shattering blow. Tom went into the garden afterwards to hit a few baseballs with his dad, but tears blinded his eyes. The children's loyalty lay with their mother, however. Fearing she might lose custody of them under Canadian law, Mary Lee ordered them all to pack suitcases secretly and keep them under their beds. Tom even slept with his baseball glove. It was like something out of the Great Escape. A week after the family gathering, she woke the children up at 4.30 a.m. and they tiptoed downstairs with their belongings to the station wagon. Their mother, pent-up with emotion, caned the car to the Canadian border. 'We felt like fugitives,' recalls Tom, which in fact they were: fugitives from their father. Mary Lee made for her mother's house in Louisville, Kentucky. Tom would only see his father twice again.

Coming south from Canada, Cruise to a certain extent reinvented himself. Certainly he dropped his Canadian twang and adopted a Southern drawl. But then, throughout his peripatetic life he had grown used to change – 'In every different place I became a different person.' A more serious problem than acclimatisation in Louisville was cash. Mary Lee had family there and even the Mapothers were sympathetic to her plight, but she was too proud to take more than the most minimal financial help. Cruise remembers those days with pain. 'One time my mother went to apply for food stamps. She saw all these people and she said "I don't care what it takes, I am not coming here again."' The shame of handing over the stamps at the supermarket where she was known was too much for her.

No money was forthcoming from her husband and during their marriage she had stayed at home to bring up the four children – Cass was still barely a teenager. Now they had to grow up fast. All the girls worked after school as waitresses, while Tom worked before school on a 5 a.m. paper round and knocked at the doors of neighbours to get work mowing lawns and clearing up leaves. It filled all his non-school hours. Their mother, meanwhile, attempted to hold down two jobs and, when possible, to work as a saleswoman at weekend electronics exhibitions: she had picked up a little about the subject from her husband.

Christmas at home was now an exiguous affair. With insufficient money to buy presents the Mapother children wrote poems and gave them to each other, and, at a more prosaic level, gave the present of a task – like making somebody's bed for a week. Not that it wasn't festive. Mary Lee still had a desire for the smell of grease paint, something she liberally applied to her son as she dressed him up on one occasion for a sketch as a Victorian lady with lipstick and eye shadow, pearls and a feather hat.

The family house was now a small bungalow in a row of similar dwellings, set back from the road by a large swathe of grass – so there was plenty for Tom to mow. Raymond Wilder, their neighbour, still lives there. He remembers them as 'good people', although by the time Tom was thirteen he already had a competitive streak. 'He was athletic and he challenged me to a game of tennis. I beat him. He threw his racquet down and stomped around and wanted to play again. But I was too old to play again.' Tom admits: 'I didn't have a lot of friends. The closest people around me were my family. I think other people felt a little nervous about me because I had a lot of energy and couldn't stick to one thing. If I worked in an ice-cream store – and I've worked in a lot of them – I would be the best for two weeks, then I was always quitting or getting fired because I was bored.'

Before he hit his teens Tom, in what was now a single-parent family, had acquired another role: that of paterfamilias. This, too, is a key to comprehending what makes him tick. Many people have suggested that his appetite for controlling others and his confidence in doing so was born of his experience with the Church of Scientology; in fact it was probably in place long before he even heard of L. Ron Hubbard. Although younger than Lee Anne and Marian, he was vigorously protective of them. Lee Anne, in a rare interview, told *Vanity Fair* about it in 1994. 'Whenever any of us girls started dating anybody we were serious about, having them meet Tom was a big deal. His opinion has always weighed very heavily with all of us.' It is said that his youngest sister, Cass, was surprised that a boy she had been dating regularly refused to kiss her. Family legend has it that Tom had threatened to kill the poor fellow if he so much as touched her.

It may have been a relief to the girls when they learnt that their brother was going to leave Louisville and continue his education at St Francis near Cincinnati. This was not just any boarding school: St Francis Seminary was run by Franciscan monks, and its prime aim was to prepare young men for the priesthood. It has been perceived by some that this move was intended to enable the newly impoverished Mary Lee to lighten her financial burden by a quarter, for the school would award the son of a Catholic of her means a full boarding scholarship. But it is doubtful that such an extreme step would have been taken on these grounds alone. Did the now teenage Tom realize the full ramifications of what that lay ahead of him? One can only presume that for a short time, at least, he did and that the priesthood, with its vow of chastity, was not abhorrent to him as a way of life. 'I've had such extremes in my life,' he once observed, 'from being this wild kid to studying to be a Franciscan priest in the seminary.'

The school was a stylish collegiate building surrounded by 150 acres, which meant that he was able to indulge in his growing passion for sport. The discipline was stern there – but Tom was made of stern stuff. Pedantic rules that gave pleasure to petty minds – certain areas of lawn were out of bounds, a pupil must place his foot on every step when ascending or descending the stairs – were enforced with a rigour that would have endeared itself to Tom Brown's Flashman. In fact for the more serious infringements of the rules – usually booze and smoking – beatings were not uncommon.

Tom shared a dormitory with twenty other pupils who were roused at 6.40 a.m. every day to follow a strict regime, the most important hour of which was Mass. Father John Boehman, who taught him, remembers clearly: 'He was certainly spiritual. I don't think a boy could come here if he wasn't spiritual. He used to sit in the front of the chapel because he was the smallest boy in his class. He kept his eyes glued on me when I conducted the service.'

Being new to the school, Tom didn't know anybody and remained somewhat of a loner. Father Hilarian Kistner, another former teacher, recalls: 'I would come over to the gym after lunch and he would be playing around with a basketball. We would play a game together shooting hoops.' The place has subsequently closed down due to lack of pupils. But their most famous alumnus has said: 'It was the best year I ever did at school.' Tom only stayed a year because he didn't feel he had a true calling. But it had been for him, as for all the pupils, a necessary experiment. Father Kistner says: 'They came to the school to find out if that's what God wanted them to do.'

Tom himself has subsequently said that he didn't become 'too close' to becoming a priest and recalled: 'We used to sneak out of the school on weekends and go to this girl's house in town, sit around, talk and play Spin the Bottle [a kissing game]. I just realized I loved women too much to give that up.' However his first wife, Mimi Rogers, perhaps with a degree of animosity, did claim that he practised celibacy for almost a year of their marriage while he decided if he wanted to go into the Catholic Church. Later she said she had been joking.

Much more revealing in the quest for what makes Tom tick is his need for a creed, for rules by which he could make sense of and live his life. The fact that Scientology replaced the Church of Rome is possibly subsidiary to the fact that – given he had neither college education nor knowledge of the great philosophers and other beliefs – he craved something that could make sense of the universe to him, and he was to find it in Scientology.

Back in the bosom of his family in seventies' Louisville, Tom seemed to have little room for friends on the outside. In 1986 he told the magazine *Rolling Stone*: 'After a divorce you feel so vulnerable. And traveling the way I did you're closed off a lot from other people. I didn't express a lot to people where I moved. They didn't have the childhood I had, and I didn't feel like they'd understand me. I was always warming up, getting acquainted with everyone. I went through a period after the divorce of really wanting to be accepted, wanting love and attention from people. But I never really seemed to fit in anywhere.' It doesn't take a genius to see that this craving for love and attention was to be sublimated in years to come when the superstar went among the crowds at the premieres of his films. Nevertheless, the image of the lone boy sitting on the steps of the house playing his guitar should be set against the fact that every week he would cross the state border into Indiana to join in a regular hockey game with boys there.

Probably nothing hit Tom harder than the lack of money. The family had had sufficient, and now they had insufficient. Desperate times called for desperate measures. His scholarship had finished and Mary Lee did not make enough to rent a house for herself and her four children so she had to forgo her pride and accept the charity of her family. Tom was sent to live with his aunt and uncle, the Barratts.

Perhaps learning from his brother that Mary Lee was at her lowest, her ex-husband made an attempt to re-enter the life of his family. He even took Tom and Cass to a drive-in movie. But he was too late. Mary Lee had met another man at one of her electronics conventions. Joe South, a plastics salesman, married her and moved the family to the genteel surroundings of Glen Ridge, New Jersey, a town set in a time warp with colonial mansions and a Queen Anne-style railway station serving as the local post office. It was a safe environment, the sort of place where you wouldn't bother to lock your car, and the perfect environment to raise a family.

Tom had mixed feelings about his stepfather: he had usurped the young man's role as chief male, but on the other hand he was happy to bet against him on football games and – surprise, surprise – nearly always lost. It was in New Jersey that Tom enrolled in his fifteenth and final school, Glen Ridge High. Visually, it was an austere concrete block – very different from the mock-Gothic buildings and rolling lawns of St Francis. But it was there that he experienced the decisive moment that would change his life for ever. Tom tried out for the school wrestling team and greatly impressed the coach, Angelo Carbo – enough for the man to suggest that a wrestling scholarship might be the best method of paying his fees at university. 'At first he had to learn a lot about wrestling not having done it before,' Carbo remembers. 'He learnt it here. It is the most demanding sport in high school and he gave it a hundred per cent. It was an advantage to be small – you wrestle fewer upper classmen.'

The notion of college appealed to Tom, who had a long-term plan to become a pilot in the Navy. This was born of his passion for the film *Midway* (released as *The Battle of Midway* in the UK), which had the stellar cast of Charlton Heston, Henry Fonda, Robert Mitchum, James Coburn, Robert Wagner, Edward Albert, Glenn Ford and Toshiro Mifune. It told the story of an epic World War II encounter between the Americans and the Japanese in June 1942. A large Japanese carrier force had attempted to break the Pacific stalemate by attacking the American-held island of Midway in the hope of engaging the American fleet and causing it irreparable damage. But, through ignorance or arrogance, they hadn't factored in the might of the Navy Air Force which, operating off just three aircraft carriers, fought a fierce and valiant three-day battle, decimating the Japanese fleet and turning the fate of the war in the Pacific in America's favour. Guts, heroism and patriotism all impacted on the teenage Cruise, who had an immediate vision of his mission in life. Ironically, it would only be realised on celluloid.

On the eve of an upcoming wrestling match with a neighbouring school, Tom found that he was a pound overweight for the category in which he was to fight. So he decided to lose it by running up and down the stairs at home. Recklessly, without fear or much forethought, he tripped and tumbled to the bottom of the stairs, fortunately not breaking his neck but tearing a tendon in his leg which put an end to his wrestling career and any hope of a university scholarship. The Chinese ideogram for 'calamity' is the same as the one for 'opportunity'. It is a more concise way of expressing the Western clichés 'Every cloud has a silver lining' and 'When one door closes another opens.' In the case of Tom Cruise, all three were to have their most potent proof.

Unable to play sport any longer, he was still anxious to make a good impression at Glen Ridge and volunteered for a part in the chorus of the school production of *Guys and Dolls*. Early in rehearsal the drama teacher was made aware of Cruise's gift for mimicry, which had been honed in the kitchen doing Mickey Rooney and John Wayne impressions for his mother. Could he catch the Brooklyn drawl of Nathan Detroit? Indeed he could, as well as assume the shady Damon Runyon character who ran a floating crap game, a part played by Frank Sinatra opposite Marlon Brando as Sky Masterton in the 1955 film.

His friend and contemporary at Glen Ridge, Tom Tapke Jr, acknowledged that Tom was good but had no inkling of the life that lay ahead of him. 'I would say he was one of the top performers in the play. He just had a lot of charisma and really absorbed himself in whatever he did. He was somewhat of a perfectionist. I remember he had a love for automobiles and I figured he might be a real good mechanic when he got older.'

However, Cruise was getting a standing ovation at each

performance, to the amazement of everybody except Mary Lee. She had always known he was a gifted performer from the early kitchen days. 'He had it in him then. But as he got older he was more into sports and it stopped completely.' Tom was seventeen when his mother and stepfather attended the first night of *Guys and Dolls*. 'I can't describe the feeling that was there,' Mary Lee recalled. 'It was just an incredible experience to see what we felt was a lot of talent coming forth all of a sudden. It had been dormant for so many years – not thought of or talked about or discussed in any way. Then to see him on that stage.'

The experience of playing Nathan totally changed Tom's life. 'I just loved it. At the schools I grew up in sensitivity was not accepted. Especially being the new kid, I felt vulnerable a lot of the time, constantly having to put up these guards to take care of myself. You didn't sit around with the guys and say: "God, that really hurt my feelings, what you said." It was more like: "Yeah, let's go out, have some beers and kick some ass." That was really frustrating to me. So the first time I did the play, all the guys came and saw it and said "Whoa, we didn't know you could do that." I felt good about it. Not just the fact that they saw it, but I felt good about it in my heart.'

It was his epiphany, and he recognised it as such. Perhaps the lines of Nathan's he had to speak each night infiltrated his imagination: 'You only get one chance to roll the dice of life. Make it wisely.' In tandem with his impetuosity was an almost eerie confidence. 'If I could just focus in and do something, I know I've got the creativity and the energy to be great.' And now he knew: he wanted to be an actor.

Another young man once bravely stood up at a lecture in London by the late Rod Steiger and asked for his advice: he would like to become an actor but he was unsure how wise that was. The audience hooted with derision but Steiger stilled them. 'That is a very sensible question and I happen to be able to answer it. If you want to become an actor, don't,' he said, adding, 'if you *have* to become an actor, you hardly need my advice.'

So it was with Tom. 'All of a sudden you are up there and you're doing something you really enjoy and people who never turned their heads or said anything before are now saying: "Gee, look at him." And I said to myself: "This is it." As soon as I started acting I felt from that point on that if I didn't go for this I would be making a terrible mistake.' In retrospect he was to tell Barbara Walters: 'I felt I needed to act the way I needed air to breathe.'

And so he threw himself upon his luck – and talent.

4

HONOUR-DUTY-COUNTRY

Unlike some twentieth-century Dick Whittington, Tom did not expect the streets of New York to be paved with gold. He arrived with a few hundred dollars that he had saved from doing holiday jobs and a loan of $800 from his stepfather, Joe South. He had told Mary Lee and Jack that he was going to give himself three years to crack it as an actor in the Big Apple. If he wasn't earning a living by the time he was twenty he would try something else. Only too aware of his steely determination, they put no obstacles in his way. 'We felt he had a God-given talent,' said Mary Lee. 'We gave him our blessing and the rest is history.' Her enthusiasm for her son's chosen profession was such that she herself drove him to Manhattan in a green Ford Pinto which Tom had purchased for $50. Thanks in part to being observed in *Guys and Dolls*, he had managed to find a female manager, but at seventeen he was too young to sign papers and so Mary Lee was obliged to give her consent as a parent.

Tobe Gibson is still in the job today, looking out for up-and-coming talent. 'The moment he came in he shook my hand and said: "Hi, I'm Tommy." I am very psychic and I said: "I think you're going to be a major star." I never heard him sing, I never heard him read, I never saw him dance. But I knew he could do it.' Tobe knew the name Mapother IV was hardly a star appellation and suggested he drop it. He agreed. 'So,' she says, 'he walked in as Thomas Mapother IV and he walked out as Tom Cruise.'

Having signed on for the status of 'out-of-work actor' he found himself doing the traditional round of menial jobs: he unloaded trucks, waited tables and for more than a year was an assistant superintendent at a building on the Upper East Side at 86th Street and Amsterdam.

The job came to an abrupt end when Cruise's patience ran out. 'People would call me in the middle of the night and say, "My heating's not working." And I replied, "My fucking heating's not working, either." '

He took classes at the Neighborhood Playhouse, a revered institution with alumni ranging from Gregory Peck to Diane Keaton, where Sanford Meisner developed what is known as the 'Meisner Technique', a step-by-step procedure of self-investigation for the actor based on the original principles of the Russian acting pioneer Constantine Stanislavsky. Harold Baldridge, who was running the Playhouse in Tom's time, placed great emphasis on risk, something that undoubtedly helped form the young actor who in later years was prepared to essay *Born on the Fourth of July* and *Interview with the Vampire*.

'The actor in training,' Baldridge taught, 'learns by doing, doing it wrong, doing it wrong probably several times wrong before he or she finds the way that works best for him or her. Learning to act is about stretching yourself, venturing into areas where most people are reluctant to reveal themselves. Most times when you get there, they are not such frightening places at all.' Tom welcomed this approach; he wanted to be pushed. Baldridge passed on the wisdom gained in his career as a director in the theatre. 'If you do nothing but perform, then you are stuck with what you know works and there might be other parts of your instrument that you could use. We give you the opportunity to go out on a tightrope saying: 'I don't know if this is going to work, but I'm going to try it.'' In fact the Meisner Technique might not have stood Tom in good stead in his early attempts at a career. It seems that he was already far too intense without the introspection. When he was up for a commercial where he had to tell kids to 'Eat the Fritos', the general consensus was that he would frighten small children. He never got any commercials. 'I guess I'm a kind of obsessive person when I'm working on something,' he acknowledged.

Cruise was unable to afford a full-time course at the Playhouse but took classes in the evenings. 'It was great,' he recalls. 'I was like an animal in the jungle. I didn't have enough money to buy food, so I'd walk to my classes. Save that $1.25 so that I could buy hot dogs and rice.' His first part didn't too much need of Stanislavsky. He played Herb in a dinner theatre production of *Godspell* in Bloomfield, New Jersey. This was the musical version of the Gospel according to St Matthew that John-Michael Tebelak had written as his master's thesis. In the famous Toronto production, starring the late Gilda Radner and Martin Short, Eugene Levy (who later found fame in *American Pie*) played Herb, who ultimately takes on the role of Jesus himself.

Tobe Gibson maintains: 'He took off immediately. The word was out that there was a hot new actor in town. Phone Tobe Gibson and get Tom Cruise.' But he grew disillusioned with his manager. She would ask him to run errands, fetching groceries or her dry cleaning, so he fired her. She pointed out that he couldn't: he had signed a five-year contract. He pointed out that he had been under-age when he signed it so it wasn't legal – and hired a lawyer to back him up, a mature initiative for one so young and a sign of things to come.

Tobe Gibson remains bitter about this. 'I was very angry. Not angry that he left. That's his privilege. The way he did it was not very nice. You plant a seed and you want to see it flourish into flower.'

A change of manager brought a new horizon. He was flown to Los Angeles to try out for a sitcom. At the end of his audition the casting agent asked him, 'How long are you going to be out here?' Tom recalled: 'I was thinking: "I kicked ass in this reading – this guy's gonna ask me for a callback." And I'm thinking, "He's probably going to want me to come and read again with someone else." So I said:

71

"Oh, about a week or so." "Oh, a week," he said. "Well, get a tan while you're here." It was just so cold I walked out and I thought to myself: "Did that really happen?" I thought it was the funniest damn thing. Tears were coming out of my eyes, I was laughing so hard. I thought "This is Hollywood – welcome, Cruise." ' Back on the East Coast a producer informed him that he was too intense and not pretty enough for television. He should try feature films.

Such setbacks might have made most mortals think about an alternative profession, but they merely quickened Tom's resolve. 'I felt that people rejecting me were there to help me in the long run. Sometimes it hurts, but I truly believe there are parts I am supposed to get and parts I am not supposed to get and something else will come along.' He was right. Franco Zeffirelli did. The exotic Italian director, famed for his work with young people on *Romeo and Juliet* (1968) and *The Champ* (1979), took a shine to Cruise, calling him '*bellissimo*' when they met, and cast him in *Endless Love* (1981), his first feature. Bruce Robinson, who wrote the marvellous *Withnail and I*, had had a small part in Zeffirelli's *The Taming of the Shrew* with Richard Burton and Elizabeth Taylor. Many of the extras were played by Oxford undergraduates, and Zeffirelli's endless pursuit of pretty young Robinson caused him to satirise the director in the character of randy uncle Monty, memorably played by Richard Griffiths in *Withnail*. Tom escaped such a fate, apart from the odd gentle pat, not least because he was only in the film for a day. The lead was played by handsome Martin Hewitt, whose official biography says he beat five thousand other actors to the part.

The *raison d'être* for the saccharine romance that was *Endless Love* was fifteen-year-old Brooke Shields, whose barely clad performance in *The Blue Lagoon* the previous year had grossed the producers $60 million. Brooke had made her name at the age of ten when naked photographs of her were displayed in Manhattan's American Fine Arts Gallery. This was a stepping-stone to her role as a twelve-year-old in a brothel in Louis Malle's controversial *Pretty Baby*. After *Endless Love*, Brooke's film parts did not improve, but she remained in the limelight by appearing in an unbuttoned brown shirt and pair of blue jeans on advertising hoardings with the quote: 'Want to know what comes between me and my Calvins? Nothing'; being married to André Agassi for a couple of years; and having that famous public spat with Tom about the correct treatment for postpartum depression.

Tom's fleeting appearance in *Endless Love* – clad only in cut-off jeans and with a high-pitched voice – was to advise Hewitt to set fire to Brooke's home so he could put it out and gain her family's approval. It misfired: Hewitt nearly incinerated the lot of them. Using his dangerous intensity, psycho Tom advised him: 'Hey, I tried that. Eight years old and I was into arson.' He earned $300 for his day on the movie, more than he would make waiting tables. He was also took off his T-shirt in the film to reveal a well-toned torso which enabled him to earn some much-needed cash as a model. One set of shots with him either shirtless or wearing some very short shorts ended up in the gay magazine *Parlee*. They also ended Tom's desire to earn money from photo-shoots.

His principles set him on the road to penury. He could no longer afford the rent on his shared Manhattan apartment and decided to return home to Glen Ridge. Before he left the city, he went to an open call audition for a new movie called *Taps*. It was 1980, Ronald Reagan had become President and patriotism was in the air, a sea-change from the emollient foreign policy of Jimmy Carter. Twentieth Century-Fox, sensing this, decided to adapt Dervery Freeman's novel *Father Sky* for the screen. The 141-year-old military academy of Bunker Hill is to be closed down and condominiums built on the site. The cadets revolt and, in the great American tradition of the Alamo, defy the construction crews with armed force and resist a siege by the military in an attempt to keep the academy going.

Fox had an ace up their sleeve in the shape of George C. Scott, the former real-life marine, who some ten years previously pronounced his patriotism in front of the Stars and Stripes as General Patton. Patton enjoyed ceremony but Scott, personally, did not: he declined his Best Actor Oscar for the role, insisting that he was not in competition with other actors. But he was prepared to play another general for the studio: Harlan Bache, who runs the academy. The other key player was the officer cadet who was to lead the revolt and, again, Fox had another Oscar winner in place – twenty-year-old Timothy Hutton, who won Best Supporting Actor in Robert Redford's debut film as a director, *Ordinary People* (1980).

The rest of the film was not that hard to cast. Director Harold Becker just had to find a couple of hundred young men who could be trained to act as military cadets. Cruise knew the odds as he looked round the thousand other actors in the rehearsal room, but felt he acquitted himself well in his brief conversations with the director and producer, Stanley Jaffe. Then he hitched home to New Jersey and, so legend has it, as he was walking up the garden path his mother called from the kitchen window saying that his agent was on the phone and he had got a part. True or not, the image is a heartening one.

Cruise's focused intensity was just right for the role of rebellious cadet Billy Harris. In fact it was worth more than that. Two weeks into shooting Becker decided to up him to a much bigger part, that of David Shawn, the true psycho in the revolt who wants to shoot it out to the last cadet standing. It was a similar experience to the one Tom had had in *Guys and Dolls*, but this time he declined: he didn't want to put another actor out of a part and was content to learn from the likes of Scott and Hutton. It was, after all, only his second film. 'I just thought "oh, fuck", I said: "Thank you very much but I don't think I want to play David Shawn." I was in a small role and that is the way I wanted it to be. I was learning so much by just being around, watching everything that was happening. They had already increased my role a lot because I had so many ideas.'

But he was no match for Stanley Jaffe. 'It was a battlefield promotion,' he recalled, 'he just blew me away with his ideas.' The producer informed Cruise that the options open to him were either play Shawn or leave the movie. Tom played Shawn. 'I am very aggressive,' he conceded. 'You've got to be aggressive – there's too much responsibility not to be. I need a creative outlet. Now I get up and work out for forty-five to sixty minutes every day. Discipline is very important to me.'

The military bit was drummed into the actors by having them go through parade ground drill, eating and sleeping with real cadets at Valley Forge Military Academy in Pennsylvania. The repeated mantra of 'honour – duty – country' was also drummed into them from the lips of their commander, General Harlan Bache.

Scott had a reputation as a moody, difficult actor to work with. There is a famous story that one of his co-stars, Maureen Stapleton, confessed to the director of Neil Simon's *Plaza Suite*: 'I don't know what to do, I'm scared of him.' The director replied: 'My dear, *everyone* is scared of George C. Scott!' But on *Taps* he was warm and willing. Although only fifty-four he drew a *Goodbye Mr Chips* sympathy from the audience, not least when his character had a heart attack and was taken to Intensive Care.

Cruise was in awe of him. 'I'm sitting with Patton and General Buck Turgidson from *Dr. Strangelove*, this brilliant actor. And Hutton had given that extraordinary performance in *Ordinary People* and just won an Academy Award. I remember being nervous, really nervous because at that point, when you're young, you just don't want to get fired. You have that "it's so much fun I can't believe this is happening" feeling. And Harold Becker was really smart, taking these young actors and putting us through four weeks of boot camp which helped us and acclimatised us to making movies and working on characters. So we had all that time to get familiar and comfortable with the environment. And he created a bit of tension, you know. I mean, I was a young actor, getting into character and not wanting to leave any stone unturned. But I remember I was nervous, man I was nervous. I thought: "This is too good to be true. I wonder what's going to happen." ' He was also pleased with his $100 daily fee which, he reported home, enabled him to dine off steak and lobster most nights.

The other new boy with a leading part was Sean Penn, but his parents had been in the business – his father a director, his mother an actress. Sean had already worked on Broadway in *Heartland*. Cruise was also impressed by Hutton and Penn since they lived in California and he had only been there once for his unfortunate TV audition. 'I really don't know if me and Penn ever slept during that movie. We'd stay up all night and just talk about the film and about acting. We were really scared and nervous and excited. We didn't know what was going to happen.'

Unlike Scott's general, Cruise's character engendered little sympathy. Shawn was a dangerous fanatic, ramming the sheriff's car and shooting to kill at the National Guard. 'A lot of the character was my childhood,' he said. 'I wasn't intense like that but the character is just fear. That's what he does when he's afraid – he fights.' He emerged creditably from his first major part. Vincent Canby in *The New York Times* wrote: 'Whenever the action of *Taps* begins to flag, we recommend that you keep an eye on the show-stopping performances of Sean Penn (in his movie debut) and Tom Cruise as two of the cadets.'

With the $50,000 he had earned from the movie, Tom took himself off to grandfather Mapother's log cabin by

Lake Cumberland in Kentucky to review his situation. His judgement, however, did not prove as sound as that of his new friend Sean Penn. The latter became Jeff Spicoli, a sempiternally stoned surfer, in Amy Heckerling's hit *Fast Times at Ridgemont High* (1982). It was written by and based on the experiences of *Rolling Stone* journalist Cameron Crowe who was later to play a major part in Tom's life directing him in *Jerry Maguire* and *Vanilla Sky*.

Hubris, perhaps, caused Cruise to take a substantial step in the wrong direction. He was inveigled, possibly by the size of his fee, by the now disgraced Canadian mogul Garth Drabinsky into an R-rated sex comedy, *Losin' It*. The director was Curtis Hanson, who later went on to redeem himself with films like *L.A. Confidential* (1997). 'I didn't know anything about agents or business or scripts,' Tom commented. 'Coming off *Taps* I felt like, "Hey, everyone wants to make a great movie. Everyone who does this loves their work. It's too hard a line of work not to love it." When I first read *Losin' It*, it was worse than the released film. I had this small-time agent who said: "Do it, do it." I worked hard, but it was a terrible time in my life.'

Tom realised the script, based on the story of four American high school boys setting off for Tijuana to lose their virginities in a brothel, was bad, but was constantly reassured that it would be all right on the night. It wasn't. 'You know you're in trouble,' he later observed, 'when it's a comedy and everybody making the movie is miserable.' So was the audience. 'I neither laughed nor smiled for the entire 100 minutes of the film,' one critic observed. The opening joke title card 'A Long Time Ago in a High School

Not So Far Away' gave a substantial hint as to the level of wit that was to follow. The boys pick up a fugitive bride, Shelley Long (the disgruntled wife of a grocery store owner), on the road to Tijuana. Lured into the brothel by pretty prostitutes, they are shocked to find their actual purchases are a good deal older and uglier, with saggy breasts. Tom just can't make out with his but – guess what? – he docs later with Shelley. So his mission is not in vain.

Known in the trade by the few who saw it as 'Porky's in Tijuana', the film was in fact made in the small Californian town of Calexico, near the Arizona state line, which has a large Hispanic population. Nobody was too keen to cross the border to the land of Montezuma's Revenge. According to contemporary accounts, Tom had rather too good a time with the birds and beer on location and back in Hollywood. In retrospect he is somewhat remorseful about this. 'I became an asshole. I was the most unpleasant person to be around.'

Always looking on the bright side, Cruise later said of his 'cable classic': *'Losin' It* is an important film for me. I can look at it and say: "Thank God I've grown."'

5

BRINGING HOME THE HOOKERS

For someone normally so focused, as Cruise was, early 1982 was the worst of times. Moving to Los Angeles at first he roomed with Emilio Estevez and then he rented in the same Hollywood apartment building as the brothers Penn, Sean and Chris (later to make his name in *Reservoir Dogs*, of 1997, but sadly to die young in 2006). 'Those were some wild times,' Tom admitted. 'My life just wasn't full. It was very difficult to find where to go and what to do. Very unsettled. After *Taps* came out I was offered every horror film, every killer-murderer part. I told this one agent I wanted to work with Francis Ford Coppola and he said: "Francis! He's not going to pay you anything."'

The most important asset in Hollywood for any actor, writer or director, apart from a modicum of talent, is a good agent. Agents are the oil that enables the industry to run. They are more responsible than anybody for getting projects off the ground and given the green light. The reason is quite simple: a studio executive gets an annual salary; an agent only gets paid when a film is happening. And the most powerful agency when Tom hit Hollywood in 1982 was Creative Artists which had been founded by Michael Ovitz when he left William Morris with three other agents in 1975. It quickly hoovered up much of the major talent in town.

A youthful agent, Paula Wagner, who had been there for less than two years, was on the lookout for new young talent and her wise eye fell on Tom. They have been together ever since, forming Cruise-Wagner Productions. Paula had been an actress on the East Coast, appearing on the stage in New York and at Yale Rep. Like Tom, she took the big step to Los Angeles and got a part in the NBC mini-series *Loose Change* in 1977. But her own agent noted she was probably better at spotting talent than performing, so she made the switch to agenting. She liked Tom and she liked his philosophy: 'I realised that if you wanted to grow as an actor you have to work with the best. Then you'll be able to have more control over what you do.'

One of the best at that time was Francis Ford Coppola. A few years previously he had scooped up Best Picture, Best Director and Best Screenplay Oscars for *The Godfather Part II*. While there was no doubt about Coppola's merit as a visionary director, unfortunately his success led to excess. *Apocalyse Now* went out of control and spiralled over budget; he virtually had to back his musical *One from the Heart* himself and, as it flopped on release, virtually bankrupted himself. Coppola had to sell his Zoetrope Studios and faced vast debts. In seven short years he had gone from movie majesty to a desperate director looking for work with few studios prepared to trust him with a budget. (A Zoetrope, incidentally, is one of those nineteenth-century horizontal spinning wheels that made images seem to move; ominously it was known as the 'Wheel of the Devil'.)

The Outsiders, by S. E. Hinton, was the Harry Potter of its day. Since its publication in 1967 it had become a classroom fixture. The author, Susie – like J. K. Rowling, she feared a female name on the cover might spoil sales – had little desire for it to be filmed. But a Fresno librarian, Jo Ellen Massakian, sent the book to Coppola, saying he was the man to do it since she and her students had liked *The Black Stallion* so much – she even included a petition signed by thirty of them. (This film had, in fact, been directed by Carol Ballard, who was a bit miffed about any interference from Coppola as executive producer.) Miss Hinton wanted $5000 for the film rights, but Coppola was so cash-strapped that he could only offer $500. She agreed, adding the amusing rider: 'You made the *Godfather* film better than the original book and I don't want you to do that to my book.' In the event, he didn't.

To thin down the numbers of actors that go before the director and producers for final choice, a casting director can see literally thousands of people. Janet Hirshenson did. 'I met all the good-looking boys in the seventeen-to-nineteen age group. Tom came along to the pre-reads for *The Outsiders*. I had seen him in *Taps* and thought he was amazing. He read five different roles and in fact got the smallest, but I was thrilled.'

Coppola had not lost his superb knack for casting as amply demonstrated with *The Godfather*. He began with Matt Dillon, suggested by Hinton, already a bit of a heart-throb from *My Bodyguard* and who had appeared in another Hinton film, *Tex*, and C. Thomas Howell who had been in *E.T.* The other outsiders were relatively unknown but several went on to fame and fortune: Ralph Macchio became the *Karate Kid*; Patrick Swayze starred in *Dirty Dancing* and *Ghost*; Emilio Estevez was in *The Breakfast Club* and *St Elmo's Fire* – and was thus focal in the 'Brat Pack', as his generation was often referred to in the eighties; Rob Lowe also did *St Elmo's Fire* but then an unfortunate video with a minor sullied his reputation for a while until he triumphed in *The West Wing* on television. And the final young man was Tom Cruise.

It wasn't surprising that Emilio Estevez was called to the final audition: he knew Coppola from visits to see his father, Martin Sheen, on the location of *Apocalypse Now*. Tom may not know it but his inclusion was very much due to Fred Roos, the man who had been Coppola's casting director since *American Graffiti* ten years previously, which Coppola produced and George Lucas directed. That film pointed Harrison Ford and Richard Dreyfuss on the road to stardom. After the brilliant casting of the *Godfather* movies. Roos was upped to Coppola's co-producer. Looking back, he says: 'I could see Tom Cruise had talent from *Taps*.'

Coppola instituted a most unusual auditioning process. He asked all of those who made the cut to act out scenes from the movie together, with the actors playing several parts. He videoed the whole process, something which remains a unique insight into the burgeoning talents of the young actors. 'For me it was a lot of fun,' he says today, 'but, looking back, for them it was a life-or-death career chance.' Matt Dillon remembers: 'It was the film everybody wanted to be cast in', and Rob Lowe recalls: 'Nearly every actor under the age of thirty-five was there.'

Some weren't lucky. Helen Slater (who went on to be Supergirl) and Kate Capshaw (who starred in *Indiana Jones and the Temple of Doom* and subsequently became Mrs Steven Spielberg) lost out to Diane Lane for the part of Cherry. Diane stayed with Coppola through *Rumblefish* to *The Cotton Club*. Only just eighteen, she proved herself very assertive in interview, recalling how she fell in love at fifteen, and even more so during the filming, telling Coppola that she wanted to chew gum during the drive-in scene – he wouldn't let her.

In the States there used to be twenty-five cent seats at the back of drive-ins for those who couldn't afford cars – free seats, actually, for the Outsiders who used to crawl under the wire – and Tom had to do the scene where he chatted up Diane and her friend. 'I know you two, don't I? You used to hang around rodeos.' But he was younger than her and, during auditions, in his sleeveless yellow T-shirt and with his teenage lock of hair over one eye, looked younger still. Tom Howell got that part. He also read for Darry Curtis, who is bringing up his two younger brothers after the death of their parents in a car crash. But that was never really on; Patrick Swayze, some ten years older, played Darry in the movie.

In Coppola's rehearsal videos Tom seems always to be smiling but, in the looks department, was eclipsed by Rob Lowe (who was mysteriously cut out of much of the final film.) However, Fred Roos observes that Tom 'was severely intense, not playing around between tests, but getting into character. He took acting very seriously.' Possibly it was this lack of joining in with the rest that caused Tom not to be part of the main pack but to drop down to co-starring billing as a gas station attendant. He did, however, get a role, unlike Mickey Rourke, Val Kilmer and Dennis Quaid.

Tom knew he was in competitive company and was just desperate to get a part, any part. 'I had been offered some leading roles but I didn't think that I could carry a film. I hadn't learned enough and felt that I would be eaten alive. So when they started auditioning for *The Outsiders*, I remember pulling Francis aside and saying: "I'll do anything it takes. I'll play any role in this." And he was nice enough to hire me.' Incidentally, the twelve-year-old playing a young panhandler at a drive-in restaurant didn't have to audition. She went on to be nominated for three Oscars for *Lost in Translation*, winning for Best Original Screenplay. She was Francis' daughter, Sofia.

Coppola flew the assembled cast to Tulsa, Oklahoma where the story was set, but he omitted to tell them that he had a major problem: there wasn't enough money to finance the film. Undaunted, he hired the gym of a local school and rehearsed his actors, videotaping them at work. This suited Tom. 'We had workshops with all the actors in which we would ad-lib and play around. I remembered feeling very good, building up my own instincts on acting and understanding more of each level. Learning more about film acting and what I wanted to do.' Rob Lowe is still in thrall to Coppola's educating skills. 'He would help us with the technique of being an actor. He might say, "You're nervous in this scene and you want to go to the bathroom." He would provide us with props and wardrobe in rehearsal so we could find the character.' Patrick Swayze states unequivocally: 'My career wouldn't be where it is now without him.'

The Outsiders, originally set in the sixties, is about gang warfare between the upmarket 'Socs' and the very down-market 'Greasers'. On location Coppola housed the Socs in expensive rooms and the Greasers in drab ones, with a much lower living allowance. Tom had the misfortune to be a Greaser. Nevertheless there was a lot of fun and games in the Excelsior Hotel when the young men were not on set. Groupies thronged to the place, as they would for visiting pop stars. Within the group pranks were not uncommon: Tom managed to get into Diane Lane's room and put jam on her lavatory seat. Several years later, after *Top Gun* had made Tom a household name, he was approached by a bellman at the Chicago hotel where he was staying who informed him he had been working at the Tulsa Excelsior Hotel when Tom and the others were there. The star put his hands to his head in shame: 'Oh, my God!'

The story of *The Outsiders* is streetfighting turned into a tragedy with a murder, a boy burnt to death and another shot by the police. Towards the end of the movie, for no very persuasive reason, the Socs and the Greasers agree to have a fight without weapons in a wood. It rained heavily that night, and the resulting brawl has echoes of Monty Python's Batley Townswomen's Guild's re-enactment of the Battle of Pearl Harbor, which had taken place in a muddy field a decade earlier. Tom fought well but broke a thumb. Nevertheless he bravely jumped up and down at the end of the battle to celebrate the Greasers' win, his hands high in the air in a pre-echo of Oprah's sofa.

Coppola didn't give him much to do in the movie, and his character was rarely in the foreground. Tom was persuaded to remove the cap from the tooth which he had broken at tennis, so his developing smile was not yet an attractive asset. But he did manage both a forward somersault and later a backward one across the front of a truck. Fred Roos maintains that Tom was so nervous about the stunt that he discharged his lunch in the lavatory. Nevertheless Roos has a very definite memory of Cruise at that time. 'We all knew he was going to be a star.'

The final film held little appeal for an adult audience, as is exemplified by the major reviews: 'A laugably earnest attempt to impose heroic attitudes on some nice small characters' – *New York Times*; 'A teary teen soap opera' – *Newsweek*. But, like the original novel, it was for kids rather than grown-ups, and it found its niche market. It was, Coppola now says, 'a *Godfather* for children'. Coppola got his $10 million from Chemical Bank, with a completion guarantee from Britain's National Film Finance Corporation and strict orders to stay on budget. He did, and the film went on to gross more than $25 million in the United States alone.

Coppola had the sensible idea of remaining in Tulsa with the same crew and many of the cast and shooting another Hinton book, *Rumblefish*, a dark tale of two dysfunctional brothers. During the shooting of *The Outsiders* he had scripted the novel with the author. He worked from a huge silver trailer with his editing equipment inside, so that he would be able to cut *The Outsiders* in the evenings. Curiously Mickey Rourke, who had been turned down for *The Outsiders*, was cast as the lead – the Motor Cycle Boy – with Matt Dillon playing his third Hinton film in a row. It was assumed that other actors would be available, as would Diane Lane and Sofia Coppola who were given roles.

But Tom chose not to be available, not even for the great Coppola. Paula Wagner had read a good script at CAA which she thought was right for his first lead. The writer/director hardly fulfilled Tom's dictum that 'to improve as an actor you have to work with the "best" – Paul Brickman's main contribution to American screenwriting was *The Bad News Bears Break Training* some six years earlier – but, there again, Brickman didn't want Cruise as his leading man, Joel. 'This guy for Joel?' he vouchsafed to his producers. 'This guy is a killer – let him do *Amityville III*.'

Possibly Tom's cause was not helped at his audition by the fact that he was still in 'Greaser' mode with oiled hair, chipped tooth and even an Oklahoma accent. The part he was reading for was a clean-cut preppy schoolboy from the affluent outskirts of Chicago. Moreover, due to his dyslexia, when asked to read by Brickman he made a hash of it. He sensed the director was about to say, 'Thanks but no thanks', and pleaded to have another try, going again from the top. This time he managed to make Brickman laugh – at the dialogue the director had written himself.

Whatever misgivings Brickman may still have harboured, Tom had a new and infinitely more powerful friend in court: David Geffen. The music business billionaire had made his fortune by spotting and promoting talent. Joni Mitchell, Crosby, Stills, Nash and Young, the Eagles and Cher all owed their success largely to him. Now another name was added to that list – Tom Cruise. Geffen spotted the considerable potential in the young actor, and *Risky Business* was produced by Geffen Pictures for Warner Bros. Thanks to him, Tom was called back a second time.

'I tested for it at six in the morning. I was shooting nights and so I flew in late, got in at 1 a.m. and I had to leave by 10 a.m. to shoot the rumble scene in *The Outsiders* that night. My hair was greasy and I was heavy. But now I was wearing this preppy maroon Adidas shirt. My arms were huge. I walk in and see this stunningly gorgeous woman sitting there looking at me and I'm thinking: "Oh, my God." Rebecca had already been cast. They wanted to see the two of us together. I tested and, to make a long story short, we didn't test that well. Paul just believed in me. I told him exactly what I was going to do. We talked about it for a long time and he trusted me.'

The gorgeous woman was twenty-one-year-old Rebecca De Mornay, and this was only her second film. Although born in southern California, she had had an unusual upbringing having attended the unconventional Summer-field School in England where pupils were free to choose whether or not to attend classes and would meet weekly to decide on the school rules. It did Rebecca no harm; subsequently she graduated 'summa cum laude' – but in German from Kitzbühel School, high in the Austrian Alps. Back in the States she studied acting at the Lee Strasberg Institute and then served an apprenticeship at Francis Coppola's then still solvent Zoetrope Film Studio, where she was co-opted as an understudy in the ill-fated *One from the Heart*. Beautiful and intelligent, De Mornay was ripe for stardom and the part of Lana, the tart with the heart, was ripe for her.

Risky Business was an original, clever and amusing script, a subtle satire on capitalism, honed by the writer/director's experience as a story analyst at Paramount and Warner Bros. It addresses all the angsts of teenagers in their last year at high school: the future, pleasing their parents, getting into university and, most important of all, getting laid. Joel's parents are going away for a few days from their house in an affluent Chicago suburb, and he manages to achieve the last when he calls up a hooker and the dreamlike Lana arrives, the answer to all his prayers. Unfortunately the cost of all his prayers is $300, which he sadly lacks, and it is not long before he is being pursued by her pimp while managing to plunge his father's Porsche into Lake Michigan. Such factors, as one might imagine, have an adverse affect on his academic work, as well as landing him in debt. Much emphasis at school is put on the Future Enterprise scheme and the alert Lana shows him the way to turn on a dime by rounding up her fellow harlots and turning his home into a brothel for the night. His wealthy

The young Tom Cruise

In *Taps* with Timothy Hutton and Sean Penn.

With Emilio Estevez: co-star in *The Outsiders*, leader of The Brat Pack and best man at Tom's wedding to Mimi Rogers.

Coppola's *The Outsiders*: Emilio Estevez, Patrick Swayze, Ralph Macchio, Matt Dillon, C. Thomas Howell, Rob Lowe and Tom Cruise.

His first hit – 'Risky Business' (1983) with future girl-friend Rebecca DeMornay.

The big breakthrough – *Top Gun* (1986) with Kelly McGillis

"I feel the need, the need for speed." Practising for the Firestone Firehawk Grand Sports Race, 1987.

With Paul Newman,
Best Actor, *The Color
of Money*, 1986

With Stanley Kubrick and Sydney Pollack on the set of *Eyes Wide Shut*, 1999

Mr and Mrs Tom Cruise (May 1987-February 1990). Born Miriam Spickler, her parents were Scientologists and she was previously married to Scientology auditor, Jim Rogers.

With Dustin Hoffman, Best Actor, *Rain Man*, 1988

With fellow vampire, Brad Pitt, in *Interview with the Vampire*, 1994.
Pitt: 'Tom and I walk in different directions. He's North Pole and I'm South.'

Jack Nicholson. Nominated for Best Actor, *A Few Good Men* 1992

Born on the Fourth of July, 1989 – with Vietnam vet,
Ron Kovic, whom he portrayed.

middle-class chums turn up in their droves and the house gets 50 per cent of the take, giving Joel a net profit of $8000. Does he get into Princeton, as his father wishes, and does he get Lana's love? In the version we see he does; in the script Paul Brickman wrote and shot he doesn't. Tom recalls: 'Instead of the scene outside where Rebecca says, "Do you want to come over?" she sits on my lap in a restaurant and it just ends on the sunset background coming up and me stroking her hair with her head on my shoulder. I say, "Isn't life grand." It was really nice. They thought it was too sardonic. Geffen Films felt it was a bummer. So we made it more specific and upbeat.'

Brickman initially refused to shoot the ending whereby Joel was admitted to Princeton. In the original script he failed. This might have been more logical since the admissions officer, improbably, arrived at Joel's house during the night of the hookers. But whether it was Joel's unique business enterprise or the fact that the academic might have been pleasured by one of Lana's colleagues is open to interpretation. Whatever, the director eventually succumbed to the pressure from the producers and Warner Bros to have a feel-good finish – just as he had succumbed in the casting of Tom as Joel. The part had been offered to Timothy Hutton, who turned it down in favour of playing the title role in Sidney Lumet's film of E. L. Doctorow's *Daniel* – an unwise move, as it transpired; his career never soared back to the heights of *Ordinary People*.

Although he didn't know it at the time, Tom had some tough competition in getting the part. Tom Hanks and Nicolas Cage were among the actors who had auditioned.

But once he got it, he nailed it perfectly to play a young man who was semi-innocent, semi-naïve but with an instinct for survival. The script owed not a little to the style of *The Graduate*, with the camera viewing Joel's parents through the boy's eyes, and Cruise's performance had the endearing, suppliant passivity of Dustin Hoffman's. Both were to act together five years later in the Oscar-winning *Rain Man*.

The movie is replete with fun moments, such as Joel eating his frozen TV dinner – frozen – or when Dad's Porsche is in the garage being emptied of Lake Michigan and fish swim from it on to the floor. And droll lines that address the central dilemma of the schoolboys: 'I've got a mid-term tomorrow and I'm being chased by Guido, the killer pimp,' wails Joel's chum Miles. The young men are persuaded to lose their various virginities because 'College girls can smell innocence.' When Joel complains to Lana that her co-harlots are wearing his mother's clothes, she calmly replies: 'What's wrong with that?' he shouts back: 'I don't want to spend the rest of my life in analysis.'

But the scene that marked Cruise out for stardom was the one where he danced around the living room clad in his shirt and Fruit of the Loom underpants, miming to Bob Seger's 'Old Time Rock and Roll'. This was seen by a vast audience, as it was used on the television advertisements for the film and canonised when Ron Reagan Jr did it on *Saturday Night Live*. In fact the musical sound track cleverly enhanced the film's appeal to both the young and the not-so-young generation. David Byrne and Tangerine Dream played the original music, and there were accompanying tracks from Prince, Phil Collins and Tom Jones. The hand of David Geffen was visible on the tiller.

Tangerine Dream proved the perfect background to one of the other highlights of the movie: the love scene between Tom and Rebecca on the famous Chicago L-train. It wasn't in the original cut – they had previously made love against a blue screen background. 'It just didn't work,' Cruise recalls. 'It just wasn't erotic. I remember it was just uncomfortable.' So Brickman had to beg for more money to do the revised version. It was worth it.

Tom's interpretation of the movie also has a serious side to it. 'It's about today's capitalistic society. Do the means justify the ends? Do you want to help people or do you just want to make money? Joel is questioning all of that. The movie is Joel's exploration of society, how he gets sucked into this wild, capitalistic ride.'

The film was widely praised by the critics and the local Chicago one, Roger Ebert, put his finger on precisely why it worked. 'Risky Business is a movie about male adolescent guilt. In other words, it's a comedy. It's funny because it deals with subjects that are so touchy, so fraught with emotional pain, that unless we laugh there's hardly any way we can deal with them. . . . I became quietly astounded when I realized that this movie was going to create an original, interesting relationship involving a teenager and a hooker. The teenage kid, in what will be called the Dustin Hoffman role, is played by Tom Cruise, who also knows how to imply a whole world by what he won't say, can't feel, and doesn't understand. This is a movie of new faces and inspired insights and genuine laughs. It's hard to make a good movie and harder to make a good comedy and almost impossible to make a satire of such popular but mysterious obsessions as guilt, greed, lust, and secrecy. This movie knows what goes on behind the closed bathroom doors of the American dream.'

It is not at all unusual for the male and female leads in a romantic movie to translate their relationship into real life and, after initial hesitation, so it was with Tom and Rebecca. Not, of course, while they were making the movie. 'During the film, we did have a strong affinity for each other,' Rebecca concedes, 'but it was, like, not the time. Tom seemed to be looking for somebody to love and somebody to love him back. He really is a pure person. There's something that's earnest and virtuous about him that is quite rare.'

Risky Business was made for $6 million and grossed nearly $65 million at the box-office. So by the end of 1983 Tom's asking price had shot up and he had embarked on his first serious public relationship which was to last more than two years. His stardom was to last more than twenty-two – and is still going strong.

6

CHILD OF THE FOREST

In terms of box-office, $63 million US gross, *Risky Business* was the tenth most profitable film of the year. It was some way behind *Star Wars VI: The Return of the Jedi*, which grossed more than $300 million and *Terms of Endearment*, which made $100 million and got an unaccountable number of Oscars, but not far behind the latest Bond, *Octopussy*, or *Staying Alive* or *Mr Mom* (with Tom Hanks).

In terms of quality, Hollywood had not, in 1983, surrendered to popcorn movies to feed the multiplexes. Mature, thoughtful films were still being written and made: Lawrence Kasdan's *The Big Chill*, about a university reunion; *The Right Stuff*, based on Tom Wolfe's perceptive book about selecting the astronauts who would go to the moon; and *Silkwood*, starring Meryl Streep – Mike Nichols' film about the plutonium plant activist Karen Silkwood who was found dead.

Films like these were manna for the critics and adult cinemagoers alike, but presented twenty-year-old Cruise with a problem. His avowed intention to work with the best was thwarted by the fact that the best were occupied with preparing films like *The Killing Fields*, *A Passage to India*, *Romancing the Stone*, *Amadeus* or *Indiana Jones and the Temple of Doom*, which had no place for a juvenile lead. So he settled for second-best – which was a mistake. *All the Right Moves* was based on an article by Pat Jordan, who co-wrote the screenplay (her first and last) with Michael Kane whose provenance was *Jaws III* and *The Legend of the Lone Ranger*. The director was Michael Chapman who had been nominated for an Oscar as cinematographer for Martin Scorsese's *Raging Bull* but had none of his master's magic at the helm. This was, in every way, a wrong movie.

The film, a predictable story of a high school football player who needs to get a college scholarship or else face a lifetime working in the steel mills, was shot in Johnstown, Pennsylvania. There was a poignant irony here: the Bethlehem Steel Corporation had recently laid off two-thirds of its workforce so there were abundant unemployed men to act as extras, especially in the stadium scenes.

Tom received his first million-dollar pay day for the movie, although it was a poor investment for Lucille Ball Productions and Twentieth Century-Fox, making only a quarter of the gross that *Risky Business* did. But Cruise's acting reputation was enhanced. I used to have a post-dinner drink with the American critics in the bar of the Majestic Hotel during the Cannes Film Festival, and both

Kathleen Carroll of the *New York Daily News* and Roger Ebert of the *Chicago Sun-Times* told me then he was the rising star to watch out for. In private, he remained very close to his sisters and mother, Mary Lee. And he was very proud that he had been able to repay the $800 loan to his stepfather, Joe South, to whom he became increasingly close. But his estrangement from his real father was to come to a tragic conclusion.

On 9 January 1984 Thomas Cruise Mapother III died of cancer. He was only forty-nine. With the exception of one meeting he had been estranged from his children for nearly a decade, since that midnight flit. It seemed that he had become something of an itinerant hippy in California, hoping to earn a living as an inventor. Certainly his appearance – long grey hair and beard – did nothing to belie that when Tom and his sisters visited him in a Louisville hospital when his condition became terminal. But he refused to tell them about himself, promising Tom that when he got better they would go out for a steak and a beer and then he would reveal all.

But that was not to be. He did reveal that he had followed Tom's rise in the film firmament, as was evidenced by the pictures of his son on his hospital wall. But he had never actually seen one of his movies. 'When I saw him in pain, I thought, "What a lonely life,"' Tom recalled. 'It was sad.'

A writer from the London magazine *Time Out*, asked Tom what effect his fractured upbringing had had on him. The actor was unsure. 'Would I have liked a happier childhood and a loving father? Would I have had it differently? Maybe I wouldn't be here today if it had been. There are no accidents. I don't know. But I don't like pain, just like anybody else doesn't. I feel it.'

Pain or no pain, his career went marching on – alongside the careers of his remarkable peer group, for 1962 had been a vintage year for future film stars. Matthew Broderick was born in March, Emilio Estevez in May, Ally Sheedy in June, Tom Cruise in July, Demi Moore and Andrew McCarthy in November. Twenty-two years later four of them went off to Washington to make *St Elmo's Fire* for Joel Schumacher, a benchmark eighties' youth film about a club of recent graduates who are finding their materialist ambitions hard to fulfil in the real world and drown their sorrows in St Elmo's bar, occasionally abandoning their drinks for pot or sex or both. The exceptions were Matthew Broderick and Tom Cruise who, having established themselves as leading men (Broderick in *War Games*), did not want to get lost in ensemble pieces.

Unfortunately, leading parts in 1984 were primarily going to another generation: Robert Redford in *Out of Africa*, Michael Douglas in *The Jewel of the Nile*, Harrison Ford in *Witness*. And even to those of a generation before that: *Cocoon* starred Hume Cronyn, who was seventy-four and Jack Gilford and Don Ameche, both seventy-seven. But there was work in the overseas fantasy world for the younger stars. Broderick ended up in Italy in *LadyHawke* as Phillipe Gaston, a medieval Frenchman who has adventures with a pair of lovers, the male one of which becomes a wolf at night, while the female is a hawk during the day. This proved quite an incompatibility problem. Tom found himself in England in an enchanted forest full of unicorns, fairies and goblins. The British director, Ridley Scott, had himself enchanted Cruise with a magical pitch about this battle between good and evil, backed up by 411 storyboards of how sumptuous the movie would look. 'It's not a film of the future or the past,' Scott said. 'It is not even a story of now. The conflict between darkness and light has been with us since the creation and will be with us until eternity.'

If the story had been as good as the storyboards then *Legend* itself might have proved enchanting, but Scott was enamoured of an American writer called William Hjortsberg – especially his novella entitled *Symbiography* about a man who dreams for a living. The two of them cobbled together their fairy tale, inspired by sources as rich as Cocteau's *Beauty and the Beast, Bambi, Snow White and the Seven Dwarfs* and *Tristan and Isolde*. Unfortunately the result measured up to none of them.

Had he made *Tristan and Isolde*, as he had initially intended to, Scott would have found the essential emotional essence that *Legend* lacked. He had long wanted to film the story of Tristan and Isolde – Tristan escorts Isolde from Ireland so that she can marry his uncle, King Mark of Cornwall, but falls fatally in love with her. Tom would have been excellent in the part. Scott commissioned a screenplay from Gerald Vaughn-Hughes, and Paramount green-lit the project. He was going to shoot it in the Dordogne in France and give the characters a roughened cowboy look. But when he and his producer, David

Puttnam, saw *Star Wars* in 1977 he felt, for some inscrutable reason, that George Lucas had beaten him to it in character design and, surprisingly, abandoned the idea. Now it has gone ahead with Kevin Reynolds directing and Scott as executive producer. Tristan is played by James Franco, who made his name portraying James Dean on American television.

But the character Ridley wanted Tom to play was the less exotically named Jack O'the Green Forest. Cruise had a great admiration for the English director's work. *Alien* had been a visual breakthrough in space films with the arresting design of the planet and the monster by the Swiss artist, H. R. Giger. Even *Blade Runner*, which appealed to few people in its first incarnation, had dazzled him with its design. Scott, bruised by its rejection, retreated into his original profession of directing television advertisements and stunned the States with a two-minute version of George Orwell's *1984* which filled the coveted January 1984 Superbowl slot. It launched the Apple Mac.

Cruise recalls that the first thing the director did when he arrived at Pinewood Studios in Buckinghamshire was to take him to Theatre 7 and show him the 1970 François Truffaut film, *L'Enfant Sauvage – The Wild Child*. It was based on a true story, the memoir of Dr Itard, who is played by Truffaut himself. In 1798 a child aged about ten or twelve emerged from a forest in central France. He was unable to speak or even walk but moved on all fours as if he had been raised by animals – as Romulus and Remus were allegedly brought up by wolves. Itard confounded expectations by eventually turning him into a verbal human.

So it was with Jack; although human, he was a child of the forest, and Tom evolved movements, jumps and alert gestures of the head that belonged more to the animal kingdom. It was an inventive performance. But while he was a natural in the part, they also had to find an ingénue who could dance and sing to play Princess Lili, his love interest. Scott wanted an unknown and after a prolonged search settled on seventeen-year-old Mia Sarapocciello, a Brooklyn girl who had never acted professionally. Prudently, she shortened her name to Mia Sara.

The plot, for what it's worth, revolved round the quest of the Lord of Darkness (Tim Curry of *The Rocky Horror Picture Show* – red skin, huge horns and cloven hooves) to kill all the unicorns in the forest and destroy daylight. He fails. To be fair, the film was ahead of its time – judging by the reception that fantasy films like *The Lord of the Rings* have recently received.

The English crew liked Tom. He was charm incarnate, giving Mia as much help as he could. Geoff Freeman, who was unit publicist on the movie, says he was rather reluctant to go out and about too much as he had had to grow long hair for the part and felt self-conscious about it. His relationship with Rebecca De Mornay continued, but she was only able to visit him a couple of times since she was making no fewer than three films that year – *The Trip to the Bountiful*, *Runaway Train* and *The Slugger's Wife*. Other than that, it appeared that he lived a fairly monastic existence with none of the entourage he has today. Geoff recalled that he would come into his office – ostensibly to go through the stills, over which he had sufficient status to have approval – but really for a chat about the movie or sport or what was happening back in Hollywood.

What was not in dispute was that the film, like all of Scott's, looked extraordinary. Scott had visited the giant redwoods in northern California where George Lucas' Ewoks came out to play but decided he wanted the control afforded him by a studio set. It took fifty builders fourteen weeks to construct the forest on the famous 007 stage at Pinewood Studios. The columns in the Lord of Darkness's home were twenty-five feet high and nine feet in diameter. For winter scenes the vast set was coated in polystyrene and decorated with fifteen hundred icicles made out of several hundred pounds of paraffin wax.

Ridley Scott pioneered the use of video playback on the film set, so that he could instantly review a take. Geoff Freeman recalls him coming on to the set on the first day of the winter shoot and looking at the screen of the monitor which was showing the virgin snow forest. 'Absolutely perfect,' Ridley observed. 'Pity we have to spoil it with actors.' Or dialogue. Here is the love scene between Jack and Princess Lili after he has shown her the precious unicorns and she has sung him a little song.

Jack: When I get to heaven, I know just how the angels will sound.

Lili: Do you flatter all the girls like that, Jack?

Jack: It's the truth.

Lili kisses Jack sweetly. He doesn't respond.

Lili: Are you afraid of my kiss?

Jack: I'm afraid you'll break my heart.

Lili: Then still your heart. . . . You are dear to me as life itself.

Jack: Only because I amuse you. . . . Like some trained bear!

Lili: That's not true! I do love you, Jack. You must believe me!

Jack: And if I do so no good can come from it. I am only a Green Man, without land or title, no name or wealth to bring you.

It might have been preferable if Jack, like Truffant's Wild Child, had remained mute for the most part.

A month before the end of shooting on *Legend*, a remarkable thing happened. The 007 stage burned down. Fortunately, the cast and crew had taken a break for lunch. It was known that the stage had poor ventilation, and there was a build-up of gas fumes which could not escape: they were ignited by a freak electrical spark, and the vast polystyrene snowscape went up in smoke. A major constituent of polystyrene is the highly inflammable hydrocarbon pentone. Tom joined the rest of the crew as they watched fire-fighters try to save some of the forest but in vain. The ever-pragmatic Ridley looked at his watch, turned to Tom and said: 'Well, I'm off to play some tennis. Do you want to meet up for dinner later?'

In the event, the disaster proved less damaging than people had at first feared. The ingenious art director, Assheton Gorton, went through Ridley's remaining storyboards with him and built the necessary smaller sections of the set on other stages. They lost only three days' shooting and a few shots.

Much more of a disaster was the American sneak preview. Ridley had brought his 150-minute cut of the film down to 113 minutes, but even that failed to hold the audience's interest. On these preview occasions an independent company hands out sheets of paper to the audience with questions such as 'Would you recommend this film to a friend?' and 'What scene did you dislike most?' In the industry they are known as the 'cards of death'. Worse still, sixteen people, a 'caucus group', are invited to stay behind to discuss the film with a trained market researcher. They become self-appointed critics, infinitely more brutal than the professional newspaper ones. As Ridley ruefully observed later: 'The fate of the film was decided by some pot heads.'

His nerve had been badly damaged by the failure of *Blade Runner*, and he agreed with Universal to cut the picture down to 98 minutes and replace Jerry Goldsmith's score with a hipper one by Tangerine Dream who had provided music for *Risky Business*, thereby emphasising to fans that it was a Tom Cruise picture. Unfortunately this had little effect. When *Legend* eventually crept out in the States it grossed only $15 million. Tom shrugged his shoulders, saying: 'If it ain't on the page, it ain't on the stage. You have to learn what scripts not to do.'

But as his reputation grew over the years, so did a renewed interest in *Legend*. A well-run fansite on the web led to a *Legend* Ultimate Edition DVD being released in May 2002 and, three years later, a two-disc DVD with not only Scott's commentary but Jerry Goldsmith's score, a song by Brian Ferry and all the missing scenes. As the authors of the site wrote: 'Thank you to all the *Legend* fans around the world who kept the faith and made their voices heard.'

7

THE NEED FOR SPEED

Here's the amazing thing about *Top Gun*, the film that elevated Tom Cruise from a star into a superstar. It was the biggest grosser of 1986 and one of the biggest of all time, and broke the world record for VHS sales on advance orders alone. But nearly everybody in Hollywood had turned it down – writers, actors, directors and, especially, the studios.

In May 1983 producer Jerry Bruckheimer read an article by Ehud Yonay entitled 'Top Guns' in *California* magazine. It was about fighter pilots at the Miramar Naval Air Station near San Diego, nicknamed 'Fightertown USA'. Only the crème de la crème were admitted to this elite establishment. 'I thought it was like *Star Wars* on Earth,' Bruckheimer recalls. His producing partner, Don Simpson, was less than interested, thinking this was some cowboy piece. But eventually he was persuaded to read it, and became as enthusiastic as Jerry.

They tried, with little success, to get established writers interested. So they had breakfast – as one does in Hollywood – with Jack Cash and Jim Epps, who had never even had a film made but had circulated half-a-dozen scripts around town. 'They pitched us eight ideas and one was *Top Gun*,' Epps remembers (Jack Cash died in 1990 of an intestinal ailment). 'I had my private pilot's licence and I thought, "this might be interesting – I might get a ride in a navy jet out of it."' He did.

'When I went to Miramar Naval Air Station everything changed. I wanted to be them. I told my wife that if I was younger I would have enlisted. Flying in an F-14 Tomcat is like nothing you have ever felt before in your life. It's like being 28,000 feet up in a little sports car, an MG. Your instinct is to hold on to something, but the lever beside you operates the ejection seat.' And it was there that he formulated what the film was about. 'The pilots spoke a language I couldn't understand, all the time spitting out these words and phrases like "He's my Rio" – Radar Intercept Officer, or "ACM" – Aerial Combat Manouvering. It's also a great athletic thing, and this was the key to the film. It's about sports. Who's the best?'

It was essential to get the Navy's cooperation to make the movie: this was before the era of computer-generated imagery in film post-production, and when it came to F-14s it was the real thing or nothing. The Navy had disliked Richard Gere's *An Officer and a Gentleman* – although it did wonders for recruiting – and so were wary of the Hollywood view of their way of life. Simpson and Bruckheimer flew to Washington to give their assurances to naval top brass. Pete 'Viper' Pettigrew, a retired officer, was assigned as technical adviser and to watch over them. As a lieutenant commander he had flown F-4J Phantoms off the USS *Kitty Hawk* in the Vietnam War and had shot down several North Vietnamese MiG-21 fighters.

Now fully versed in the subject, Cash and Epps were convinced they had an exciting, commercial movie but, as Epps sadly relates: 'Paramount didn't like it. Their response was: who wants to see a movie with too many planes?' The studio had funded the initial development of the script, but now the top executives cooled on the idea. This was especially galling for Simpson as he had been President of Worldwide Production for Paramount until he was eased out in 1983, and now it was his former assistant, Jeffrey Katzenberg, who was in his job and telling them he was putting the movie into turnaround. (Turnaround is one of those technical Hollywood terms, meaning that the studio which nurtured and paid for your project suddenly turns against you and decides to hang you out to dry from a very high clothes line.)

Simpson was a man known for his excess – whether it be drugs or alcohol – and was also known never to take no for an answer. So, at a meeting with Katzenberg and the studio boss, Michael Eisner, he fell to his knees and begged them to change their minds. Eisner, in a rare moment of compassion, said to Katzenberg: 'If they're this desperate, we've got to let them keep developing it.' So Cash and Epps continued rewriting the script until they reached the seventh draft when, Epps recalls, 'The movie died.'

So that was the end of *Top Gun*. Or would have been had

not Eisner and Katzenberg left Paramount for Disney at the end of 1984. Ned Tanen, who had been President of Motion Pictures at Universal until 1982, after a spell producing Brat Pack movies, returned to the fold as President of Paramount Motion Pictures.

Normally when a new guy takes over he kills all the existing projects of his predecessors in order to make his own reputation. But Ned had already proved himself. Besides, he found the cupboard was bare. He knew – everybody knew – that Simpson and Bruckheimer could pull commercial rabbits out of their hats with the most improbable stories. Humble girl welder becomes star dancer? Yes, with *Flashdance* in which they made Pittsburgh look like Las Vegas and coated the movie in fifteen musical numbers, the most notable being 'What a Feeling!' And *Beverly Hills Cop*, in which a humble Detroit detective tears apart Tinseltown. The role was intended for Sylvester Stallone, who pulled out at the last minute – so the producing duo hired Eddie Murphy, guaranteed to appeal to the broad spectrum of American cinemagoers. The result was $250 million at the box-office. So when Tanen met them for lunch he simply asked: 'What have you got?'

They outlined *Top Gun*.

'How much?' was his next question.

'Fourteen million dollars.'

'Go and make it.'

At that point, one might think, all their troubles would be far away. But, if the word in Hollywood is to be believed, both John Carpenter and David Cronenberg turned down the chance to direct, Matthew Modine passed on the leading role and Val Kilmer bluntly refused to be in the picture.

Simpson and Bruckheimer had already noticed that much British directing talent lay in commercials. Having seen Hugh Hudson make a good job of *Chariots of Fire*, they hired Adrian Lyne, also a commercials director, for *Flashdance*. Another British commercials director was languishing in LA, down on his luck. His movie *The Hunger*, with Catherine Deneuve as an Egyptian vampire and David Bowie as her lunch, seemed to have brought his feature film career to a halt with reviews such as 'agonizingly bad' and 'a nearly unwatchable lesbian vampire flick'. They don't come much worse than that, so with Tony Scott conceding that 'for four years I couldn't get arrested' he returned to ads. One was for the new Saab 200 Turbo, and Scott shot it with his usual aplomb racing the car against a jet plane.

After their success with Lyne, the producers decided to risk him – they needed someone who could handle plane shots inventively. Moreover his brother, Ridley, could help the connection with Tom Cruise. After the maladroitly written *Legend*, Tom was ultra-cautious about stepping into another role until he was happy with the script, and told Simpson, Bruckheimer and Scott that he wouldn't sign for the leading role of Maverick but instead would work with them for two months on the script to try and get it right.

'I think they were kind of taken aback at first,' Cruise recalls. 'I just wanted to make sure that everything was going to go the way we talked about.' Pete Pettigrew, the technical adviser, is more precise about Tom's initial recalcitrance. 'He wasn't sure he wanted to be in the movie but we tried to convince him that it was a movie about excellence, trying to become better at what you did which was a very difficult job – not a movie about killing people.' Even Cruise succumbed to the ultimate seduction. His boyhood ambition had been to be a pilot, and although becoming a movie star had somewhat thwarted this dream his love of prowling the skies remained constant. He got on his motorbike and shot down the San Diego Freeway to Miramar. There he spent a lot of time with the fighter pilots, trying to work out what they were made of.

'They just stuck me in a plane and said, "Don't touch that, you can touch that, don't touch that." Then they just said, "Have a nice flight, sir" and closed the lid on me. I had this great pilot called Griz who really gave me a ride. We screamed along about fifty feet above the ground. He said "Now don't you tell anybody I'm doing this for you, do you hear?" "All right, man." He let me take over the stick after a while. I thought it was going to be the greatest thrill and it was. It went beyond that.'

Griz was, in fact, Dave Baranek, who became a role model for Tom's Maverick. He liked Tom. 'I taught him how to climb up on to an F-14, told him about flying one and helped in the details of what he had to say. He was polite and he was eager. He wanted to hear more and more about the business.'

Meanwhile, negotiations were still going on with the Navy at various levels. There obviously had to be a love story in the script, and Cash and Epps had Maverick having an affair with a woman instructor. The commander of the

Miramar base found that unacceptable. 'We don't let our officers date one another.'

It looked as if they had reached an impasse. But Tony Scott set up a meeting with him and inquired if any civilians came into contact with the pilots. The commander informed him that the Ran Corporation evaluated them. Thus Kelly McGillis was transformed from a naval officer into a Ran employee, Charlie. (Ally Sheedy, incidentally, had turned down the role.) McGillis was five years older than Cruise and so had a measure of authority. She had also enjoyed a big hit in *Witness* opposite Harrison Ford the previous year. But, as Dave Baranek ruefully notes: 'Our teachers did not wear fish-net stockings.'

Peter Pettigrew (whose name was subsequently borrowed by J. K. Rowling for a rat-like member of Gryffindor House in the Harry Potter books) was amused by some of the requests the Hollywood team managed to get past him. Although pilots are officers with their own rooms, they insisted: 'We have to have a locker room scene. We have to have the analogy to sports. There are things we can say there that we can't say anywhere else. Besides, we're paying a million dollars for Tom Cruise and we have to show some flesh.' Worst of all, thought Pettigrew, was the notion of the pilots competing for the Top Gun Trophy – the very *raison d'être* of the movie. 'If there was a Top Gun Trophy, no one would ever graduate,' he observed. 'They would all crash in pursuit of it.' But Pettigrew had a nice sense of humour. When questioned by Washington as to how the movie was going, he responded: 'Right now I'm just trying to prevent them turning it into a musical.'

He was less accommodating on the death of Goose, Maverick's mate who had to die so Maverick could feel responsible. A lethal crash on the deck of an aircraft carrier was out of the question. It was eventually agreed that the F-14 could go into a flat spin. The pilot would be outside the centre of the spin, but his co-pilot behind would find himself unable to open his canopy because of the spin and thus unable to eject. Unlike similar scenes in some other movies, this one was realistic – it is not possible to eject through the canopy.

The film was to open with a spectacular dogfight between F-14s and MiG-28s, but this had to be rewritten to accommodate the rules laid down by Robert Manning of the Navy Department. The director wanted to shoot it over land. No. 'That would have made it over Cuba,' Manning pointed out. 'We said it had to be over international waters. And we insisted that the Navy pilots would not fire until they were fired upon.' In this respect the Navy held all the cards – or, rather, planes. Not just the F-14 Tomcats but also the MiGs. It was not possible in 1985 to borrow the latter from the Russians. Although not quite at war with them, Reagan had just daubed them the 'Evil Empire' and it was the super-patriotic spirit of his presidency that the film reflected. The MiGs themselves were played by converted Northrop F-5 Tigers, the planes that were used to simulate MiGs in training exercises in Air Force Aggressor Squadrons. There was no doubt about whom the military thought their next war might be against.

A team of actor-pilots was assembled. Now that the

show was on the road with Tom Cruise, all the young actors in Hollywood were keen to be recruited. Charlie Sheen insisted, 'I have just *got* to be in this movie', but, at eighteen he was considered too young. Cruise, at the tender age of twenty-three, had casting approval.

Tony Scott studied the way Bruce Webber cast male models in his commercials, perhaps unwittingly attracting the homo-erotic charges that some would later level at the film. Anthony Edwards had the serious mien of the ill-fated Goose; others were more gung-ho, such as Tim Robbins, Rick Rossovich and Tom Skerritt from brother Ridley's *Alien*, and even the recalcitrant Val Kilmer. After he had again declined a part, according to Kilmer: 'Tony Scott ran after me down the corridor and blocked the elevator shouting "You gotta do it!"' In a previous interview Kilmer revealed he had only agreed to be in the film because Paramount exercised an option they had on him, but in either event he ended up as Maverick's main adversary in the film, Iceman. Meg Ryan was rescued from the daytime soaps where she was playing Betsy in *As the World Turns* and became Mrs Goose, later Widow Goose.

The actor-pilots were put through a four-day survival course. 'We went through ejection seat training,' Tom remembers with a wince. 'You had to take your mask off and they simulated the effect of high altitude without oxygen. And we had to tread water for fifteen minutes in a full flight suit.' It had been Scott's intention to shoot his actors in the rear cockpits of the F-14s, but this proved almost impossible – the camera's anamorphic lens simply shattered because of the powerful G force. So he had to admit defeat and shoot in mock-ups on the ground. But an exception was made in the case of Cruise. One of the F-14s was expensively customised to minimise the G force, and six Super-35mm cameras were strategically placed in the cockpit.

Tom had reason to be a little nervous. 'I had two pilots, Bozo and Feebs. We had a two-hour briefing before we went up and sometimes did three flights a day, which was pretty exhausting. I would get in the back seat and Bozo would control the camera on my face. It's amazing the power you feel sitting in a supersonic machine. I was sitting there, switching the radio on and pulling the switches so the engine starts up when, all of a sudden, this hazard light comes on. I yelled to Bozo, "This hazard light keeps flashing" and he said "Oh, that thing. Just switch it off. It never works." And I thought, "Oh, my God – what *does* work?"'

The Navy had given Tony Scott two aircraft carriers to play with: the USS *Enterprise* and the USS *Ranger*. The deal was that if they were going about routine exercises there would be no charge, but for non-essential man-oeuvres the film people would pay. No luxuries were added for the stars when they did their tour of duty on board. 'An aircraft carrier is a prison with the threat of drowning,' states Cruise. 'In fact, the rooms are not even up to prison standards. I don't know how those guys do it. Nine months! I had a nice room but no-one slept, not with 50,000lb planes landing on my head all night. And when the planes stopped they would be working on the vessel, drilling away. It sounded like I was at the dentist. Rick Carter took a picture of me when I fell asleep with my head on his make-up case. He blew it up saying that this was proof that someone got some sleep on the carrier. But I'm glad I went through it. We had some good laughs.'

Tony Scott lived up to his Saab pedigree and shot the Tomcats slickly and sensuously, rolling their paths through an ochre sky. Such was his quest for perfection that one evening when he was looking for a vital shot on board the aircraft carrier he begged the captain to alter course so that the sun would be in the right position to backlight the characters. His request fell on uncooperative ears; it would be too costly to do such a manoeuvre. Scott looked to his producers who said they were unable to authorise this $10,000 spend instantly. Luckily Tony had his cheque book in his pocket, and there and then made out a cheque to the US Navy for that amount.

Despite the innumerable rewrites on the script, the story didn't break any new boundaries of invention. Maverick set out to become Top Gun and did so, on the way competing with Iceman, falling for Charlie, finding out the truth about his dead father, downed in 'Nam, and, himself, downing a couple of MiGs. But, like *Titanic* fifteen years later, this film was less a story than an experience. The charisma of Cruise, the macho exploits of clean-cut young American patriots and a thundering score from Georgio Moroder ('Take My Breath Away' won the Oscar for Best Song) made this one of the hippest, high-concept movies of all time. Sales of Ray-Ban 'Aviator' sunglasses shot up by 40 per cent after its release in May 1986. Certainly nobody went to see it for the dialogue.

Viper (their instructor): I flew with your old man. VF-51, the *Oriskany*. You're a lot like he was. Only better . . . and worse. He was a natural heroic son of a bitch that one. . . . What I am about to tell you is classified. It could end my career. We were in the worst dogfight I ever dreamed of. There were bogeys like fireflies all over the sky. His F-4 was hit, and he was wounded, but he could've made it back. He stayed in it, saved three planes before he bought it.

Maverick: How come I never heard that before?

Viper: Well, that's not something the State Department tells dependents when the battle occurred over the wrong line on some map.

Although it had its moments, like this one in the classroom.

Charlie (their other instructor – Kelly McGillis): Excuse me, Lieutenant. Is there something wrong?

Maverick: Yes ma'am, the data on the MiG is inaccurate.

Charlie: How's that Lieutenant?

Maverick: I just happened to see a MiG 28 do a 4G negative dive.

Charlie: Where did you see this?

Maverick: Uh, that's classified.

Charlie: It's what?

Maverick: It's classified. I could tell you, but then I'd have to kill you.

But the film was test screened it was discovered that the affair between Tom and Kelly was weak, so Tony Scott had to take his camera into the bedroom and film a short but passionate love scene between them.

Top Gun soared effortlessly over the small arms fire of the critics and into the record books. Peter Biskind in his 1998 book *Easy Rider, Raging Bulls* gave his own analysis of what gave the film its dazzling appeal: 'Don Simpson was to gay culture what Elvis Presley was to rhythm and blues, ripping it off and repackaging it for a straight audience. The blockbusters Simpson made with Bruckheimer were star vehicles comprised of little more than a series of movie moments set to a pounding score. Simpson took gay culture, with its conflation of fashion, movies, disco, and advertising and made highly designed, highly self-conscious, high-concept pictures like *Flashdance*, *Beverly Hills Cop* and *Top Gun.*'

Well, if it was that easy why didn't every producer slap together the ingredients and make themselves hundreds of millions? Slightly overlooked are the timing and polish of the film, the near-perfect casting and, yet again, the searchlight intensity of Tom Cruise's performance. The greatest praise comes from the man himself, Dave Baranek. ' I cannot think of another actor who would have done a better job. He had vulnerability but showed enthusiasm and a sense of confidence. Maybe too much confidence sometimes – but that's what they wanted.'

As far as the homoerotic bit was concerned, that was more subtly addressed in Quentin Tarantino's satirical performance as a movie bore, Sid, in *Sleep With Me* (1994). 'You know what one of the greatest fucking scripts ever written in the history of Hollywood is?

Top Gun. You think it's a story about a bunch of fighter pilots. It is a story about a man's struggle with his own homosexuality. You've got Maverick, all right? He's on the edge, man. He's right on the fucking line, all right? And you've got Iceman, and all his crew. They're gay, they represent the gay man, all right? He could go both ways. Kelly McGillis, she's heterosexuality. She's saying: go the normal way, play by the rules. They're saying no, go the gay way. That is what's going on throughout that whole movie. He goes to her house, all right? It looks like they're going to have sex, you know, they're just kind of sitting back, he's takin' a shower and everything. They don't have sex. He gets on the motorcycle, drives away. She's like, "What the fuck is going on here?" Next scene, she's in the elevator, she is dressed like a guy. She's got the cap on, she's got the aviator glasses, she's wearing the same jacket that the Iceman wears. She is: okay, this is how I gotta get this guy, this guy's going towards the gay way, I gotta bring him back, I gotta bring him back from the gay way, so I'll do that through subterfuge, I'm gonna dress like a man . . . The REAL ending of the movie is when they fight the MiGs. They are this gay fighting fucking force, all right? And they're beating the Russians, the gays are beating the Russians. And it's over, and they fucking land, and Iceman's been trying to get Maverick the entire time, and finally, he's got him, all right? And what is the last fucking line that they have together? They're all hugging and kissing and happy with each other, and Ice comes up to Maverick, and he says, "Man, you can ride my tail, anytime!" And what does Maverick say? "You can ride mine!" Swordfight! Swordfight! Fuck-in' A, man!'

Sid's memory went into homoerotic overdrive with regard to the final exchange. What Iceman in fact said was: 'You can be my wingman any time' and Maverick replied: 'Bullshit, you can be mine.' Moreover, such an interpretation would doubtless have come as something of a shock to Meg Ryan aka Mrs Goose who, certainly on screen, betrays no awareness of her husband's lack of heterosexuality. It is possible that Quentin's character was expressing such an interpretation based more on hope than on forensic fact – and also for some laughs.

What is not in doubt is that Cruise, with his producers and director, had put together a Jet Set which was a counterpoint to the Brat Pack – an appellation that had been applied to his generation in a cover story in *New York* magazine in June 1985 by David Blum. It was a club to which Cruise was very keen not to belong but he was, to a certain extent, roped in by association. The article cited *Ordinary People* and *Taps* as Brat Pack movies, even declaring that the latter had changed Hollywood for ever, which it hadn't – but they were too serious in content to be bunched with later films that did have the common theme of the problems of being young in America: *The Outsiders* (1983), *Breakfast Club* (1985), *St. Elmo's Fire* (1985), *About Last Night* (1986) and *Pretty in Pink* (1986).

The core of the pack consisted of that 1962 generation: Emilio Estevez (dubbed leader by Blum), Ally Sheedy, Demi Moore and Andrew McCarthy plus a younger member, Rob Lowe, and an older one, Judd Nelson. Matthew

Broderick later played the lead in *Ferris Bueller's Day Off* (1986), a teen angst comedy from the pen of John Hughes, the leading writer for the Pack. Blum saw the ringleaders – Estevez, Lowe and Nelson – as hanging out at the Hard Rock Café in Los Angeles, enjoying some of the excesses of alcohol and sex that they portrayed in their movies and partying all night. Thus they were the modern equivalent of the Rat Pack of yore, featuring Frank Sinatra, Dean Martin and Sammy Davis Junior.

Tom hated the appellation and thought it was nonsense. Yes, he had had a small role in *The Outsiders* and yes, he admitted Emilio Estevez was his best friend, but Cruise wanted to be taken much more seriously – the fact that he had casting approval on *Top Gun* was indicative of that – and was hell-bent on a career that would take him far ahead of the pack. In his personal life he did not want to be associated with roistering – that was a thing of the past, on *The Outsiders*. He had broken up with Rebecca De Mornay on his return from England and, for a while, was content with his own company. 'I spend a lot of time alone. I mean a *lot* of time alone. But I've spent time alone my whole life and it doesn't bother me. I feel lonely at times but I just don't want to get into a relationship if it's not right. I'm not the kind of person who just does things to do them. It takes time to get to know people.'

During a break from *Top Gun* he went to a dinner and sat beside an actress called Mimi Rogers. She wasn't well known; her TV series *The Rousters* and *Paper Dolls* had been flops. But she was beautiful and, after an unsuccessful marriage to a Scientology counsellor, Jim Rogers – she must have been relieved, at least, to have got rid of her maiden name, Spickler – she was now dating again, having had relationships with Tom Selleck, Bobby Shriver of the Kennedy dynasty and, currently, a friend of Tom's. Tom fell for her, despite the fact that she was eight and a half years older than him, and bided his time. 'I like bright, very sexy women,' he said. 'And strong, someone who I'm not going to run over, someone who's going to stand up to me. She's also got to have her own thing going. I don't want someone living for me.'

Having spent an evening with Mimi at the Toronto Film Festival, I can vouchsafe that she has all those qualities and more, coated in the most gentle demeanour and with the sort of twinkling laugh that makes men melt. She is like a character out of a Jane Austen novel. She also had another link to Cruise, playing the romantic lead opposite Tom Berenger in the next film that Ridley Scott made, *Someone to Watch Over Me* which was filmed in New York and Los Angeles. Mimi was the beautiful heiress who, under a witness protection programme, was guarded by a married cop (Berenger) who, inevitably fell for her. The lush film was book-ended by Gershwin's magical lyrics, sung at the beginning of the film by Sting and, at the end, by Roberta Flack.

The other Tom was similarly captivated by Mimi. When the coast was clear they began to date, something that became public in late 1986. He fell in love with her – 'I'd never been in love before' – and, on 9 May 1987, they got married at a house Tom was renting in upstate New York. It was an understated event. His sister baked the wedding cake. His mother, Mary Lee, thought Mimi top-notch: 'I couldn't be more blessed. She is exactly the kind of woman I always hoped Tom would marry.' And the leader of the Brat Pack, Emilio Estevez, was best man.

8

POOL WITH PAUL

After his film *Raging Bull* was released at Christmas 1980 the director, Martin Scorsese, was flattered to receive a fan letter from Paul Newman saying how much he liked it. The fact that the star began the letter 'Dear Michael' in no way detracted from the praise. 'I've had *The Deer Hunter* attributed to me a lot,' Scorsese ruefully recalls – that film was actually directed by Michael Cimino.

Scorsese next heard from Newman four years later. The actor wanted to do a sequel to *The Hustler*, his acclaimed 1961 role as 'Fast' Eddie Felsen, a small-time pool hustler who challenges the legendary 'Minnesota Fats' for his world title. Was Scorcese interested in directing it? He was – subject to script. It turned out that Newman had been working on it with Walter Tevis, author of the original book and a follow-up, *The Color of Money*.

But Scorsese didn't much care for the results. 'If I wasn't

involved in the original idea of the script, then it wouldn't be something I could turn up early in the morning for. I didn't feel the character of Fast Eddie was strong enough or dramatic enough. I felt it had to go in another direction.' So he brought in the novelist Richard Price, who had written a screenplay, *Night and the City*, based on the 1950 Jules Dassin film about a con man turned corrupt wrestling promoter. 'I don't want to do remakes,' Scorsese explained – eventually the script was turned into a drab film by Irwin Winkler. 'However, I liked Richard, and his script had a very good street sense, and wonderful dialogue.'

Price recalls his first encounter with Newman. 'We were in Malibu – me and Marty Scorsese – the two New York guys on the beach. Marty's sitting there with his jacket and his nasal spray and I was smoking a cigarette, hunched over coughing. And then Newman comes out, all tanned up, Mr Sea and Ski. It was the two New York clowns with the Hollywood platinum.'

'My tastes don't run to shooting sequels,' Scorsese confessed, 'but I love Paul Newman's work – especially in *The Hustler* – and I liked the ambience of that film. But I suggested to Newman starting fresh – taking the Felsen character fresh and working a whole new story around him twenty-five years later. You see, I don't know anything about pool. I don't like what's *on* the table, but what's *around* the table, the intrigue, the manipulations.'

Although the three men quickly agreed on a plot – 'We kind of hammered together a plot line that day,' Newman recalls, 'and we committed to it' – the sixty-year-old superstar had an instinct for what the public expected when they saw him, and Price's first version of Fast Eddie was too dark and too unlikeable. 'Newman loves playing the antihero,' the writer explains. 'Like a combination of all the Hs: Hustler, Hud, Hombre, Harper. He likes playing a character that you can't bring yourself to hate. He was looking for redeemable features to come in a little earlier. He just didn't like the guy. Marty and I like mean things – the meaner the better, because of the shaft of light in the end. And while Newman wanted to explore aging – the fear of losing it – he just thought the character was too hard.'

Once the Felsen character had been customised to fit the star, a sorcerer hustler, his apprentice, the flakey pool genius Vincent Lauria, was more easily crafted. Right from the outset Paul Newman had wanted only one young man for the part – Tom Cruise. Thus did the greatly rewritten script land on Tom's lap as he was waiting for his next sortie from the deck of the USS *Enterprise* in the Pacific Ocean.

He had promised himself a break at the end of this arduous ten month shoot. But now he had a dilemma. Should he pass up the chance to work with two of the legends of his childhood? It was a no-brainer. The irony was that they needed him far more than he needed them. Newman had had a terrible time on *Harry and Son* in 1983, which he co-wrote, produced, directed, acted in and generally made a mess of. 'I threw caution to the wind and, as far as the workload, I really regretted it. You can't do your best work when you're beat. Never again.' The casting of the uncharismatic TV actor Robby Benson as his son was a substantial part of the problem, and Newman's mood was not improved by flying across the continent from Florida to

Los Angeles for the Oscars, only to sit and listen to his name not being read out as Best Actor for the sixth time. The movie took less than $5 million at the box-office.

Scorsese had managed to do even worse commercially with *King of Comedy* in 1982. It cost $25 million to make and returned barely a tenth of that. Despite the presence of Robert de Niro it was a deeply uncomfortable film, attempting to be both comedy and tragedy and ending up as neither. 'When it was shown on the first night at the Cannes Festival, I went backstage with Sergio Leone and he looked at me and said: "Martin, that's your most mature film." I don't know if it was his way of saying he didn't like it. I guess that comes to mind because my friends and I have had a running joke about slow movies, where the camera doesn't move, as being "mature".'

Although *Top Gun* was not yet finished, Cruise's star was in the ascendant. But even after he came on board they had trouble getting funding for the film. Although Twentieth Century-Fox had made *The Hustler*, they were unhappy with the script. Columbia also passed. Jeffrey Katzenberg and Michael Eisner, perhaps mindful of their decision at Paramount to reject *Top Gun*, finally agreed to back it – but only if Newman agreed to a pay cut and both he and Scorsese put up a third of their salaries as collateral against an overspend on the $14.5 million budget. Newman had hoped to lure Jackie Gleason back to reprise his role as Minnesota Fats but the seventy-year-old actor declined the part, saying it was too small. He died two years later.

'Luck plays a part in a pool hall – but for some players luck itself is an art,' intones Scorsese in his voice-over that begins *The Color of Money*. Felsen is now a liquor sales-man, and Vincent Lauria is pretty well a reincarnation of his younger self. Felsen teaches the flakey youngster how to hustle, to use his psychology to study his opponents in order to take advantage of them, to understand when to lose is actually to win. He takes Vince under his wing with the cooperation of his feisty girlfriend, Carmen (Mary Elizabeth Mastrantonio), and the three of them set off for a high-stakes nine-ball tournament in Atlantic City. Symbolically he gives Vincent a Balabushka pool cue, worth tens of thousands of dollars.

For Felsen, money is God and 'Money *won* is twice as good as money earned.' But he is deluding himself. He beats Vincent in the tournament, but when the younger man reveals that he threw the game in order to bet on Felsen and make $8000 Fast Eddie's world crumbles. He realises that the exultation of victory meant more than money. The apprentice has now become the sorcerer and morphed into a more unfeeling, cruder, uglier person than his mentor.

Tom set about the physical side of his part with his usual perfectionism. He played pool twelve hours a day in various New York halls and then trained with former pool world champion Mike Siegel, who was the technical adviser on the film. Siegel is able to isolate the element of Cruise that sets him apart from other actors. 'He can turn his hand to almost anything. He is able to watch and then immediately do it. He can do it in anything – racing, cocktails – he has a gift of picking it up so fast, it's amazing.'

Tom had two apartments when shooting the movie in Chicago. In the lower one was a pool table. Siegel says that they would drink until four in the morning and then go back and play pool. Not the conventional picture of Cruise, who today is largely teetotal. 'He learned to play pool better in six weeks than I did in five months twenty-five years ago,' Newman observes. Scorsese recalls: 'Tom played all his own shots except one – the slow-motion one when he hits a ball that goes over two other balls. He could have done it but it would have taken a further two days, and I didn't want to spend the time.'

For the most part, the film was shot in grimy pool rooms and bars in Chicago. Newman insisted that they rehearse for two weeks, something neither Scorsese nor Cruise had done before, and the young actor found the experience 'a revelation. When I was doing *Taps*, I must have seen *Raging Bull* five times in one week. And now I am working with Scorsese and Paul fucking Newman. What surprised me about Scorsese is the joy he had. Joy in the characters and the behaviour of the characters. He got off on the characters. Scorsese is an actor's director – details, details, details.'

His input is evident from the first time we see Vincent, playing an electronic games machine in the pool room bar, and the sheer braggadocio of his body language tells you that here is a cockerel who has more than the confidence of youth. When he kisses his girlfriend, Mary Elizabeth Mastrantonio, it is with a feral intensity with which we have never seen Cruise embrace a woman before. And, as he takes John Turturro to the cleaners on the pool table, he manipulates his cue like the marshal of a marching band, a wizard who knows that this is his magic wand.

Newman recalls that Scorsese's most valuable advice to him was to underplay the humour – 'Try not to be funny.' Cruise's relationship with Newman in rehearsal was more laid back. 'He immediately made me feel comfortable, but he didn't go out of his way to make me feel comfortable. I realised he was already working on the character but it didn't feel manipulative, it was just very easy. We were sitting there, just talking, and suddenly he was doing the scene.'

Until the action reaches Atlantic City it is a deliberately dark and dirty movie, with the streets of Chicago covered in filthy slush. There are only so many ways you can shoot innumerable games of pool and Scorsese did them all, his camera sometimes skimming across the table like a ball, crabbing with the players or fast tracking in and, at one stage, performing multiple circles round and round a close-up of Newman's head. The director paid less attention to Tom's hairstyle, with his dark locks rising vertically in a wave like Jack Lord in *Hawaii Five-O*. It seemed to rise higher as the film progressed.

During the course of filming, Paul Newman learned that he was going to be presented with an Honorary Oscar at the Academy Awards on 24 March 1986, presumably to compensate him for the six times he had sat there, nominated but not the winner. He declined to travel to Los Angeles but agreed to speak from the set in Chicago, masking his disappointment that it was not quite the real thing. 'I certainly want to thank the members of the Academy and I'm especially grateful that this does not come wrapped as a gift certificate to Forest Lawn [the

California cementery],' adding pointedly, 'my best work is down the pike in front of me and not in back of me.'

For Tom Cruise it was the best of times: he was working with men he profoundly respected and from whom he could learn. 'I could call Newman. He would never say: "This is how it is, kid." He'd say: "I don't know. It's a different time now. But this is how I did it. You have to find your own way."' Paul also extended the hand of friendship to a man nearly forty years younger. Six years previously Newman's son, Scott, had committed suicide from an overdose of drink and drugs. He was just twenty-eight. Scott had been Paul's only son – he has five daughters, two by Jacqueline Witte, his first wife, and three by his second, Joanne Woodward. Scott had felt resentful about his father's divorce. The boy tried to go into film acting but was not a success, and so he turned to excess. His father felt haunted and not a little guilty about his son's death.

Now here was a younger man with no father, upright and ambitious and eager to learn. The two of them played endless games of pool with each other while waiting to shoot. And Newman, aware of Cruise's 'I feel the need – the need for speed', introduced him to the world of automobile racing. Newman's passion for the sport had led him to make a feature about it, *Winning*, in 1969. Three years later, at the age of forty-seven, he took an eighteen-month break from films to concentrate on his racing. He was good, driving his Triumph TR6 to victory in four Sports Car Club of America National Championships in Class D. In 1977, completely against his wife's wishes, he entered the Le Mans twenty-four-hour race with team-mates Dick

Barbour and Rolf Stommelen — at fifty-four he was the oldest competitor — and came second. 'Racing is the best way I know to get away from all the rubbish in Holly-wood,' he told Tom.

Tom had asked him during filming: 'If we're still friends at the end of this, could you get me into racing?' Newman responded by renting a racetrack near their location and letting Tom bomb round the course in his Porsche. At the end of the shoot he arranged for Tom and Don Simpson to have five days' intensive training at a racing school with his partner, Jim Fitzgerald.

Scorsese, who at forty-four was closer in age to Cruise, provided entertainment of a less frenetic kind. He and his wife, Barbara De Fina, who was producing the film, kept an open dinner table for him. 'I never had such Italian food! I felt taken care of,' cooed Cruise.

Tom desperately needed the counsel of these more experienced new friends. *Top Gun* was just about to open and word was beginning to build in the industry, in the press and on television and radio that Tom Cruise was going to become the hottest star on the block. And the prospect intimidated him. 'I felt lonely and isolated. I didn't know what was going to happen.' From 12 May 1986, when *Top Gun* opened, Tom Cruise lost the peace of privacy and would never again be able to go out in public without attracting attention. He rationalised his situation as care-fully as preparing for a part, because from now on all the world was going to be a stage for him. Part of it was a fear that he might 'piss it all away,' that he might succumb to the heady pleasure of celebrity. MTV was just starting, and

the appetite for icons had never been stronger. He acknowledged: 'I don't quite know how to handle all this stuff.'

For a man who was not yet twenty-four, he arrived at a
mature decision. He would buckle down. He would not
take the easy route. He would take the harder route. And he
would learn. So instead of all the *Top Gun 2* offers that
were coming his way with vast pay cheques, he set his sights
on working with Dustin Hoffman in *Rain Man*.

The Color of Money duly opened to a raft of rave
reviews and an ultimate US gross of $52 million which
was high for a Scorsese film. In fact it was his biggest hit to
date – helped, no doubt, by his star casting. Vincent Canby
wrote in *The New York Times*: 'Mr Newman appears to be
having a ball as the aging but ever-resilient Fast Eddie. It's a
wonderfully funny, canny performance, set off by the
actor's intelligence that shines through the character without upstaging it. Mr Cruise works successfully against his
pretty-boy looks to find the comic, short-sighted nastiness
that's at the center of the younger man.' He added: 'The
film's revelation is Miss Mastrantonio.'

And here Cruise's contribution is not to be underestimated. He brought such energy to his part that Mary
Elizabeth Mastrantonio rose a few notches above the
performance anyone had seen from her before or since.
It brought her her only Oscar nomination. Since then,
however, her roles have been in largely moderate movies.
Maybe producers have a problem with her name; how
prudent of Tom to elbow Mapother IV.

Newman finally got his Best Actor Oscar on his seventh
nomination. Naturally he didn't attend the ceremony –

pride and the fear that his presence was a jinx on his likelihood of success stopped that. Nor did he permit his publicist, Warren Cowan, to run an Oscar campaign. It was perhaps as well that he didn't attend. The presentation of the Best Actor Oscar was a hilarious shambles. Seventy-eight-year-old Bette Davis got a standing ovation as she came on but, as the ceremony was running late and her timing was not hitting the clips of the nominees, the director, Marty Pasetta, cut off her microphone, only turning it on again when she announced Newman as the winner. Paul's pal Robert Wise, who had directed him in *Somebody Up There Likes Me* came on stage to accept it on his behalf, but no sooner had he begun to speak than Miss Davis interrupted him and decided to tell the audience who Wise was. She took so long there was no time for Wise's speech, so the mike was unplugged for the second time that evening. Newman, watching in Connecticut, was gently amused. 'I'm on a roll now,' he said in a television inter-view the following day. 'Maybe I can get a job.' His co-star Tom Cruise was not to make his first appearance on the Oscar stage until two years later, when he presented the Academy Award for Best Actress to Jodie Foster for *The Accused*.

Tom's intention to work only with the best came about in the most remarkable way. The one actor he had idolised throughout his short career, Dustin Hoffman, renowned for his character roles, had agreed to play an autistic *savant* in a film property owned by Peter Guber and Jon Peters. Dustin's career, which must mark one of the most meteoric climbs in Hollywood history, had fallen into a black hole with Elaine May's disastrous *Ishtar* in 1982. In what appeared to be an attempt to re-create a Bob Hope/Bing Crosby 'road' movie, Hoffman and Warren Beatty (who was also the producer) played two second-rate lounge singers on a tour of North Africa who become embroiled in a mythical coup. It was meant to be a comedy, but laughs proved very thin on the sand and the venture was more renowned for its budget ($40 million) than its box-office ($4 million). Hoffman's reputation was strong enough to survive this, but he actively needed a part that would remind people of his prodigious acting versatility, ranging from Ratso Rizzo in *Midnight Cowboy* to Dorothy Michaels in *Tootsie*. So he asked his agent, Michael Ovitz, founding father of Creative Artists, to find him one.

Fortunately the über-agent was aware of a developing project in the Peter Guber–Jon Peters Company about an autistic man and his brother. Tom Cruise too was looking for a mature and meaty role, and he was with the same agency. So, in the way Hollywood was beginning to be run, Ovitz put together a tight package. However, the script was far from cooked, and it would be a year and many writers and directors later before the camera rolled.

Tom, in the interim, turned his attention to religion. Although he had been brought up a Catholic and had even attended a seminary, he needed something more. Many people in America are not content with the Christ story but are looking for a more recent and accessible religious leader who lays down challenging, clear-cut rules. As a consequence many men have put themselves forward to fill that need. In 1827 Joseph Smith Jr, a penniless farmer, claimed to have met an angel named Moroni who gave him some golden plates. Using special stones set in silver bows he translated them into the Book of Mormon, bringing the news that God has evolved from man and man can become a god. That Church now has 5 million members. In 1952 the Reverend Sun Myung Moon, an immigrant from Korea, founded the Unification Church. Christ had evidently asked him to complete his task on earth, although not everyone was welcome. Moon said the Holocaust was God's revenge on the Jews for killing Christ, and referred to gays as 'dung-eating dogs.' The Reverend Moon likes mass wedding ceremonies – he claims to have married 450,000 people on 12 February 2000 and to have 4.5 million followers. Less populous was the People's Temple, founded by the Reverend Jim Jones in the 1950s. To an extent it achieved its aim, as 914 followers set out on their journey to the Planet of Bliss on 18 November 1978 by committing suicide – not all of them voluntarily.

Tom's eye, however, fell on the Church of Scientology. The founder of Scientology, which was formally established in the United States in 1954, was Lafayette Ron Hubbard, a former naval officer and a popular writer. In 1950 Ron Hubbard gave an outline of his new science of mental health – Dianetics – in the Spring journal of the Explorer's Club. It was made available to a much wider audience in the May 1950 issue of *Astounding Science Fiction* (the magazine's cover bore an image of a hairy alien with piercing yellow eyes who was said to be the evil Duke of Kraakahaym from the Empire of Skontar). The object of Dianetics was well intentioned – to make you a healthier, happier person. By two-person question-and-answer therapy the 'auditor' would seek out painful memories – 'engrams' – in your subconscious and this evidently helped people improve their lives. It was quite a long process, as you had to get rid of engrams from previous lifetimes before you reached the eighth level and could be pronounced 'clear'.

In book form, *Dianetics* sold amazingly well; *Newsweek* reported that two months after it was published not only had 35,000 copies been shifted but 500 Dianetic groups had been set up across the States. Hubbard later said that he had conducted years of intensive research into the nature of human existence before arriving at Scientology. He had found the soul in a human being, and Scientology was an applied religious philosophy that promised to improve the condition of the human spirit, which he called the 'Thetan'.

All of this had considerable appeal, especially for young people. They went along to Scientology centres to be tested for stress by an 'E-meter'. This consisted of two cans, which the person held, attached to a metal box with a dial on it. The E-meter, Ron insisted, could read your mental state. Like a lie detector, it probably responded to perspiration and pulse in the fingers. Hubbard demonstrated this device in a Wichita, Kansas hotel in 1952 by taking a member of his audience, getting him to hold the cans and pinching him. The needle flickered. Then Hubbard asked the man just to imagine the pinch, and the needle flickered again. This, he said, proved that his invention was capable of measuring emotions and was able to give the auditor a deep and marvellous insight into the mind of the 'pre-Clear'.

A further benefit of Scientology was that it helped people to overcome doubt and ignore rejection. That is why it proved popular with some actors, notably John Travolta, whose star was in the ascendant after *Staying Alive* and *Perfect*. 'Before Dianetics, if people said negative things to me or about me, I would cave in easily,' Travolta says. 'Being a man, that wasn't a very appealing quality. Some people would say, "The boy is too sensitive." But many times I had suppressive people around me who would cave me in on purpose. I was sort of like a minefield.'

Auditors would frequently have to clear engrams from previous lives, getting through several levels in the process of reaching clear. This took from, on average, one to two years – and was far from cheap. It was claimed that one Scientologist had witnessed Vesuvius destroy Pompeii in AD 79, another had been a fish and yet another a walrus. Several people had been Jesus Christ, and others had been Walter Raleigh, Queen Elizabeth I and the Venerable Bede.

But most outstanding was Lafayette Ron himself, who claimed he had visited heaven. He later stated this was a humorous allegory. When he took to life at sea as he grew older, he spent time circling the Canary Islands off the coast of North Africa as part of the Hubbard Geological Survey Expedition.

The reason Ron had settled for life on the ocean wave was simple: many governments were not too keen on Scientology, fearing that their credulous citizens were parting with regular sums of money for a process that was neither scientific nor logical. The Australians were first. The report of the Australian Board of Inquiry into Scientology was published in October 1965. It ran to 173 pages and was pretty straightforward in that typical Aussie fashion: 'Scientology is evil; its techniques evil; its practice a serious threat to the community medically, morally and socially; and its adherents sadly deluded and often mentally ill.' The Church was outlawed in the state of Victoria, but in 1983, the Australian High Court finally recognised Scientology as a religion.

In 1968 the British Minister of Health announced a ban on Scientology students coming to Britain. He agreed with the Australians that Scientology was socially harmful: 'It alienates members of families from each other. Its authoritarian principles and practices are a potential menace to the personality and well being of those so deluded as to become its followers. Above all, its methods can be a serious danger to the health of those who submit to them.' Not just Scientology students were banned from coming to Britain – so was Ron himself, whom the Home Secretary classified as an 'undesirable alien.' This ban was lifted in July 1980 after a petition was raised by 120 British MPs.

In July 1977, 134 FBI agents stormed the Scientology offices in Washington and Los Angeles, taking away 48,149 documents. In August 1978 a Federal Grand Jury in Washington indicted nine Scientologists on twenty-eight counts – largely consisting of espionage in government offices. Mrs Hubbard got five years in jail and her co-defendants slightly shorter terms. Operation Snow White revealed the extent of their infiltration. In response the Church executives expelled the staff, closed the unit and introduced safeguards to try to ensure that no similar events would occur again.

Although Cruise says he choose to join Scientology after reading about religions in books, it is impossible not to believe that he was subsequently influenced by his then wife Mimi, who was not only a Scientologist herself but the daughter of Scientologists and had actually been married to Jim Rogers, who was a Scientology Counsellor. Kirstie Alley, who shared an apartment with Mimi when they were starting out, was another prominent convert. Scientology has worked well for Cruise. He says, 'There are tools that you can use to help to understand yourself more, understand the world and things that you can do to help people. The incredible study technology that L. Ron Hubbard developed has been very helpful to me in my life.' He even claims that it cured his dyslexia.

Despite the exhortations from Dustin Hoffman to keep the faith and stay on board, it looked less and less likely that *Rain Man* would go into production for at least three months. Tom does not like kicking his heels, so he quickly committed to a movie to fill the gap – *Cocktail* – and approached the part with his customary thoroughness, studying barmen. 'You serve all the pretty women free drinks, because that gets the guys coming into the bar. If a girl is in there on a date, you make sure her boyfriend feels like a god, because the better he feels at the bar, the bigger tip you're going to get. You're the extractor – not the bartender, the extractor. It's all about tips and it's all about money – flat out.' It was a personal story from the pen of Heywood Gould whose screenwriting credits included *The*

Boys from Brazil and *Fort Apache: The Bronx* and whose books included a biography of the architect Sir Christopher Wren. The novel itself was somewhat dark and disenchanted, as Gould admits: 'Working behind a bar I learned quickly that you become cynical and jaded. I also realised that I had to get out of that lifestyle before it killed me.'

The producing partners, Robert Cort and Ted Field, optioned the book while it was still in manuscript and asked Gould to write a screenplay. Not everybody shared their enthusiasm and the script remained in limbo with Frank Price, the head of Universal, and the Oscar-winning James L. Brooks almost committing to it, but not quite. This was Cort and Field's good fortune. Jeffrey Katzenberg at Touchstone Pictures, part of the Disney empire, could see how the story could be lightened up so as to be more like *The Graduate* – everybody in Hollywood wanted to find another Graduate – and he knew just the man to play the lead, the young star of Touchstone's *The Color of Money*.

Even if it was a short shoot, they could only have Cruise if they paid him his full fee of $3 million. So economies had to be made in the rest of the casting: Bryan Brown, best known for marrying Meggie (Rachel Ward) who fell in love with Father Ralph de Bricassant (Richard Chamberlain) in *The Thorn Birds*, and Elizabeth Shue, who had just emerged as Ralph Macchio's girlfriend in *The Karate Kid*, were hired.

Tom Cruise plays a discharged serviceman who intends to hit New York and make his millions. It is the late eighties and elsewhere in the city Michael Douglas is shouting, 'Greed is good.' Despite a diet of self-help books and mind-numbing evening business classes, Tom cannot cut the mustard. Bryan Brown hires him as a fellow barman and, before you can say prestidigitation, they are twirling vodka bottles like drum majorettes. Sadly they fight over a girl and so Tom leaves for Jamaica where he both serves and has Sex-on-the-Beach. The recipient of his favours is Elizabeth Shue, but when Bryan arrives with a rich wife Tom wants one, too, and shoos out Elizabeth in favour of his own rich woman. It doesn't work out, the nadir of the relationship taking place at the opening of a Manhattan sculpture exhibition where Tom brings crashing down both the sculptor and his central exhibit. He realises the wealthy way is not for him, a view reinforced when Bryan commits suicide because he has lost all his money in commodities, and returns to Elizabeth who is carrying his twins (inside her).

This is a pretty lame tale, with lashings of music ranging from Elvis to Robert Palmer layered over montages to fill up the gaps. Tom shows his expertise at basketball, (six or seven hoops in a row, one thrown backwards), horse riding (along the beach) and having meat loaf mozzarella and chicken à la king thrown over his head and groin respectively by the enraged Miss Shue. Brown, for some reason, begins to speak in tongues after he is married, beckoning his wife with the words 'Sweetheart, come hither' and suggesting they dance with the phrase 'Let's decimate the dance floor.' Cruise himself gave a convincing performance in an unconvincing film.

In the words of Tom's agent, Paula Wagner, the critics 'eviscerated' the movie. But every Hollywood cloud has a silver dollar lining and on the Saturday morning after the Friday opening Jeffrey Katzenberg of Disney called to congratulate him: *Cocktail* had had one of the biggest openings in Disney history. On a personal note the studio president informed him that he was now able to 'open' a movie. 'And in some weird way,' Tom recalls, 'that really changed everything. That became, as far as the business side, a defining moment in terms of me getting certain pictures made, like *Born on the Fourth of July*. I didn't even really grasp what it meant at that time.' His fans turned up to the tune of $78 million and *Cocktail* was the seventh most popular film of 1988, sandwiched between *Die Hard* and *The Naked Gun*.

Less harmoniously, war broke out off the set between professional barmen, each of whom claimed to have taught Tom to spin the spirits. This was hardly surprising as he claimed to have visited thirty-four bars in Manhattan to do his research. When 'barstar' Myke Gorecki of Baywatch Café claimed in *Cheers* Magazine that he had trained Tom, John 'JB' Bandy wrote an angry letter saying that he had had no part whatsoever in the movie. Bandy had trained and choreographed Cruise and Brown and got a credit. Bruce Rampick of Lucy's Retired Surfers Restaurant and Bar in New Orleans said Cruise had trained in the bar he used to own in Manhattan. Phil 'Dog' Lockhart of the Beer Hunter Sports Pub and Grill in Rancho Cucamonga wondered why any bartender would brag about training the bartenders for *Cocktail* as 'most of the tips and pours they did wasted a lot of liquor.' Nevertheless John 'JB' Bandy sued Michael 'Magic Mike' Warner when he claimed that he had conducted the training – his claim for damages being his earnings as a bartender/consultant, which had increased tenfold since he had been canonised as Cruise's trainer.

The dispute remains unresolved in the world of the twirling dervishes.

9

DRIVING WITH DUSTIN

There are few more consummate examples of how the Hollywood system works – meticulous, tenacious, ego-driven, spending profligately on research and development – than *Rain Man*. From an idea that was pure but a script that was weak, it was shepherded through the development process with various people adding their talents to the story until a movie was produced that attracted critical acclaim, earned eight Oscar nominations (four winners) and took $172 million in the USA alone. It then became the number one movie in every country it played in throughout the world.

It would never have happened without Bill Sackter who in 1920, at the age of seven, was placed in the Minnesota State School for the Feeble-Minded and Epileptics. He remained there for more than forty-five years before becoming a ward of state. A young student, Barry Morrow, and his wife, Bev, petitioned for his guardianship. Barry was due to take up a job at the University of Iowa School of Social Work and insisted Bill come with them. The School gave Bill a coffee shop to run and, true to Morrow's faith in him, he became popular with students and faculty alike. He died in 1983 at the age of seventy, but Wild Bill's Coffee Shop is still there and Bill himself found fame in a 1981 television movie about his life, written by Morrow, in which he was played by Mickey Rooney. Both Morrow and Rooney won Emmies.

Morrow gained a degree of fame for this achievement and also for setting up a mall of small shops next to the coffee shop, all of them operated by people with disabilities. He was invited to Texas by the Association for Retarded Citizens and there he met Kim Peek. To Morrow's amazement, Peek was able to tell him the author of every book in the university library, correct the zip codes on the membership list and give him detailed driving instructions to almost anywhere. Thus *Rain Man* was born.

Morrow came up with the story of two brothers, Charlie Babbitt, a tough young Los Angeles businessman, and Raymond Babbitt, a retarded *savant* in a sanatorium, who only discover each other when their father dies. The Emmy-winner was now versed in the way to get a TV programme made and pitched it to Stan Brooks, head of television at Guber-Peters Productions. The President of the company, Roger Birnbaum, was at the meeting and declared the idea to be 'The best story I ever heard.' It was worth a feature film.

Peter Guber, later to head up Sony, was unenthusiastic

but let Birnbaum have his head. He and Morrow took it to Warner Bros, but they turned him down as they had something similar in development – *Forrest Gump* (a film the studio dropped after the success of *Rain Man* – Paramount made the hit film ten years later). Undaunted, Birnbaum managed to get Robert Lawrence, President of United Artists, to hear Morrow's pitch. He bought the idea within fifteen minutes.

After the script had been worked on for eight months with input from Birnbaum, Michael Ovitz of Creative Artists was brought in and Barry Morrow found himself at dinner with Dustin Hoffman and the director of Guber-Peters' world-wide hit *Beverly Hills Cop*, Martin Brest. At the end of the meal Hoffman pronounced: 'We're going to do this movie together and it's going to be great.' But when Hoffman said *this* movie, he actually meant a rewritten version of the script, and, to Morrow's chagrin, two new writers – Richard Price and Michael Bortman – were hired to script their versions.

Dr Darold Treffert, Clinical Professor of Psychiatry at St Agnes Hospital, Wisconsin and an expert on Savant Syndrome, who was the consultant on the film, was pretty horrified by the turn the story had now taken. 'Savant Syndrome is spectacular in its own right,' he points out. 'It does not need to be embellished. That script had in it more typical Hollywood scenes – Mafia mobsters, narrow escapes and a chase scene in which Charlie and Raymond roar out of a burning barn on a motorcycle fashioned by using some of Raymond's *savant* mechanical skills.' More worrying was the ending. 'In the original script there was a happy ending. Raymond has changed so much that he does not return to the institution. He moves in with his brother, they go to ball games together and live happily ever after. While that makes a nice story, it is also an unrealistic one.'

Ovitz, meanwhile, proposed another of his clients – Tom Cruise – as the younger brother, Charlie Babbitt. Tom accepted with alacrity and, in September 1987, joined Hoffman (Raymond Babbitt) and the screenwriter and the director in adjacent beach houses in Malibu to work on the script – only now the writer was Ron Bass and the director Steven Spielberg. Hoffman had had 'artistic differences' with Martin Brest. One of them apparently was that Brest didn't like the idea that Hoffman, the title character, did not appear for the first fifteen minutes. Dustin retorted that Cruise was the biggest star in the world, quite capable of holding the movie for forty minutes if need be.

Experts were flown in. When Hoffman met Kim Peek and his father, the boy demonstrated his encyclopaedic memory by churning out facts about baseball, the Bible, British monarchs – everything under the sun. Unfortunately Kim had been born with encephalitis and had an enlarged and slightly distorted head. The team did not want to make a film of the *Elephant Man* variety, so Hoffman came up with the idea that his character should be an autistic *savant* with perfectly normal looks.

Spielberg told Tom: 'This film is basically a love story. And the most important thing to give it dramatic quality is that there have to be obstacles. If Raymond is a sweet, retarded man there are none. He must be difficult, he won't let you touch his stuff, he won't let you touch him, he doesn't want to have anything to do with you.' His instinct was to prove correct, but he was unable to stay with the project as it would run into his obligation to George Lucas to make *Indiana Jones and the Last Crusade*.

The search was now on for a third director. Ovitz brought on board Sydney Pollack, who had had something of a fraught time directing Dustin in *Tootsie* (although it had brought both of them Oscar nominations). Unfortunately Pollack liked to work with his own writers, so out went Ron Bass and in came Karl Luedtke and David Rayfiel. They decided the love story was actually between Tom Cruise and his American attorney girlfriend. But this version did not appeal to either the actors or the studio, so Pollack went off to make the ill-fated *Havana*.

Ovitz did not become the most powerful man in Hollywood for many years, by failing to get his own way. He wanted this project made, and it would be made. Completely undaunted by the fact that Barry Levinson (who had made a brilliant writer-director debut with *Diner* and gone on to direct Robert Redford in *The Natural*) had turned down *Rain Man*, preferring to direct *Good Morning, Vietnam* with Robin Williams, Ovitz tried to persuade him to change his mind. And Ovitz's powers of persuasion are pretty formidable. So, with only seven weeks to prepare the movie Levinson at last agreed to come on board and Ron Bass (a former lawyer – Stanford, Yale, Harvard – who is one of the few writers in Hollywood to employ a team of ideas people and researchers) came back to work with him.

Hoffman and Cruise had not been idle in the meantime. Both avid researchers, they had visited *savants* and autistic *savants*. Joseph Sullivan of Huntington, West Virginia was able to multiply 341 by 927 without paper and pencil. Try it. The answer is 316107, and Joseph was able to arrive at that in fifteen seconds. They also borrowed his obsessive, ritualistic behaviour for the film. Joseph ate cheese balls with a toothpick – so now does Raymond Babbitt. Equally Raymond's memorising of a phone book and licence plates, and even his fit when the kitchen fire alarm goes off, are all taken from Joseph's life. There was humour in the encounter, as well. When Hoffman asked him if he knew the Gettysburg address, Joseph replied: '4 Water Street, Washington DC.' The scene where a waitress spills toothpicks from a box on to the floor and Raymond immediately knows how many there are (246) did not come from Joseph; it was something that a pair of *savant* twins, known only as George and Charles, were able to do.

Now it was time to work on the Cruise character. Morrow had written him much older – Hoffman was pushing fifty and Cruise was only twenty-five, but it is improbable to have a twenty-five-year age gap between brothers. Initially Bill Murray had been approached, but wanted the Raymond part. Spielberg had been anxious to customise the part for Cruise and imparted his wisdom to Levinson. 'He debriefed me at a restaurant in Westwood and I gave him everything, all my notes, everything I had developed,' Spielberg says. 'I just poured them out to Barry. What he used or didn't use was his call. My last words to him were that the film would be a hundred million-dollar winner.' Spielberg was wrong – the film grossed $400 million worldwide.

Charlie Babbitt was initially, in Morrow's version, the bullying boss of a cold call centre. But Levinson wanted to move him further upmarket and deeper into debt, so he awarded him a floundering Lamborghini franchise – a far cry from John Updike's downtrodden Rabbit who had to make do with Toyotas. The trouble with Charlie was that he was inherently dislikeable, mean to his staff, mean to his brother and, initially, swaggeringly solipsistic. Tom knew this was a tough call. 'I enjoy pressure. When you come from a divorced family, you assume a lot of pressure at a very young age. I'm used to that. It's going to be challenging. But I wouldn't have gotten involved if I didn't think we could do it. This character is always five steps ahead and not thinking about what's going on. It's just move, move, move.'

The art of getting audience empathy with a fundamentally nasty piece of work is to put another character on the screen who has been able to see through his shortcomings and find something to love in him. The American lawyer figure was too austere for this so Ron Bass changed her to a young Italian girl, innocent but instinctive. She was Charlie's assistant and verbal conduit to the Lamborghini factory back home, and also his girlfriend. Being foreign, she could also act as an audience within the film, giving vent to her emotions when Charlie is callous to his brother. The Neapolitan Valeria Golina's biggest role to date had been as Gina Piccolapupula in *Big Top Pee-wee*, the second in a film series with Pee-wee Herman which was also to prove the last after the eponymous actor was found playing with himself in a cinema. She did not disgrace herself in the part.

Rain Man was nearly called 'No Man'. Barry Morrow went through a list of childish pronunciations of male names – Charlie was a baby when his brother was institutionalised – and that was the one for Norman. But his children didn't like it. However, they did approve of the one for Raymond.

After four years, six writers and four directors they finally had a story acceptable to all. As Tom humorously observes: 'You know what they say – the fourth guy up is the home-run hitter.' The father whom Charlie hasn't seen since he left home in his teens dies in Cincinnati, Ohio. All he leaves Charlie are some rosebushes and a 1949 Buick Roadmaster convertible. Three million dollars has been left to an unnamed beneficiary who, it transpires, is the brother he never knew he had, Raymond. He pretty well kidnaps him from the institution, Wallbrook, he has been in since Charlie was two in order to hold him to ransom for half the 3 million. Raymond, an autistic *savant*, refuses to fly or take major highways or travel in the rain. There is a rapport in Las Vegas when Raymond's *savant* skills earn Charlie enough to pay his debts, and Charlie realises this is the 'rain man' whom he always thought was an imaginary friend. Back home he wants to try to care for Raymond, but realises this is impossible. Raymond cannot exist in the outside world. But Charlie will visit him at Wallbrook.

Cruise had always been in awe of Hoffman, as he had of Newman. 'I always think "What are they going to be like?" Just in terms of rejection, because I'll be working with them. But Hoffman and Newman both make you feel good about yourself and confident in your work.' Hoffman had a reputation for intense perfectionism on set – he did warn Cruise that he was not going to look him in the eye when in character – but, there again, so had Tom.

'At night, Tom was constantly knocking on my door. He'd say, "Why don't we do it this way?" And he'd do my lines so well he could have played *my* part as well. He would have been terrific as Raymond,' Hoffman recalls. 'I started out by being his mentor but, in the end, Tom was as much directing me as I was directing him. He's such a moment-to-moment actor. He's in the moment. He doesn't have an intellectual idea of what he wants to do. He's coming off the gut and that makes him a pleasure to play ping-pong with. He's a Christmas tree, lit from head to toe.' He was also, post *Top Gun*, a bigger star than Dustin. On street locations the elder of the two observed: 'It was the first time I was ever acting on a set where I was just anonymous. As far as the crowd was concerned it was "Tom! Tom!" It was a nightmare.'

Ron Bass had to finish the final draft before a planned Writers' Guild of America strike. He talks dramatically of pushing the final handwritten pages through Levinson's door hours before the strike began. It did mean there was no writer on call for rewrites, which are commonly necessary on a film of this order. There was great debate on why the two brothers didn't just get on a plane and fly back to Los Angeles. The audience would probably have accepted the fact that Charlie wanted to get the 1949 Buick Roadmaster back home, but the perfectionists on the film wanted something more specific. Raymond had a fear of flying and one of the film crew pointed out that the Australian airline

Qantas was the only one in the world never to have had a crash which led to this memorable exchange:

Charlie: Ray, all airlines have crashed at one time or another, that doesn't mean that they are not safe.

Raymond: Qantas. Qantas never crashed.

Charlie: Qantas?

Raymond: Never crashed.

Charlie: Oh, that's gonna do me a lot of good because Qantas doesn't fly to Los Angeles out of Cincinnati, you have to get to Melbourne! Melbourne, Australia in order to get the plane that flies to Los Angeles!

In fact Qantas had had several crashes in its propeller days but not with its jet service, which remained untouched until 23 September 1999 when a jumbo jet crashed on landing in Bangkok. The airport exchange, incidentally, was removed from the in-flight version by all airlines – except one.

It is almost impossible to say which actor had the more significant part. Hoffman adopted the clenched body and cocked head that many autistic *savants* have, and developed the tidy, short-stepped walk and jerky gestures that almost made his character more puppet than person. Pauline Kael in the *New Yorker* dismissed it as a 'one-note performance.' Presumably she had seen autistic people who changed completely and became healthy, open humans. They don't.

Cruise's Charlie, as Barry Morrow noted, 'drives the car and dramaturgically drives the movie.' He also had to give it all its energy, as Raymond's clockwork progress through the story has little or none. In this, Cruise splendidly transmutes his innate intensity into steaming frustration. Valeria Golina's character Susanna, very shrewdly written by Bass, appears to be (and is) emotionally distraught by what is taking place between these two brothers – such a chilly fraternal relationship could never happen in Italy – while she is, subtly, slipping the audience the plot points. The actress could see the merit in Cruise. 'He's protective and strong and still innocent. His most attractive feature are his eyes. Not their colour; their "regard." The way he looks with them. They're very alive.'

Every film has to revolve around an axis, a turning point, and in *Rain Man* it takes place in Las Vegas, a city of endless optimism. Barry Morrow intended to test his idea of a *savant* counting cards and beating the table by taking Kim Peek to Reno in Nevada. Morrow was not a gambler himself but bought a book on beating the system. He started to explain the technique to Kim, but the boy stopped him. 'I know how to do it,' he said, as they were driving away from a filling station. Morrow protested that he didn't, but Kim then told him that, while Morrow had gone to the bathroom and then to the motel shop, he had digested the ninety-seven-page volume. Morrow tested him and found his claim was true. But Kim, despite much persuasion, refused to play cards in the casino since he knew he would win and felt this was unfair. He did, however, slip a quarter into a slot machine – that was fair – pulled the lever and won $80 on his first attempt. 'There must be a design to this,' Morrow muses, 'but I won't know it in my lifetime.'

Raymond has no such morality. Not only does he count

cards for Charlie until the casino bans them, but he makes an assignation with a hooker. Not that he is aware of her profession. But something has stirred inside him, and he permits Charlie to touch him and dance with him in preparation for the date. It is another memorable moment in a film rich with memorable moments, and the onset of comprehension and compassion on Cruise's face is the stuff of artful movie acting.

Further proof that Raymond is opening up, just a little, comes as Susanna gives him a kiss in a lift. 'What was it like?' asks the lawyer who is deciding whether he should go back to the institution. 'Wet,' he replies. The lawyer was played by the director, Barry Levinson – when the actor who had been cast in the part didn't finish his previous picture in time, Hoffman suggested to Levinson that he give it a go. It was another piece of the good fortune that graced the shooting of the movie. Since Levinson, unlike an actor coming in, carried the whole story and back-story in his head, he was able to improvise with Hoffman and Cruise. Tom becomes visibly and verbally incensed by accusations that he cannot look after his brother. Levinson says that he was provoked into this by unexpected questions. It might just have been good acting.

At the end of the film, when Raymond is leaving to return to the institution, it is apparent that one of the brothers has changed. But it is not the autistic one. Cruise's Charlie has learnt that making money and treating people like shit is not the best way to exist; responsibility, compassion and love are greater virtues. 'Charlie learns how to live life through Raymond,' says Tom. 'That's beautiful.'

The preview audiences were cool on the film and icy on the ending. So was the studio. Levinson was prevailed upon to shoot a happy ending with the two brothers living harmoniously in Los Angeles, maybe going to the odd baseball game. That, after all, is the correct way to end a Hollywood movie. But the director and his cast obdurately resisted this. They had learned enough about autistic *savants* to know that Raymond lacked the capacity to live in the outside world. The person who wrote on his sneak preview card: 'I was hoping the little guy would snap out of it' was perhaps more representative of the easily corralled preview audience than the discerning cinemagoer. There are a lot of them out there and, to quote Kevin Costner, 'If you build it, they will come.'

The reviews, however, were more than 90 per cent positive, and the word travelled that *Rain Man* was something different – but also something the same. Sometimes a screen male pairing can be greater than the sum of its parts, whether it's Walter Matthau and Jack Lemmon or Paul Newman and Robert Redford. The audience loves the chemistry. So it was here – hence the vast international box-office.

Hoffman, of course, won the Oscar. In an Academy tradition stretching back to John Mills in *Ryan's Daughter* and beyond, whether it was Cliff Robertson in *Charly* or, later, Geoffrey Rush in *Shine*, anyone playing a mentally disturbed role tends to be preferred. *Rain Man* also won Best Picture and Best Original Screenplay for Morrow and Ron Bass. There was no nomination for Cruise. But, Barry Morrow remembers well, when he came off the stage at

The Shrine Tom was the first person to congratulate and embrace him. Barry Levinson also won for Best Director. He has a hook on why Cruise is somewhat overlooked on such occasions. 'Tom is at a disadvantage. He's got such a pretty face his abilities are underestimated. And he's not working a rebel image, which is associated with being a good actor.'

No man under the age of thirty had ever won the Best Actor Oscar. Time was on Tom's side. Time and talent.

10

BORN IN THE USA

Although it may be heresy to say so, especially in a film book, there are more important things in life than show business people giving each other prizes; in fact, most things are more important. So to put the Oscars for *Rain Man* in context, one of the most powerful consequences of the film's success was to open people's eyes to Raymond's illness and kindred conditions. Dr Darold Treffert, Clinical Professor of Psychiatry at the University of Wisconsin Medical School, claims: 'That 1988 movie, in its first 101 days, accomplished more towards bringing Savant Syndrome to public awareness than all the efforts combined of all those interested in this condition for the past 101 years following Dr Down's 1887 description of this disorder.' John Landon Haydon Down, a Cornishman, was a brilliant physiologist who in 1858, to the amazement of his peers, became resident physician at the Earlswood Asylum for Idiots in Surrey. There he devoted himself to the hitherto gravely neglected study of mentally retarded children. After ten years' research he identified Down's syndrome – also known as mongolism – and kindred infant mental illnesses.

After the release of the movie and his father, Fran's, subsequent book *The Real Rain Man*, Kim Peek, the thirty-five-year-old who could do seemingly anything with his mental arithmetic and had recall of some 7600 books, was to become well known through television. He developed greater self-esteem and capacity to communicate his message: 'You don't have to be handicapped to be different. Everyone is different.' He continues to make presentations across America – Fran calculates that to date they have travelled 1.1 million miles and Kim has spoken to 2.6 million people. As recently as 2005 a documentary was made about him and Daniel Tammet, the twenty-six-year-old Londoner who created a sensation with the 'Pi in the Sky' when he recited, from memory, Pi to 22,514 decimal places. This was done on Einstein's birthday and took place in front of Einstein's blackboard at the Museum of the History of Science in Oxford. The two *savants* were accorded the accolade of appearing on the *David Letterman Show*.

This is not to say that Cruise appeared in the film in the furtherance of all this. He most probably had no idea what the consequences would be but, possibly as a result, went on to make another film that would have a vast beneficial impact. There is little doubt that Ron Kovic, the marine sergeant who was wounded in Vietnam and returned home a paraplegic, would not have such a high profile and platforms to air his anti-war views had it not been for Tom Cruise's decision, while he was at the height of his fame, to play him in the movie, *Born on the Fourth of July*.

Kovic's righteous indignation has been reignited by the Iraq war. In 2006 he pronounced: 'As I now contemplate another January 20th [the day he was shot and paralysed] I cannot help but think of the young men and women who have been wounded in the war in Iraq. They have been coming home now for almost three years, flooding Walter Reed, Bethesda, Brooke Army Medical Center and veterans' hospitals all across the country. Paraplegics, amputees, burn victims, the blinded and maimed, shocked and stunned, brain-damaged and psychologically stressed, over 16,000 of them, a whole new generation of severely maimed is returning from Iraq, young men and women who were not even born when I came home wounded to the Bronx veterans' hospital in 1968.

'I, like most other Americans, have occasionally seen them on TV or at the local veterans' hospital, but for the most part they remain hidden, like the flag-draped caskets of our dead, returned to Dover Air Force Base in the darkness of night as this administration continues to pursue a policy of censorship, tightly controlling the images coming out of that war and rarely ever allowing the human cost of its policy to be seen.'

Kovic had been in the vanguard of anti-war protesters, notably at the Madison Square Garden Democratic Convention of 1976, but since the release of the Oscar-winning movie sixteen years ago he has become a legend, a rallying point for dissent. Commentators have spoken of him being in the great tradition of Gandhi and Martin Luther King, his hero. Indeed, when Bush was about to lead the nation into war in Iraq Kovic invoked King in speeches across the country to students, activists and even National Guardsmen, advocating non-violent protest and placing blame for the terrorist threat squarely at the feet of the Bush administration. 'The leaders, the president . . . they are the ones who have brought on September 11. It is their violence that brought the violence to our nation, and it's their violence that we must stop, and stop for ever.' He even flew to London in 2003 to lobby Bush and present letters of protests at 10 Downing Street.

There is a perplexing question mark hanging over *Born on the Fourth of July*. Why did Cruise want to do it in 1989? After all, the American presence in Vietnam had been removed by Congress sixteen years previously and Hollywood had already made hundreds of Vietnam movies, from *The Green Berets* of 1968 to Michael Cimino's inspired *The Deer Hunter* of 1978. The spirit of these movies, except John Wayne's, was anti-war, but that was not naturally representative of the initial mood of the country. (I made BBC documentaries about John Wayne and Clint Eastwood for the American Bicentennial in 1976, and the former was gracious enough to invite me for a holiday in the Pacific on board his converted minesweeper, *Wild Goose*. The ship was covered in regimental plaques and messages of thanks from those who thought their cause had been given a voice by his film *The Green Berets*.) But by 1988 even Sylvester Stallone had moved *Rambo* to Afghanistan: since 1979 there had been a US military presence there thanks to the National Security Adviser, Zbigniew Brzezinski.

The truth is that Ron Kovic's memoir was all prepped (with a script by Oliver Stone, Dan Petrie directing and Martin Bregman producing) and ready to shoot in Puerta Vallarta in Mexico in the summer of 1978. But not with Tom Cruise – not surprisingly, as he was only sixteen and still at high school. Al Pacino was due to portray Ron. He even grew a moustache. But when Kovic had his final meeting with him he immediately noticed the star had shaved it off: the project was dead. The official reason was that promised West German finance had not come through, although some of the participants were more sceptical.

'Al got cold feet,' says Stone. 'If he'd gone ahead any money problems would have been taken care of. It was a heartbreaker for everyone involved. I just gave up at the thought that the studio wouldn't make a $6 million film, not one starring Al Pacino. I became semi-comatose and Ron became a complete basket case.'

Within two days Kovic had to clear out of his expensive suite in New York's Drake Hotel and, having whiled away his nights at the late Steve Rubell's disco, Studio 54, suddenly found he was no longer welcome. He needed money and managed to get a job as technical adviser on Jane Fonda's *Coming Home* (1978), the story of a woman who has an affair with a man not unlike Kovic in a vets' hospital. Miss Fonda, who had earned the sobriquet 'Hanoi Jane' for denouncing American troops as war criminals in North Vietnam in 1972, can never be accused of consistency in her views – she later married the super-patriot Ted Turner. *Coming Home* attracted prizes but only small audiences (it took $32 million in the USA) and had the paradoxical effect of putting the kybosh on Kovic's book – perhaps for ever.

Stone was more consistent. Later, in 1986, he made *Platoon*, very much an account of his own war in Vietnam for which he had volunteered. This was considered an unusual act for a middle class white: there was a consensus that Vietnam was a white man's war fought by poor blacks. Stone had been decorated in 1967 for his charge on an enemy foxhole. 'Something went crazy in my head,' he remembers. 'I was pissed off because I knew the guys who had been killed and I had been smoking a little dope that morning.' His film took more than $170 million in domestic gross and he was decorated again, this time with the Best Director Oscar.

Kovic, as single-minded in his business life as he was in his politics, never gave up. In 1987 he told Bregman he was going to sell his book to European television for $25,000. The producer saw this as the vet selling his birthright for a mess of pottage so he called Tom Pollock, boss at Universal, and advised him to buy now. Pollock had once been Stone's lawyer, and a deal was quickly concluded with Kovic.

The studio must have realised this was a slightly passé project politically, and so would stand or fall as a human interest story. (The whole 'domino theory' that panicked the United States into intervening in Vietnam was no longer sustainable. The Russians had left Afghanistan and Gorbachev's *perestroika* and *glasnost* had opened up the Soviet

Union. Before the film even opened, on 9 November 1989, the Berlin Wall would fall.) So the film certainly needed a big star to support it. The usual suspects were considered – Sean Penn, Charlie Sheen, Nicholas Cage – but none of them could truly 'open' a picture. As it happened, Tom Cruise and Paula Wagner were both pondering the need for Tom to fly solo on a major project – he had partnered Paul Newman to an Oscar in *The Color of Money* and was about to be seen doing the same for Dustin Hoffman; now he had earned a clear run at the podium by himself. As it happened, Paula Wagner was also Oliver Stone's agent – Hollywood, near the pinnacle of the mountain, is very small – and Tom was just twenty pages into the script when he committed.

Oliver Stone, more than once bitten, was very nervous that he might lose this very big fish. 'I remember Oliver just, calling, calling, calling,' Cruise laughs. 'Finally I had to say: "Oliver, you just don't know me. Back off. Just let me do it. Just know it, if you say 'Do it, ten times,' I'm going to do it twelve times. If the call time is 6.00 am, trust me, I'll be there at 5.30. You don't have to worry. Everything's going to be organized. I'm committed to you. I'm committed to the film and by the end I will give you everything that I have. Trust me." And, from that moment, there was a bond that I felt with him.'

Ron Kovic, on the other hand, affected to be unimpressed by the landing of the top-drawing box-office star of 1988. He wasn't sure that Cruise was up to it. His Damascene moment came when he was waiting for Cruise to come to his house. Looking out of a first-floor window, he saw the star elaborately slide out of his car and into a wheelchair and struggle to get up the kerb. Soon they were doing 'wheelies' together in the back garden – and wheeling into shops. 'I remember I was going around with Kovic and I was in the wheelchair,' Tom recalls. 'I went into this high-tech gift shop and the girl comes up to me and says: "Excuse me, sir, I'm sorry but could you please stop rolling around on our carpet or I'm going to have to ask you to leave." I said: "Why?" She said: "Your tyres are leaving marks." I could not believe it.' He left the shop incandescent with rage. When they were outside he asked Kovic why he had not had a go at the woman. 'You've only had a month,' the vet replied. 'I've had twenty years.'

Together they paid several visits to the Veterans' Association Hospital in Long Beach, where Cruise listened intently to the stories of other crippled people and they used the paraplegic workout room in the basement. The only thing that marred these fact-finding visits was the American cult of celebrity: the star would find himself spending more time signing autographs than learning about the disability he was to portray.

Tom also recalled how he would bring his wheelchair to his bed and climb in with his then wife, Mimi Rogers, as if he were paralysed. 'There were times when I came home and I would have long talks with Mimi and you just can't help but think: "This could be me."' (By the time the film premiered at the end of 1989 he would be hand-in-hand with Nicole Kidman, so things must soon have begun to deteriorate.) One of the tragedies of Ron's story was that he would never be able to procreate nor to have conventional sex: he was numb from the waist down.

A true patriot, inspired by the films of John Wayne, Ron left the small town of Massapequa, Long Island and volunteered for the Marines. In his second tour of duty in Vietnam, his unit attacked a village where the Viet Cong used the cover of women and children whom his unit killed. In a confused retreat against a glaring sun he saw a VC coming for him and shot him. It proved to be a colleague, Wilson. The colonel refused to accept his confession and on a later mission he was nearly killed himself by a bullet through his spine. After a nightmare period in the filthy and understaffed Bronx Veterans' Hospital he returned home a hero, wearing a Purple Heart and a Bronze Star. But from the moment he visited his student sweetheart, Donna, on her Syracuse campus, where she was instrumental in the anti-war movement, he began to have doubts and eventually joined Veterans Against the War to disrupt the 1972 Republican Convention which re-elected Nixon. Having written the book about his experiences, he was welcomed as a keynote speaker at the 1976 Democratic Convention in New York. This is the story of a man who has been to hell but, sadly, not quite back. The Christian patriot yells to his parents: 'God is as dead as my legs.' Take away the political and military reasons for his paraplegia and it remains the cry of someone who screams: 'I want to be a man again.'

Oliver Stone shot the movie in his customary in-your-face style, plunging us into the horror with his Steadicam and spelling out the messages. Tom has to get his tongue round dialogue such as: 'Ever since I was a kid I wanted to serve my country. I wanted to go to Vietnam and I'll die there if I have to.' The sentiments, as could so many in the film, could come from Kovic or Stone.

Using the technique he had honed on *Platoon*, Stone engaged retired Captain Dale Dye to put the troops (Cruise included) through a two-week boot camp so they would know what it was like to dig a foxhole and sleep in it. Probably the most important piece of casting after the star was that of his parents. Their faces must carry the pain, sympathy, incredulity and shattered values of middle America. Again Stone went back one of his previous movies – *The Year of the Dragon* – and cast Raymond Barry and Caroline Kava who, through their gentleness, expressed their repressed emotions with extraordinary power.

But the crux of the film is Cruise, who is in nearly every shot. He knew it wasn't going to be easy. 'Artistically it was the most challenging role I've ever had.' But he was ready for the challenge and rose to it with instinct, intelligence and magnificence. 'My head was shaved, I'd lost weight, I was exhausted and I got into that mind-set. I saw it in Ron's eyes. You couldn't fake it. You had to go there. When Ron got angry he just wanted to explode. And I found it hard to disassociate those moments. It just became the world. And Oliver wanted it, created it, lived in that world. I'm not saying it's the healthiest thing to do, but it was the right thing to do and the only way to play that character. I felt it was a defining time for me.'

It is doubtful if he will ever again be offered a role of such rich texture and plangent despair. Quite simply, he plays it perfectly. The innocent jingoism of a small-town boy eager to make a reputation even in the cannon's mouth. The confident sergeant in 'Nam who, on learning that a rookie is from Venus, Georgia, informs him that 'This is my second tour and I haven't seen a Georgia boy hurt yet.' (Later, he was accidentally to shoot him.) The helpless horror of this and seeing the women and children they have killed. Stone is not afraid to close in on Cruise's eyes to communicate a sentiment. The cries from the heart in the Dickensian bedlam of the Bronx hospital, with guts on the beds and rats on the floor. The self-deluding determination to walk when he has been told there is absolutely no hope. The agonising show of dignity and self-reliance when he comes home. The mad debauchery of Mexico, where mescal offers him temporary balm and whores can do little for him, ending in a lunatic wheelchair fight in the desert with Willem Dafoe. The realisation that 'they had lied to me; they tricked me into going to war – the leadership of this government sickens me'. Finally, his finest hour when he has found his purpose in life and can define his life through that purpose. It is an overwhelming sweep of compelling emotions.

Cruise didn't win the Oscar. Daniel Day-Lewis did for *My Left Foot* – another wheelchair part. But Tom was nominated, and Oliver Stone won Best Director for the second time in four years. A greater reward, perhaps, came from Ron Kovic who towards the end of filming gave Tom his Vietnam Bronze Star on his birthday, 3 July. He knew what the film star had done for him. 'Young kids can sit in the same theatres we sat in thirty years ago with their popcorn and watch the movie the way we watched John

Wayne,' Kovic says, 'and they're going to see Tom Cruise and it's going to change the way the way they think about war. And maybe they won't have to be hurt like I was. I feel like I have turned a terrible tragedy into a triumph. No matter what happens with this film, I have won.'

11

TRACKING NICOLE

It is truth universally acknowledged that every male Hollywood star in possession of fame and fortune must, when he has achieved the clout, make a motor racing film. For example James Cagney, *The Crowd Roars* (1932); Pat O'Brien, *Indianapolis Speedway* (1939); Mickey Rooney, *The Big Wheel* (1949); Clark Gable, *To Please a Lady* (1950); Kirk Douglas, *The Racers* (1955); Elvis Presley, *Spinout* (1966) and *Speedway* (1968); Paul Newman, *Winning* (1969); Steve McQueen, *Le Mans* (1971); Al Pacino, *Bobby Deerfield* (1977); Tom Cruise, *Days of Thunder* (1990); Sylvester Stallone, *Driven* (2000).

They are rarely particularly successful. One of the reasons for this is that, as the late Formula One world champion, James Hunt, noted, people go to motor racing to see crashes – and movie crashes aren't real. The fact that in *Days of Thunder* the director managed to get two stunt cars into the real Daytona 500, the most famous stock car race in the world, for the first forty laps might have been good for some exciting shots, but could hardly induce excitement in audiences. Also, most sports films suffer from the fact that there is an artificial, pre-planned outcome: we know who's going to win. People attend most sports for precisely the opposite reason – because they *don't* know who is going to win. Only films that capture the iconography of a sport – baseball films often work for this reason – manage to supersede these inbuilt flaws.

Paul Newman can be blamed, in part, for *Days of Thunder*. As already noted, he had introduced Tom to the track while making *The Color of Money*, letting him train with his Nissan team mate, Jim Fitzgerald. Enthused, Cruise dragged Don Simpson along to the Bob Bondurant School of High Performance Driving, just north of San Francisco, for an intensive course. Bondurant was of the opinion that the 180mph Cruise was proficient enough to turn professional. And then he started racing Nissans for Newman's team. But it was while the two men were having a burn-up round the Daytona International Speedway Track, where the National Association for Stock Car Auto Racing (NASCAR) holds the Daytona 500, that the muse descended on Cruise and he knew the time had come for him to make a motor racing film.

He penned a fairly simple plot, probably rightly since stock car racing lends itself more to *Boys' Own* stories than to Proust. Cole Trickle – where do they get these names? – (Cruise) arrives on his motorbike at the track at Charlotte,

North Carolina where Harry Hogge (Robert Duvall) has arrived to see if it's worth coming out of retirement to prepare Cole and build him a car for the Daytona 500. You bet it is: Cole burns up the track like a coiffured meteor. He beats mean rival Rowdy Burns (Michael Rooker) in the next race but they both end up in hospital, subsequently having wheelchair races down the corridors. Dr Claire Lewicki (Nicole Kidman) is a brain surgeon who cures Cole but, alas, she will not allow Rowdy to race again. Cole does, and he wins the big one.

Tom rounded up his *Top Gun* producers and director Tony Scott to make the movie but, although it is consistently entertaining and well timed, it only made half as much as the former. Two things slightly surprise the vigilant viewer. The first is that the Hippocratic Oath prohibiting sex with patients can have no purchase in Daytona since Dr Lewicki is between Cole's sheets as soon as she has mended him. The other is the way Rowdy's wife Jennifer (Caroline Williams) says 'Hi, Tom' when she greets Cole. Evidently there were no resources for a retake or even a redub.

Offscreen there was a certain amount of drama. Cruise was caught speeding – 66mph in the 35mph streets of Darlington, North Carolina. But the kind cop, because he was dealing with a star, dropped the charge to that of careless operation of a vehicle and fined him only $125.

There is scant evidence of the genius Robert Towne, who was brought in to collaborate on the script, save for the way one joke is set up using the Hollywood technique of 'laying the pipe'. First Hogge and the car crew pull a stunt on Trickle whereby he is searched by a policewoman who slips her hand down his underpants and on to his beef bayonet. He is shocked but it proves to be a set-up – she is a stripper dressed as a cop. When those self-same mates come to visit him in hospital Hogge introduces Trickle to Dr Lewinski and Trickle, thinking this is a similar jape, unerringly guides her hand to the same spot.

Robert Duvall is obliged to reminisce about the old days and the deaths of drivers, informing Cole, the rookie, that there is a tradition that no racing driver ever attends another's funeral. In this he is less than correct: at Ayrton Senna's state funeral in Sao Paulo his fellow drivers escorted the coffin.

That apart, Towne gives a philosophical underpinning to this seemingly straightforward story: 'Cole Trickle is the embodiment of the competitive zeal and talent that believes blindly in itself. Until that critical turning point of the story, a mind-bruising crash. It is then that the young protagonist must discover how much he can control his own fate. His story becomes the struggle of a driver to replace his belief in his own infallibility with the true courage of a man who recognises that, even if some things are beyond his control, he must go on to face them if he is to race, to win, to live his life.'

Indeed, Dr Lewicki tells Trickle: 'You're scared; it's called denial.' But there is scant evidence of this in his subsequent behaviour – except, perhaps, on the cutting room floor. Instead his life is now suffused by his passion for the doctor herself. It is of interest to speculate – and it can only be speculation – why Cruise chose Nicole Kidman for the part. He had seen the frizzy-haired young Australian in the movie *Dead Calm*, which she made when she was only nineteen – rather young for someone who a couple of years later would be asked to be credible as a senior hospital doctor who could make life-or-death evaluations from brain scans. Or did the sight of Nicole have some further effect on Tom?

Dead Calm was the tense, unnerving story of a mass murderer, Billy Zane, who, having killed and dismembered the crew of the *Orpheus* in the Pacific, boards the yacht which Nicole is sailing alone, her husband having gone to check on the *Orpheus*. Zane rapes her and she succumbs, in the hope of surviving. What follows is a deadly game between psychopath and gutsy teenager as she tries to outwit him. Nicole is plausible, powerful and pulchritudinous in the part.

Mimi Rogers, meanwhile, had made a quantum leap from television actress to the lead in a Columbia feature, *Someone to Watch Over Me*, directed by Ridley Scott whose brother, Tony, had subsequently helmed *Top Gun* and *Days of Thunder*. Her co-star Tom Berenger, the cop who had to watch over her and did rather more, was later to appear in *Born on the Fourth of July*. Mimi looked classy and alluring but the chemistry between them was less so, possibly because the director seemed to spend more time on the look of the film – Mimi's bedroom with its four-poster was a mirage of voile and muslin shot through smoke – rather than the romance. The late Adrian Biddle, Scott's regular cameraman, once vouchsafed that when shooting *1492: The Conquest of Paradise*, the director would spend all day at sea filming the eddies and ripples of the schooner's sails in the ever-changing sunlight – he had to be reminded at the end of the day that Christopher Columbus and his crew had some dialogue to deliver.

So *Someone to Watch Over Me* was a flop and Mimi's big break was never to be. She was clearly supportive to Tom in helping him with the part of Ron Kovic – Mimi had actually volunteered for hospital work with the mentally ill and veterans of the Vietnam War – and nervously supporting him at the racetrack. But fissures seemed to be appearingin their relationship as Tom began to spend more time in their East 13th Street apartment in New York (in a block that also accommodated celebrated Brits such as Keith Richards and Phil Collins) while Mimi preferred their Los Angeles home. It was thought that they tried Scientology counselling to keep their marriage going. Even when Tom stayed in LA the papers reported that they had substantial rows which caused him to sleep elsewhere, sometimes with his friend Emilio Estevez. After the marriage was over, Mimi was to claim that they didn't make love for a year while Tom was contemplating becoming a priest. Later she withdrew this remark, saying it had only been a joke. Not a particularly hilarious joke, one feels.

Tom was on the cover of *Time* magazine and *Rolling Stone* in January 1990 in anticipation of him winning the Best Actor Oscar for *Born on the Fourth of July*. To put an end to the rumours of estrangement Tom told *Time* how much he loved Mimi and confessed, to *Rolling Stone*: 'I couldn't imagine being without her or being alone. I care about my wife more than anyone in the world. She's my best friend. I love her.' The same month he filed for divorce.

Ten years later Nicole Kidman was to undergo virtually the same experience. But during that decade they were, beyond a peradventure, Hollywood's golden couple.

Was it love at first sight? Nicole was at the Tokyo Film Festival promoting *Dead Calm* in the autumn of 1989 when she was informed by her agency, ICM, that the producers of an American film about motor racing to be called *Daytona* would like her to read for a role. She was surprised and knew she wouldn't get it – whatever it was – but relished the thought of a free first-class trip to Los Angeles. She even made a booking to fly on to London the following day to visit her sister Antonia, whom she hadn't seen for some time.

Nicole duly presented herself at Paramount on the appointed day and was escorted into a room where she was introduced to Jerry Bruckheimer, Don Simpson, Tony Scott and Tom Cruise. The star greeted her warmly, put her at her ease and invited her to read a passage – although it wasn't actually from the film. She was nervous but was a good enough actress – she had been persuasive in the television series *Vietnam* and quite brilliant in the subsequent *Bangkok Hilton* – to hide it and give an authoritative performance. It was broken by Tom breaking into laughter, and soon she started laughing too. That was it. But before she left for the airport the next day Jerry Bruckheimer called to say they would like her to be in the film. But it wouldn't be called *Daytona*, it would be *Days of Thunder* –

and, in fact her character had not been created yet, but they would work on it. She would be Tom's love interest.

Nicole has a breathless recall of that meeting with the star. 'I thought: "Oh, my God, he's this huge movie star." He was like this huge powerhouse. He sort of filled the room. He sat down and started talking and got really intense. He started using his hands and his eyes started to sparkle. I couldn't believe the energy coming out of this person. I thought he was an incredible man, totally self-confident about who he was and what he wanted. The kind of person who inspires confidence right off the bat. The moment I laid eyes on him I thought he was just the sexiest man I had ever seen in my life. He took my breath away. I don't know what it was. Chemical reaction? Hard to define. Hard to resist.'

Tom's reaction was more succinct. 'Pure lust.'

Whatever their feelings for one another they tried to suppress them in public during the shoot, although many suspected a romance and there were, inevitably, paparazzi photos of Tom leaning into Nicole's car and kissing her. Robert Towne said he knew Tom's marriage to Mimi was over when he had dinner with Tom and Nicole at the start of shooting.

After the film wrapped, the couple went for a two-week holiday in the Bahamas. Nicole certainly came from a different background from Tom's. Her father, Dr Anthony Kidman, was an eminent biologist who had written books on psychology which her mother, Janelle, a nurse and social worker, would edit. Nicole was actually born in Hawaii (on 20 June 1967) – which handily gave her dual American-

Australian nationality and enabled her to work in Hollywood – but grew up in Sydney where, apart from her
acting, she enjoyed the healthy outdoor life which is the
birthright of young Australians. So she proved the perfect
mate for Tom – swimming with whales, windsurfing and
scuba diving. He even introduced her to skydiving while
they were shooting *Days of Thunder* – not a fact he
mentioned to the film's insurers. It was an experience that
appealed to the athletic Nicole. She later declared: 'It's an
amazing sensation. Not as good as sex – but almost.'

Days of Thunder failed to emulate the success of *Top
Gun* at the box-office. Director Tony Scott ruefully remembers: 'The Paramount executives said that Tom could
sit behind the wheel of a racing car and smoke a cigarette
for a hundred minutes and we'd make a huge amount of
money. They were wrong.'

Nicole and Tom's first public appearance together was at
the Academy Awards in March 1990. She held one of Tom's
hands and his mother, Mary Lee, the other. This was
received with general approbation save by an Australian
soap star, Marcus Graham, who was under the impression
that *he* was living with Nicole at their apartment back in
Sydney. Alas, no more. She was to move with Tom to the
penthouse suite of the Bel-Air Hotel, then a $5 million
mansion in Pacific Palisades, his Manhattan apartment,
and, eventually, a ranch and seventy-seven acres in Colorado and a home in Sydney to which they could commute in
his private jet.

Anxious to demonstrate that her prowess as an actress
was not dependent on her boyfriend, Kidman accepted an

offer from director Robert Benton to star in *Billy Bathgate*. This was E. L. Doctorow's thirties' tale of a young teenager entering the gangster world of Dutch Schultz. Dustin Hoffman plays Dutch while a newcomer, Loren Dean, was Billy – his career was not enhanced by reviews that described his performance as being of "colourless vapacity" – and Nicole was a rich married woman who had affairs with them both. The film did her career no harm – some thought she stole the show – but it had a wordy and cluttered screenplay by Tom Stoppard. Benton could have benefited from studying the scripts of *Goodfellas* and *The Godfather Part III*, which had recently been released.

During the Christmas break from the film Tom rented a place in the Colorado town of Telluride, which took its name from the phrase 'to hell you ride' which railroad workers would shout at departing miners in the previous century. The owner of the house had been told that the tenant – it cost $2 million – was a rich studio executive, but in fact it was for Tom and Nicole's wedding which took place on Christmas Eve. Tom was twenty-eight and Nicole twenty-two. His mother and sisters were there and he flew her parents in from Sydney. Dustin Hoffman (who was staying with his wife, Lisa, and their four children) was best man and presented the couple with a pair of balls – 'his' and 'hers'. They had recently shown an enthusiasm for ten-pin bowling. 'When I was younger I thought I'd be a political journalist because my father is very interested in politics,' Kidman confessed. 'Or maybe a lawyer. I thought I'd never marry. I'd be like my idol, Katherine Hepburn, doing everything for my art.'

Tom had not worked for a while – Scientology had now become his dominant religion and he spent some time with John Travolta while Nicole was on location in North Carolina – but had been reading scripts and found one that might give him and Nicole a belated honeymoon (she and Dustin had returned to work soon after the wedding.) It was something that Ron Howard, once of *Happy Days* but now the acclaimed director of films such as *Splash* and *Cocoon* had given him some years previously and was called *Sure as the Moon*.

The story was based on the life of Howard's great-grandfather, who had left an impoverished existence in Ireland to cross the Atlantic and join the Great Land Rush of 1893. Although conventional wisdom has it that Europeans stole all the land from the Native Americans, in 1893 Congress bought 6 million acres of Oklahoma from the Cherokee for $8 million and President Grover Cleveland instituted a race among the 100,000 people who competed for the 40,000 lots.

Tom's great-great-grandfather had not been in the race but had emigrated from the west of Ireland, and Nicole's great-great-grandparents had grown up in the town of Ventry on the Dingle Peninsula in County Kerry where the Irish sequences were to be shot. It was time to go home.

Cruise put in a call to Howard, who was shooting the firefighting film *Backdraft* on the lot at Universal. It is said that Ron was surprised to hear from him since Tom had turned down a part in that movie – unlike Robert De Niro, Kurt Russell, William Baldwin, Donald Sutherland, Scott Glenn and his first movie love, Rebecca De Mornay. It is also said that when Ron asked his cast to quieten down since it was Tom Cruise on the phone, Kurt Russell, reflecting the general actor envy of the star, said 'Oh, Tom Cruise. Let's all take ten.'

Howard was delighted. The fact that Cruise had come on board meant that Sid Sheinberg and Lew Wasserman of Universal Pictures, where Ron and his partner Imagine Films Entertainment had a deal, would at long last greenlight this personal project. However, when Ron and Tom met and the latter informed him that his wife would be rather good for the female lead, Ron had to confess he had never seen any of her work. But was unlikely to be an impediment. Screenings were rapidly arranged for him and, to no-one's amazement, Nicole got the role of Shannon Christie. Tom and Nicole were invited to go on the Oprah Winfrey show – shades of events to come – where they sat on the sofa and hugged and assured the hostess that working together would present no problem as they wanted to be together twenty-four hours a day.

Having cemented his cast, even during shooting Howard was having problems finding a title for the film. It went from *Sure as the Moon* via *Distant Shores* to *The Irish Story*. Eventually he erected a board on the set so the crew could come up with suggestions. One wag wrote 'Tom and Nicole's Excellent Adventure', and he wasn't far off the mark. They had a caravan as big as a castle (some said it had marble floors), with deep freezes from which their own chef could choose their menu. Inside it, they played endless games of cards and chess and backgammon. When in Dublin they had a court set aside at a private club where they would compete furiously in a daily game of squash.

But most furious of all was the horse riding, especially the big Land Rush chase. Nicole was already a proficient rider, which provided Tom with the sort of challenge he relished. Throwing safety to the winds and once again ignoring the film's insurers, they tried to ride like Derby winners, both taking many falls in the attempt. There remains a degree of doubt over who was the faster. Nicole's camp maintained they both attained speeds of 37mph, while some of Tom's people felt he managed 39mph to her 35mph.

It is not chronicled who was holding the stopwatch, but what was in evidence was that the script followed the established template for a Tom Cruise film: he masters something and becomes the best at it – flying planes, driving cars, playing pool, mixing cocktails – comes out a hero and gets the girl. In this instance he was a poor Irish boy who finds Shannon, emigrates to the States, loses her but then secures both her and 150 acres of Oklahoma.

The Cruises hired three bodyguards to protect them in Ireland, although that summer IRA violence turned to the UK as members of the Conservative government were killed with bombs in the House of Commons and the Carlton Club. It was improbable that the IRA would want to take out a prominent American Catholic, since most of their funds came from his country via NORAID. Nicole possibly had more to fear; just before they began their European location, the IRA shot what they thought were two off-duty British soldiers in Holland. The couple turned out to be Australian tourists.

Large black screens were erected in front of the Dublin locations – to protect them less from the IRA than from the public. Tom and Nicole had become very camera shy; on occasion, films were removed from the cameras of civilian spectators. In the Dingle Peninsula, away from prying eyes, Tom and Nicole canoodled on the set with such ardour that some of the crew debated as to whether they should throw a bucket of water over them.

For the part, Tom had to learn an Irish accent. He listened to recordings of Sean O'Casey reading from his play *Juno and the Paycock*. He also had two dialect coaches: one to give him an Irish accent and the other to make sure that that accent would be comprehensible to American audiences. Some critics would say that his accent was wrong, but they must have been experts in the Kerry brogue of the late nineteenth century.

Howard shot the film on Panavision 65mm the better to capture the Irish vistas and the Land Rush. An extra 5mm was added for the sound track and John Williams' score so that it could be shown as 70mm in cinemas. It was the last time 65mm was used on a film.

Far and Away (the final title selected) was not well received. At the 1992 Cannes Film Festival, where it was shown in the presence of the Cruises, there was a degree of audible derision from some of the host audience as the film entered its third hour. This was especially ungrateful as Nicole had ascended the red-carpeted steps of the Palais du Festival radiant in a strapless aquamarine gown, looking every inch the reincarnation of Grace Kelly. For the record, *Far and Away* was estimated to have cost $30 million, of which almost a third went to the Cruises in fees, and grossed $60 million in the States and the same again worldwide.

The movie's lack of success had no detrimental effect on the careers of Tom and Nicole, however, and seemed further to cement their marriage. She confessed: 'I was never going to get married until I met Tom', and he stated: 'I say to myself "Thank God I made the right choice in marrying her and was fortunate enough that she said yes." I knew she was for me. I absolutely knew. I just knew it. I just knew I couldn't live without her.'

However, unlike Richard Burton and Elizabeth Taylor who made half a dozen films together, they were not to work on the same picture again until they underwent the bizarre and possibly destructive experience of falling under the spell of Stanley Kubrick.

12

TWIN BRIEFS

What does a leading actor do when he finds his performance as a nineteenth-century Irish working man does not appeal to his wide international fan base? The sensible thing is to play *himself* again. Cary Grant created Cary Grant and rarely strayed very far from that character. What is one of the safest roles in which to play yourself? Play a litigation lawyer. The two professions are very similar. Lord Gardiner, a former Lord Chancellor of England, always said he became a barrister after Oxford because he didn't think he could hack it as an actor. There is fierce competition from members of the Bar Theatrical Society, even from judges, to get a part in the annual production in the Old Hall in Lincoln's Inn, and members wear their club ties with pride − as if to say they could have become professional actors.

So Tom reverted to type and played a lawyer not only in

his next film, but in his next two films – *A Few Good Men* (1992) and *The Firm* (1993). Further insurance came from the fact that both were already hits: the former on Broadway and the latter as John Grisham's bestselling book. His judgement reverted to type as well: the two movies would make more than $300 million domestic gross between them and re-establish Cruise as the one of the world's most popular film stars. Besides, his performance as Lieutenant Daniel Kaffee in *A Few Good Men* is one of the most outstanding in his career, ripping through a range of emotions that propelled the movie.

At the time Nicole had her doubts about *Far and Away*. 'In retrospect I probably shouldn't have done another movie with him so quickly. I should probably have done more by myself to be seen independently. To work with Tom Cruise is a great thing, but I don't want to be in every film with my husband because it becomes a little myopic.' So she tried out for all the main female roles going – *Ghost*, *Silence of the Lambs*, *Sleepless in Seattle* and both roles in *Thelma and Louise* – but didn't get them.

She was not, as yet, hot and was out of work for nearly a year. 'Rejection used to be very difficult to take but, as an actor, you learn to deal with that. My mum calls me tenacious. People can say things and it will hurt me but I think my determination is there.'

Tom, on the other hand, could walk into pretty well any part he wanted. What he in fact did was to walk into the Music Box Theatre on West 45th Street in New York and watch the hit production of Aaron Sorkin's play. Tom Hulce was playing Lieutenant Kaffee, but such is the law of

the Hollywood jungle that, although he had been nominated for an Oscar for playing Mozart in *Amadeus* six
years previously, his film career in the interim had not
shone. And from the moment immediately after seeing the
play that Cruise lifted the phone and said to the man who
had sent him to it, director Rob Reiner, 'Yeah, let's make
it', Hulce's chances of transferring to the silver screen were
less than zero. 'It was a wonderful character piece,' says
Cruise, 'with this young man escaping the shadow of a
famous father [a legendary prosecutor who became Attorney General]. I thought the character was tremendous and
the writing was tremendous. It would be a challenging
movie to make and I wanted to go on the ride with Rob.'

The third security blanket for a quality commercial
movie was that it should be made by the clever production
boutique Castle Rock. Rob Reiner, son of Carl who was up
there with Mel Brooks and Woody Allen, was not only a
director but a writer and actor – for eight years he played
Michael 'Meathead' Stivic in *All in the Family* – and
therefore very much an actor's director. William 'Nobody
knows anything' Goldman had decades of writing experience behind him and passed his advice on to Sorkin, who
got the screenplay credit. Despite affecting to be averse to
Hollywood, Bill Goldman has an understanding of the
system that is both analytical and philosophical. Andy
Scheinman, credited as a producer, is short, wiry and sharp
as a tack with ideas spilling out of him like shrapnel. These
were the men to bring home the bacon.

The genesis of the play came from Sorkin's older sister,
Deborah. She had just graduated from law school and

wanted to get some trial experience, so she joined the Navy Judge Advocate's department. To her amazement she was assigned to Guantanamo Bay – the 45 square mile area of Cuba owned by the Americans that is getting rather a bad reputation at present – to deal with a 'Code Red' violation: in effect, an illegal punishment visited on a soldier by other soldiers. Sorkin reckoned the government had set an in-experienced counsel to handle the case so that there would be a plea bargain and it would be kept out of the public eye. He also saw a potentially compelling courtroom drama, rich with conflict and moral decisions, in which rookie lawyer Kaffee/Cruise would be sent on a similar defence assignment. A man has been assaulted by two of his fellow marines under a possible 'Code Red' violation which comes from on high, but he has died. Kaffee has to find the guts to buck the plea bargain and follow a paper trail of evidence that leads right to the door of the commander of the base, Colonel Nathan Jessep.

Reiner's masterstroke was to get Jack Nicholson for this role. No other actor could radiate such volcanic danger. It is a small part – he is on the screen for less than 15 of the 138 minutes – but a vital one. In the read-through Nichol-son delivered his role at full throttle, especially his final explosion in the witness box where he addresses Cruise as 'You snotty little bastard'. Kevin Bacon, who played the prosecuting counsel, recalls: 'Jack just blew the roof off in rehearsal. Movie actors usually save it for their close-up, not the first reading. Nobody had more fun. He *is* the party.'

As Reiner hoped, 'He set the tone for the rest of the cast.

He's the greatest slugger of all time.' And Tom knew he was back in the top league. 'Jack is a legend. He's exciting to work with and perfect for this role.'

It was a wordy piece by anybody's standards and Reiner remains, if anything, more impressed by Cruise. 'He worked so hard. He wanted to be perfect. He never shirked for a second. He'd hang around after we'd finish rehearsals like a schoolboy. He'd say: "Let's work on this, let's orchestrate it. I want each one of these monologues to be perfect so I can give you exactly the right tone for each moment." He was absolutely brilliant. I think it is some of the best work he has ever done.'

Tom, in turn, appreciated Reiner's technique. 'Rob allows the actor to create the character, for it to be *his* character.' Kiefer Sutherland, playing a distinctly dodgy and adversarial platoon commander, concedes: 'He was so prepared and did such beautiful work that I could not have given the performance I did without Tom pushing it like that.'

Cruise also had the disconcerting habit of running from his large and luxurious trailer to the stage when called by the first assistant director. Kevin Pollak, who played his deputy, would watch him go past and think there was nothing for it but to run, too, to make the scene on time. Reiner had cast this former stand-up comedy performer with a purpose: 'Kevin's natural comedic rhythm and timing lifted Tom.'

Also lifted and sitting alluringly behind her starched white shirt were the breasts of Demi Moore, born Demetria Guynes in Roswell, New Mexico, where aliens may or may not have landed. Although Demi had been considered an A-list star since *Ghost* a couple of years earlier, her interim films had not been much of a success. It was undoubtedly a help having Paula Wagner as her agent and she auditioned for the part of the lieutenant commander who wanted to conduct the defence, winning it over Linda Hamilton, Elizabeth Perkins and Helen Hunt.

She and Pollak were fine foils to Cruise in the most significant scene of the movie. It happens on a rainy night in DC. They are waiting for Tom in his apartment. Things have gone badly wrong in court that day. One of the accused changes his testimony and admits that his co-defendant, a lance corporal, ordered the 'Code Red'. Significantly, he did not get the order from the lieutenant they had hoped to nail. Tom arrives back drunk and despondent.

The art of acting drunk on film is not to use the 'clinging to the lamp-post' stagger of the stage but to try to act as sober as you can – as a man arriving home drunk might do to his wife. But here a soaking and soaked Cruise wants to let his colleagues know he has been on a bender, even to the extent of pulling a half-finished bottle of Jack Daniel's from his coat pocket. He appears ready to throw in the towel, acknowledging his inadequacy. When Demi suggests they put Colonel Jessep on the stand, he responds with heavy sarcasm: 'I forgot, you were sick the day they taught law at law school. What do we have for the losers? Yes, it's a court martial for Lieutenant Kaffee. After falsely accusing a highly decorated marine officer of conspiracy and perjury, Lieutenant Kaffee will have a long and prosperous career teaching typewriter maintenance at the Mumbo Jumbo Club for women.' He sweeps the piles of legal papers off the table where they were going to work on them, and Moore sweeps out of the apartment.

The irony has turned first to anger and now to reflective remorse. When he asks his assistant lawyer, Pollak, whether his father was proud of him, he is of course asking himself the same theoretical question since his own father is dead.

Tom Cruise sees this father fixation as absolutely crucial to his character: 'His father is held in such high regard and is so imposing on his own life that he feels almost frozen that he cannot accomplish what his father did. He's also striving to find his own life. Where does he belong in the puzzle? He has to confront who his father was and who *he* is and really make his own decisions.'

The actor had, of course, no tenable relationship with his own father which he could relate to. 'Kaffee's relationship with his father was probably a lot saner than the relationship that I had with my father. Because with my father there wasn't a lot of communication. My father, actually, unlike Kaffee's, was not very successful at living life. I loved him, you know. But there's people that lack an ability to live life. I mean, life just pummels them, and they die. A lot of people, they just get hit. So much that their perspective on life is altered and they can't even come up for air.'

Kaffee boldly ignores what his father might have done in the circumstances. He decides to go with Demi and put the colonel on the stand, reckoning that the man is so in love with the perfect chain of command he cannot bear others to think orders did not emanate from him. 'I think he *wants* to say it,' says Kaffee, knowing it will be his job to provoke him into doing so. This is despite the fact that on the way into court Demi Moore's JoAnne Galloway does a complete turnaround and warns him: 'If you don't get him, I'm Special Counsel for Internal Affairs and you could get in serious trouble.' Somebody who was not politically correct might think, 'Typical woman'.

But he does get him. The movie ain't over until big Jack sings, and his final aria is delivered with such thunder and fury that you expect him to explode like Mr Creosote in *Monty Python's Meaning of Life*. When, under arrest, he bids farewell to the rookie lieutenant with the words, 'I'm going to pull the eyes out of your head and piss into your dead skull', one is left in no doubt that this is precisely what will happen the next time they encounter one another.

As ensemble playing goes, *A Few Good Men* is, in the words of another Jack Nicholson movie, as good as it gets. Reiner has set the bar as high as he dares and nobody dares fall beneath it. The Academy ignored Tom and dutifully nominated Jack as Best Supporting Actor, but the younger generation could spot the flourishing talent of one of their own and at the MTV Awards he was nominated not only for Best Male Performance but also as Most Desirable Male – an unusual category.

Of course, with Nicholson you have the greatest eye-rolling, eye-balling, eye-popping movie star of all time. When he wasn't on set – he was only called for ten days – people, Reiner included, would do impressions of him.

Cruise even included one on the screen. 'He eats breakfast "three hundred yards away from four thousand Cubans that are trained to kill me".' Whilst demonstrating the star's versatility as an impressionist, it does point up an underlying flaw in the film that moderated the reviews. There is no real threat from Cuba at Guantanamo Bay. If there were, a hundred US Phantoms would be there within minutes. As it is, the gates are opened every day to let Cuban civilian workers come into the base which, at the time, the United States used for training. That the commander of this place should be destined to become Director of Operations at the National Security Council – as Cruise is warned – strains credulity more than a little, even if he were not palpably insane. The point and the pleasure in this film is that it is an old-fashioned courtroom drama which douses the audience in its charm offensive.

Although still in his twenties, Cruise realised he now had enough clout to get films made and enough insight and instinct to know what sort of films he wanted to make. It was a logical step to set up a company so that he could employ people to find, write and develop projects for him. Thus with his agent, Paula, he set up the Cruise-Wagner Co. so that he would have more control over his own movies – and, incidentally, make more money from them. At the time every studio liked to have 'bed-and-breakfast' companies on the lot who would usually have a first-look deal with the studio boss. Thus a constant flow of material would be coming into the studio, thanks in part to the young people employed by these companies to scour Hollywood and beyond for script, and books and even just ideas.

They were known as 'golden retrievers'. This was where Tom and Paula were now headed.

Warner Bros had an especially good relationship with Clint Eastwood, for instance, whose Mal Paso Productions has a small bungalow on the lot. Clint would drive on in his truck most days, modestly presenting his ID card to the security man on the studio gate. After the overwhelming success of *E.T.* in 1982, Lew Wasserman and Sid Scheinberg, who ran Universal, built Steven Spielberg a beautiful $3 million adobe complex on the corner of the lot. There Spielberg works to this day. It is where his company, Amblin', has its staff. No written deal was done with Spielberg; Lew and Sid just hoped he would make a lot of films for them. And he did.

Paramount, which is sited on the other side of the Hollywood Hills from the other two, in an almost residential neighbourhood east of Hollywood, was not having so much luck. In November 1992 they realised they had only one movie ready for Christmas release. The chairman of the company, the exotically named Brandon Tartikoff, resigned. In his place came Stanley Jaffe, who just happened to have produced *Taps* and also was represented by CAA, who brokered a deal whereby Cruise-Wagner would come on the lot and have an exclusive multi-picture deal with Paramount.

Part of the bait was John Grisham's novel *The Firm*. The Mississippi lawyer's first novel, *A Time to Kill*, got some good reviews but was not a bestseller. However, Paramount had kept their eyes on the author and bought the film rights to his next book before it was even published.

Their hunch was right: *The Firm* became a number one bestseller. And Tom was right for the part of Mitch McDeere, a young lawyer caught up in a web of corruption. John Goldwyn, who was president of Paramount's Motion Picture Group, went out of his way to stress: 'This is not an actor's vanity deal. Tom Cruise is an important asset to have at a studio and having teamed with Paula with her extensive film-maker relationships, I'm confident in very short order there are going to be some very formidable projects in the works.'

His confidence was well placed. Although not all his future films were for Paramount – the old studio contract system is long dead, and stars will go where the property or the deal is most attractive – Cruise was to make more than a billion dollars for Paramount in the years to come. *Variety* observed: 'Paramount is hoping that Tom will become their Clint Eastwood. Their hope is that he will star in, direct and produce films for them and become a franchise like Clint has become.'

At the same time Nicole's post-*Far and Away* drought came to an end in *Malice*, a film written by the *Few Just Men* writer, Aaron Sorkin, produced by Castle Rock and directed by Tom's *Taps* director, Harold Becker. The film suspends credulity right from the start when Alec Baldwin, a top surgeon, becomes a lodger in the New England home of a married couple, Bill Pullman and Nicole. What does he spend the other $190,000 of his salary on? one is given to wonder. But he turns out to be a confidence trickster in cahoots with Nicole, their scam consisting of him – believe it or not – wrongly removing her ovary so that she can sue his hospital. Some people will stop at nothing and this film certainly didn't. All the acting is fine: Alec Baldwin is bad, Nicole is sexy and bad, Bill Pullman is good and dull. But the plot twists a little too vertiginously ever to come down to reality. So it displeased the critics but not the public, who put it into profit and Kidman back on the map in her own right.

It was a mere blip on the career of Aaron Sorkin. He went on to write *The American President*, again for Rob Reiner and Castle Rock. Michael Douglas is the widowed President who falls in love with lobbyist Annette Bening. This political comedy found great favour with the critics but less so with the public, its US gross being on a par with its budget. But Mr Sorkin thought, 'Why do all that research into the White House and the daily routine and problems of the President and not put them to further use?' Film enthusiasts may recall that Michael Douglas's aide in *The American President* was A. J. MacInerney, played by Martin Sheen. Sorkin decided to promote him to President Josiah 'Jed' Bartlett, and four years later he had created *The West Wing* for Warner Bros – a television drama which has left the writer like a pig in clover for the rest of his days.

Paramount wanted Kevin Reynolds, who had made a huge box-office hit with *Robin Hood: Prince of Thieves*, to direct *The Firm*, but he wanted too much money. They were slightly edgy about offering up their second choice, Sydney Pollack, to Cruise since he had messed him about on *Rain Man*, but the star did not hold that against him. Pollack, although one of the most agreeable men in Hollywood, had a track record like a metronome. Having won an

Oscar for directing *Out of Africa*, he went on to make the lacklustre *Havana*, which took less than $10 million in the States. He had rewritten the female lead in *Havana* especially for the Swedish actress Lena Olin, which might be seen as a mistake. What his films did have in common was length. *Havana* ran for two hours twenty minutes, *Out of Africa* for two and a half hours, and he beat his own record with *The Firm* – two hours thirty-four minutes.

Robin Wright Penn was inked to play Tom's wife in the film but found herself pregnant, so the part went to Jeanne Tripplehorn – a difficult name for a star, who was known on the set as Trippy. She herself appears not to have thought her name career-limiting – the old studio chiefs would have changed it overnight – judging by the name she gave her child by *ER*'s Leland Orser: August Tripplehorn Orser.

Tom pretty well starts off this film where he left *A Few Good Men*, as he does a courtroom cross-examination of a partner in the Memphis law firm who wish to hire him. They are, as we immediately glean from the menacing presence of Hal Holbrook, a corrupt bunch, and Tom soon finds himself caught between the devil of Gene Hackman and the deep blue eyes of FBI man Ed Harris. He is compromised by being set up with a girl in the Cayman Islands, but after the 154 minutes of gripping Grisham intrigue (it would have been more gripping if more economically told) he and Trippy move on to a less fraught existence. After 501 pages of Grisham's novel the young lawyer was washed up and left a fugitive in the Caribbean but Hollywood movies don't end like that.

Filming went smoothly, but after the wrap there were a couple of problems. Cruise had a contract that said his would be the only name above the title in trailers and posters. Gene Hackman wasn't too keen on this, so he had his name removed altogether. Also Karina Lombard, the Tahitian actress who played the bait for Tom to have sex-on-the-beach (see *Cocktail*) with, complained that he didn't discuss their love scene before they did it. She may be right: it is one of the most tepid sex scenes in cinema history. Karina also had a moan about Nicole's continual presence on the set. But none of these grievances prevented *The Firm* from being the fourth biggest draw of 1993, after *Jurassic Park*, *Mrs. Doubtfire* and *The Fugitive*.

Tom, who had never been to university, now received the acclaim of America's leading academic institution, Harvard. In 1795 a group of twenty-one undergraduates set up an elite society called the Hasty Pudding Club (so called as they took it in turn to provide puddings at their meetings) which spawned America's oldest theatrical society – akin to the Cambridge Footlights. To be voted their Man of the Year was a great honour – Bob Hope, James Stewart and Clint Eastwood were among previous recipients – but it meant you had to have a considerable sense of humour to take being roasted by the students. Tom was teased about his height, kissed on the stage by men in drag, and obliged to put on pink pumps and a bra with a bright red satin Harvard insignia on each cup. 'I know for certain that this award has absolutely nothing to do with the fact that I have just played two Harvard graduates,' he told them with a straight face.

Karina was less generous in moaning about the continual presence of Nicole Kidman. In retrospect it is apparent that the Cruises were trying to have a baby, which had proved unsuccessful. During the film's Christmas break Tom flew down to join Nicole in a condominium in Florida which they had bought a couple of years earlier. It was largely used by his mother and stepfather, but it provided them with a residency in the state which was a precondition of adoption. Also, Florida law held that once a mother had promised her child for adoption she could not, on birth, change her mind. Few states were as strict as this. So on 22 December 1992 a young mother who already had two children but didn't have the resources to rear a third gave birth to a girl, and after Christmas the Cruises returned home with Isabella Jane Kidman Cruise.

'I was twenty-five when we adopted her,' says Nicole, 'and for a week I thought; "I'm terrible. I can't do any of it right. It's terrifying being responsible for this tiny being." Then, suddenly, it all clicked. It was so weird.'

13

BRAD THE IMPALER

Nicole Kidman gave birth in the spring of 1993, sweating her way through prolonged pain to ultimate pleasure in a most convincing way. She was playing Gail Jones in the film *My Life*, written, produced and directed by Bruce Joel Rubin who had made his mark in commercial cinema by writing *Ghost*. To simulate giving birth on screen may have been a cathartic act for an actress in Nicole's position – or a privately sad one.

Here again Rubin was dealing with a man who dies, something of an obsession of his as we know from *Ghost* and *Jacob's Ladder*. But this time there are no trips into the hereafter. It is a solidly earthbound construct. Bob Jones (Michael Keaton) has only months to live and fears he will never see the son that his pregnant wife is carrying. So he makes a video about himself which has its good and bad moments. Good when he turns the camera on himself and shows his son how to cook and play sport, less good when we discover he is not who he says but ashamed of his Ukrainian origins.

There is much spirituality in the film, but it is not helped by the fact that Keaton's career had been on something of a downward spiral since his two *Batman* films. Kidman, on the other hand, is wholly convincing as the wife who must hold his hand on his journey out of this world. Sadly, it didn't give the needed fillip to her career, only just covering its costs – but it did no harm either.

Tom, having wrapped on *The Firm* and knowing that it was likely to be big, was presumably at home holding the baby. He and Nicole attended the Golden Globes (the awards from the obscurely constituted Hollywood Foreign Press Association) in January, and naturally there was considerable press interest in Isabella. 'Seeing Nic with Isabella I see a whole different side to her,' Tom said. 'Sometimes Nic forgets to turn the baby-speaker off and I'll just sit there and listen to them. Those are the little moments in life when you stop and think: "I want to make sure I'll remember this forever. I'm a daddy. Being a father is what I have always dreamed of only a hundred times better. She has changed my life."'

One of those changes was to make him less driven. He was happy to turn down movies such as *Indecent Proposal* since it involved gambling, of which Scientologists disapprove (Woody Harrelson heads to Las Vegas to make his fortune and ends up having to rent out his wife, Demi Moore, to Robert Redford at a million dollars a night) and Quentin Tarantino's *Pulp Fiction* since it involves drugs, of which they also disapprove. Fellow Scientologist John Travolta was not similarly inhibited and took the part. His justification was that everyone who took drugs in the movie died.

Tom was awarded a star in Hollywood's Walk of Fame, rare for one so young – he was only thirty-one – and hired a large boat to sail with his family down the coast of Italy. It would take something more than the prospect of playing yet another eager lawyer to lure him in front of the camera again, since his deals on his last two films had brought him tens of millions of dollars. Did his old friend and mentor, David Geffen, sense this? Had the time come for Tom to stop playing the (frequently redemptive) hero and essay an anti-hero? It was too soon, and would be harmful to his image, if he were to portray a truly evil man. But what if he were to play a character who was *not* a man?

Vampire movies have been a cinema staple since Friedrich Wilhelm Murnau's silent *Nosferatu* in 1922. Vampires were part of Hungarian and Romanian folklore in the eighteenth century, but in his 1897 novel *Dracula* the Irish author Bram Stoker established the template for the breed with all their recognisable or, rather, unrecognisable characteristics – they cannot see themselves in mirrors nor cast a shadow. Bela Lugosi, appropriately a Hungarian actor, established himself as Count Dracula in Hollywood in 1931, and variations on the tale have surfaced annually right up to the bloodsuckers who annoy Buffy in the present day. Young Tom Cruise-like lawyers joining the legal department of Twentieth Century-Fox are taught the 'Buffy Clause' on their first day at work. This is because the writer

Joss Whedon, who had made the studio a mint with *Angel*, was offered *carte blanche* to do what he wanted next. He had never cared for the *Buffy the Vampire Slayer* film he wrote, made by Franny and Kaz Kuzui (whose associate is a friend of the author – hence this story) and starring Kristy Swanson, so Joss foisted on a willing world Sarah Michelle Geller and the rest is television history. Except for one thing: vampires, since they do not exist, are not subject to copyright. But the character of Buffy is. And Fox found they had to pay the Kuzuis a sum not far from $50 million for using the character. Not a mistake their lawyers are likely to make again.

No such problems curbed the fertile imagination of the New Orleans writer Anne Rice, whose novel *Interview with the Vampire* sold more than 10 million copies in 1976. Her original take on the traditional theme was that the story was told from a vampire's point of view. Her tragic inspiration had been the death of her daughter, Michele, from leukaemia at the age of five. In the book little Claudia becomes a vampire and thus obtains eternal life – or did in the first draft.

So David Geffen suggested to Tom that he might be interested in playing Rice's evil vampire Lestat, and his timing was absolutely right. Curiously for a such a huge bestseller, her book had been kicking around Hollywood for sixteen years with various writers having a crack at the screenplay. Geffen, when he obtained the rights, handed it back to Rice and suggested she do it herself, which she did. She had based the character of Lestat on the Dutch actor Rutger Hauer, who did the 'Pure Genius' Guinness com-

mercials. When the producer told her about the casting of
Lestat she announced: 'I'm puzzled as to why Cruise
would want to take on the role. He's a cute kid, on top
of the world and on his way to becoming a great actor but
I'm not sure he knows what he's getting into. He should do
himself a favour and withdraw. He's too mom and apple
pie.'

The words gift-horse and mouth certainly spring to
mind. Miss Rice was as good a judge of film casting as
she was at writing screenplays. In adapting her novel she
had managed to achieve the near impossible: a vampire film
without any thrills. No wonder, pre-Cruise, many Hollywood A-list directors – from Spielberg to Polanski – passed
on it. The job went to the Irish director Neil Jordan, who
had done well in the States with *The Crying Game*, the
'chick-with-a-dick' movie, earning himself an Oscar for the
screenplay. However his last excursion into the superna-
tural, *High Spirits*, with Peter O'Toole in a haunted castle,
had been something of a catastrophe. Jordan recalls finding
Cruise pretty special. 'I had never met Tom. I went to his
house and got a this-guy-is-really-good feeling. We discussed it and played with it a little bit. I could see the
extraordinary power that he would bring to it and I could
see how he would approach that icy place with tremendous
authenticity.'

The main cast was completed with Brad Pitt as the nicer,
narrator vampire Louis. He was not nearly so big a star
then, but had made his mark by sleeping with either
Thelma or Louise in a motel room and then doing a bunk
with their money. Eleven-year-old Kirsten Dunst, who had

had a small part in *Bonfire of the Vanities*, was Claudia and River Phoenix should have played the non-vampire interviewer Daniel, but tragically he died of a drug overdose in Johnny Depp's club, the Viper Room, a month into shooting. He was only twenty-three. Christian Slater, who took on the part, gave his fee to Depp's favoured charities.

In present-day San Francisco, Louis tells his life story to Daniel. Two hundred years ago he had a plantation in Louisiana. Lestat, who according to Neil Jordan finds Louis 'a beautiful creature he wants as a companion', bit him to make him eternal. The two became companions – in a memorable scene Lestat squeezes the blood out of a rat into his wineglass – and Lestat bites little Claudia, who becomes their vampire daughter. Louis and Claudia take off for Paris, where the little girl is murdered by a vampire called Santiago – bu coincidence, the same name as the marine who is murdered in *A Few Good Men*. On his return to present-day America, Louis meets once more an injured Lestat who gets a much-needed injection of new blood by biting Daniel. If this sounds like the plot of an opera, that is not too far wide of the mark. It was turned into a musical by Elton John and Bernie Taupin, with songs such as 'Crimson Kiss' and 'Make Me As You Are'. Unfortunately it ran for a mere thirty-nine performances on Broadway.

Tom took his preparation for playing a vampire extremely seriously. The surface attributes were easily acquired: a flowing blond wig, fangs and a softly spoken English accent. But it was the inner vampire that he needed to discover. 'People don't do things because they think they're evil; they do things because they think they're right. It just so happens it was evil to others. So it was really important to understand that and to understand Lestat's loneliness. He really does love Louis. He really does love Claudia. He thinks what he is giving them is this wonderful gift of eternal life. They can join him in what he believes to be the greatest adventure ever.'

Neil Jordan observes: 'In a strange way the life of a vampire is not that different from a massive Hollywood star. You're kept away from the harsh daylight. You live in a strange kind of seclusion. Every time you emerge a ripple runs through people. Lestat would enter a room and it was like an invisible stone had been dropped into a pool.' Cruise certainly endows Lestat with his own charisma in the movie – and more. 'As an actor it's very challenging because you really have to root this character in emotional reality so you're not playing attitudes. I always thought it would be wonderful to show Lestat's sense of humour because he's such a bright character. You've lived that long, you've read every book, you can play any instrument you wish.'

With Tom and Brad and vampires it came as little surprise that the film had an opening weekend that took $36 million, but word of mouth was not strong enough to make its US box-office sky-high. Even so, $105 million, with a little more than that earned worldwide was pretty respectable. The critics were divided, but there was in general more praise for the scenery and the music than for the plot.

Anne Rice changed her mind about the movie and took out two-page advertisements in *The New York Times* and *Vanity Fair* praising the film-makers. 'I was honored and stunned to discover how faithful this film was to the spirit, content, and the ambience of the novel, *Interview With The Vampire*, and of the script for it which I wrote.' This did seem a little bit like patting herself on the back. But she graciously changed her opinion of Cruise: 'I thought Tom captured Lestat perfectly. He got the incredible strength of Lestat. He got the sense of humour of Lestat. He got the boldness of Lestat who is a strident powerful personality.'

The only discordant note was a confirmation that Brad Pitt and Tom Cruise had not become best buddies. Pitt puts it in elliptical language. 'Tom and I walk in different directions. He's North Pole and I'm South. I always thought there was this underlying competition that got in the way of any real conversation. It wasn't nasty by any means, not at all. But it was just there and it bugged me a bit.'

14

MISSION ACCOMPLISHED

In 1992 Sherry Lansing became the first woman to break the male stranglehold on the Hollywood studio system when she became president of Paramount Pictures Motion Picture Group, with the power to decide which films the sixty-two-year-old studio would make. She was to hold the post for the next twelve years. Producers on the lot said Lansing was most susceptible to heart-warming movies such as *Forrest Gump*. Although she did make an astute investment in Fox's *Titanic*, her policy veered towards the risk-averse with a predilection for remakes such as *The Stepford Wives*, *Alfie* and *The Italian Job*, none of which did very good business. However her presidency did coincide with Cruise-Wagner moving into the old Howard Hughes offices on the lot with a team of ten people to go through the innumerable scripts Cruise was sent every week and to work on new creative ideas.

According to Wagner, it was Tom who called her up one day in 1994. 'I've got this great idea for a movie – *Mission: Impossible.*' He would most probably have known that the rights were owned by Paramount, but nobody had seen the wide-screen potential in this small-screen TV show. The television series *Mission: Impossible* had been co-produced by Paramount and Lucille Ball's company, Desilu, and in its seven years on CBS had been a huge earner for the studio. What Paramount knew it needed for Tom was the American equivalent of a James Bond and this series had it in spades, not in the character of the boss of the IMF but in his daredevil action man, Ethan Hunt. (IMF, incidentally, stood not for International Monetary Fund but for Impossible Mission Force.)

Mission: Impossible had been the brainchild of Yale graduate Bruce Geller, who, having had a couple of flops with his Broadway musicals, went west to Hollywood for the less glamorous but more financially rewarding work of writing for television series such as *Have Gun Will Travel*, *The Rifleman* with Chuck Connors and *Rawhide* with Clint Eastwood. He knew that to the armchair viewer familiarity meant compatibility. People liked to see the same team each week and even relished the same set-up. Thus James Phelps was offered a new job every Sunday evening by listening to a tape that began, 'Good evening, Mr. Phelps. Your mission, should you decide to accept it . . .', outlining the mission and concluding with the caveat 'as always, should any of your IMF force be caught or killed, the Secretary will disavow any knowledge of your actions. Good night, Jim.' The tape would then self-destruct in five seconds, going up in the proverbial puff of smoke.

This was the masterstroke of Geller's creation: the IMF were a bunch of loose cannons, with no back up from the cavalry if things went wrong. Did Jim ever turn down a mission? Not in seven years he didn't. He always went upstairs to select the team by pulling photos out of his cabinet. They were nearly always the same: Willy Armstrong – strong and silent; Barney Collier – technological boffin; Cinnamon Carter – intelligent cheesecake; and Rollin Hand (played by Martin Landau, who was replaced after four years by Leonard Nimoy aka Mr Spock because Landau wanted too much money). The photos got the episode off to a speedy start and also enabled Jim to show the viewers any guest stars who might be on board and, frequently, some of the villains. IMF members liked to put on latex masks to disguise themselves as villains, so it helped to know what they were going to look like.

Missions included capturing nuclear warheads, retrieving a wire recording which had vital information on it and unfixing rigged voting machines in the country of Valeria. Such places were a source of pleasure to *MI* aficionados. The Cold War was still at its most trenchant in 1966, with Leonid Brezhnev breathing fire from the Kremlin, and CBS did not want to upset the Eastern Bloc. So a whole slew of new nations joined the global map – Valeria, Santa Costa, Veyska – and, even better, new languages. Thus delicious phrases such as *Belten Attachen* (do up your seatbelts), *Fumin Prohib* (no smoking) and *Neurlogkal Institut* were the lingua franca of those Europeans who attacked the IMF.

There was a writers' strike in 1988 and ABC Television crudely tried to circumvent it by recycling old *MI* scripts. It was not a success. Bruce Geller was not around to witness this debacle. Ten years earlier he had flown his Cessna into Buena Vista Canyon near Santa Barbara, California, killing both himself and his wife.

Tom Cruise was only four when the series was first transmitted, but became acquainted with it in his teenage years since it was eternally rerun on cable channels. He was a great fan.

He was thirty when he started preparing his film of *MI*, but mature beyond his years having been tutored for nearly a decade by the top flight of directors, writers and actors. 'I enjoy producing pictures like this,' he said. 'I like big pictures – it's a real challenge. The trick of these movies is to keep the narrative going and reveal character along the narrative.'

He was wise not to hire a director he had already worked with. Tom was now the boss and that relationship might be forgotten in the heat of the shoot. Brian De Palma, although he had had a dip with *Bonfire of the Vanities*, certainly demonstrated he knew how to create screen tension in *Dressed to Kill* and had already successfully brought a TV series to the big screen with *The Untouchables*. Also he was a writer himself, having worked with David Koepp on the under-rated Al Pacino movie *Carlito's Way*.

Tom knew this project would only work with a clever script and spent millions on writers, first bringing in Steve Zaillian, who had adapted Thomas Keneally's novel *Schindler's Ark* for the movie *Schindler's List*, to work on the story with De Palma, then David Koepp who, besides *Carlito's Way* had written the screen adaptation for *Jurassic Park*, an intelligently scary picture. Koepp is probably the best action writer at work in Hollywood today (*War of the Worlds*) and he relished Cruise's challenge: 'He's incredibly persistent and focused and he'll drive you completely insane because he keeps coming at it and at it and at it. But then you realise because he's gone at it, you're going to go at it. We wanted to make a plot that was complex. We wanted a movie you'd have to bring your brain to. The character trait in Tom you notice first and that leaves the longest and clearest impression is his directness. He doesn't dodge things.'

Then came Robert Towne, who had actually started out writing TV series such as *The Man From UNCLE*. Fellow writers regard his Oscar-winning script for *Chinatown* as near perfection – his private eye goes through a densely layered plot like a corkscrew, and those in the business know him as one of the best script polishers in Hollywood – often uncredited, as in Brando's death scene in *The Godfather*. He had written *Days of Thunder* with Tom and adapted *The Firm*, and the two men, despite being nearly thirty years apart, had found a creative rapport – Towne's love of unravelling complexity was matched by Cruise's instinct for the dramatic. Cruise knew precisely the blend of action and intrigue he needed in the script for *Mission: Impossible*. 'It's just what I want when I go to see a movie like this.'

Despite the bevy of writers, much of the film was faithful to the television series. It had Lalo Schifrin's memorable theme tune. Schifrin had actually written a different theme tune for the first episode of the series but Bruce Geller didn't care for it and replaced it with some music Schifrin had written for a chase sequence. The film began with James Phelps in his first-class British Airways seat, and a stewardess handing him a cassette which contained his orders delivered in the time-honoured runic of the original. The tape even went up in a puff of smoke, something that perhaps should have been a matter of concern to the cabin crew. Then a crook-nosed man is trying to get some vital information out of a murderer. He does so and rewards him with a glass of poison. Crook-nose rips off his latex mask and, by golly, it's Tom Cruise! Such masks make frequent appearances on many characters throughout the movie, although we never see them putting one on. However, cinematic technology has improved to the extent that we now see the masks being taken off in one movement. On television they had to do it in strips, with many cutaway shots.

The Mission – or McGuffin as Hitchcock referred to it – being the *raison d'être* for the action, but really an excuse for an adventure, is to trap a traitor who is set up to steal a top-secret 'NOC list' of deep-cover American agents. Things go terribly wrong as we move from Kiev to Prague to the CIA HQ in Langley, Virginia, to London and, by train, under the English Channel. But they go terribly right for us with a cornucopia of thrills and spills, double and treble crosses, traitors who are in fact good guys and vice versa. As Robert Towne said: 'What is involved is writing a story to fit the action.' And if the audience don't follow it the first time, they can always pay to see it again.

Action sequences here included a lavish embassy ball with an IMF man in a runaway lift, an exploding fish tank, the lowering of Cruise on an eighty-foot wire into a CIA vault, Tom doing his *Outsiders* somersault on a speeding train and then hooking an enemy helicopter to it. When the train enters a tunnel, things end with quite a bang. Tom wanted no stand-ins or stunt man and stood in front of a green screen on the back lot at Pinewood, buffeted by the air flowing from wind machines. Tom is well-known for doing all his own stunts but, according to De Palma, was less than keen in doing the scene where a vast aquarium in a restaurant explodes, cascading tons of water onto the diners. It was a one-take situation. 'I'm only an actor, Brian,' the director maintains he said. But he was persuaded to do so, although De Palma adds: 'I swear he could have drowned.' This seems improbable. Although the restaurant was established in Prague, the actual stunt was done under controlled conditions in Pinewood Studios. It takes quite a few minutes to drown. It was more likely that he would have been battered by the flood and the film glass. In fact he did hurt his foot. The hardest thing about being lowered into the computer room was that Cruise had to starfish out his limbs and not dare lower them for fear of setting off an alarm. This wasn't done by editing and different angles. The first assistant director, Chris Soldo, remembers: 'If you look at the scene uncut it is amazing. He was just under such control with his body.'

Cruise confessed: 'It was just a joy to work with the actors and to create roles for them.' With himself as the newly named Ethan Hunt – 'Hunt' is obvious and 'Ethan' came from the John Wayne character in *The Searchers* – there was no real need for any other top star names, especially as there was no romance. Jon Voight had played the Ron Kovic character in Jane Fonda's *Coming Home*, but since then his career had tailed off a bit. Cruise revived it by making him Jim Phelps. He also cast a couple of Brits – Kristin Scott Thomas and Vanessa Redgrave. Sadly, the former gets killed in the first act – her performance was much more persuasive than that of the miscast Redgrave. Similarly, the French actress Emmanuelle Béart was curiously colourless (a love scene between her and Tom was shot but subsequently removed from the movie) whereas Jean Reno, the marvellous Spanish-Moroccan character actor with the hooded eyes who made his breakthrough in Luc Besson's *Nikita*, enchanted the screen with his every move. Ving Rhames (Ving is short for Irving), the African-American graduate of New York's High School of Performing Arts and well-toned star of *Pulp Fiction*, was to become Ethan's main man as Luther and remain with him through the next two *Mission Impossible* films.

Although De Palma had his preferred director of photography and assistant directors, Tom re-engaged almost the whole stunt crew from *Interview with the Vampire* under Lee Sherward: Keith Campbell, Gary and Greg Powell, Dinny Powell, Chrissy Monk, Jamie Edgell, Dean Forster, Keith Campbell, Graeme Crowther and Sarah Franzl. This was going to be a big stunt film and he wanted a top stunt team who would do almost anything. There has always been a lobby to award an Oscar for stunts, but the countervailing arguments are that stunt artists would undoubtedly kill themselves in an attempt to outperform each other and also, that if a stunt is any good the audience shouldn't notice that the actor has been replaced by a stunt artist. There are so many stunt people filmed by the second unit on a Bond film, where actors rarely do their own stunts, that the main unit sometimes refer to themselves as the 'dialogue close-up unit'. But Tom did several stunts on *MI* – not just the aquatic restaurant scene and the Spiderman descent in Langley – and gained great respect from the British stunt crew. With his need for speed and passion for everything from sky to scuba diving, he felt most relaxed hanging out with them between takes.

The exterior location shoot in Prague did not go as smoothly as they hoped. 'Prague ripped us off. They're still getting used to democracy,' said Tom. 'But we made some mistakes with our negotiations and that we have to take responsibility for.' In fact he had a meeting with Czecho-slovakia's legendary president, Vaclav Havel, the poet and playwright who had been imprisoned by the Russians for his dissidence but led his country when it found its freedom in 1993. After pleasantries had been exchanged – Havel had been a friend of director Milos Forman as a young man – it was suggested to him he could perhaps put a stop to the overcharging. He effectively passed the buck, suggesting they have a word with the prime minister, but the mayor of Prague and various avaricious entrepreneurs were the continuing recipients of big bucks from Paramount. Robert Towne was impressed by the thirty-two-year-old produ-cer's tenacity. 'Tom was really under the gun with this picture. It was the kind that could have gone over a hundred million dollars just by batting your eyelashes the wrong way. We were working in countries where the governments and civil service were barely under greater control, with a script that wasn't finished and a lot of high-tech shit to shoot. It was a lot to handle.' The shoot at Pinewood Studios in a country where the civil service is under greater control proved much smoother with, as mentioned in the introduction, a visit from the future king of England and his mum.

Cruise and De Palma (twenty-two years his senior) found an effective modus operandi and kept any creative collisions behind closed doors and away from the set. 'Of course you have arguments,' said Cruise. 'How can you make a movie and not have arguments?' But De Palma was emphatic in what he wanted and it was his desire to end the movie with a bang – the exploding helicopter – that prevailed over Towne's more cerebral conclusion. This seemed out of kilter with the style of the ice-cool IMF and alienated many critics. Not the public, though: they loved it.

With a film of this order a studio may throw into its marketing as much money as goes into its production budget. This is a science. Paramount had set 22 May 1996 as the opening date for *Mission: Impossible*, in order to get the blockbuster summer holiday audiences. *Top Gun* had opened on 16 May exactly ten years earlier. But for all of 1996 the studio had been what is known as 'tracking' the film, which means identifying how aware people were of it and how interested they were. Thus the studio was able to see where it needed to increase the marketing spend –

maybe in television, maybe in young people's magazines. Some research companies are bold enough to make box-office predictions on the tracking but these are somewhat speculative save, surprisingly, in Japan.

First, though, the critics had their say. The early reviews read like a death warrant: 'An infinite trailer that is all effects, no affect.' (Richard Schickel, *Time* magazine); 'It's the worst kind of convoluted thriller – it can never unravel satisfactorily because there's nothing simple at its center, just more confusion' (Mick LaSalle , *San Francisco Chronicle*); 'The film is painful in at least one way – its waste of good actors' (Stanley Kauffmann, *New Republic*); 'Humorless, charmless and flat' (Hal Hinson, *Washington Post*). There was a little consolation in a positive reaction from *The New York Times* – 'A sleek, whooshingly entertaining update of the vintage television series,' wrote Stephen Holden. But *Times* readers barely coincided with Tom's audience.

The film was released on the due day, a Wednesday, in 3012 cinemas to run up to the Memorial Day holiday the following Monday. By midnight that Wednesday Paramount knew they had an enormous hit on their hands, the computers reporting takings in excess of $10 million. The film would go on to do $181 million domestic and $275 million overseas ($27 million in the UK), making a world-wide gross of $456 million. *GoldenEye*, Pierce Brosnan's first Bond film, had received rave reviews six months earlier and, although it was the most successful Bond to date, took $125 million less than *Mission: Impossible*.

Why, then, the disparity between the critics and the

international audiences? Many of the former approached the film from the wrong angle. The plot was too complex and convoluted for in-depth analysis. What they might have concentrated on was the relationship between Cruise and his public. The one thing they wanted to see their favourite star do was overcome impossible odds, and this he gave them in spades.

The best American adventure films owe a lot to the philosophy of Joseph Campbell. His book *The Hero with a Thousand Faces* (1949) is a study of the myth of the hero. He used James Joyce's word 'Monomyth' to explain that not only did most heroic tales have a common pattern, but that the hero's journey could be a metaphor for the culture as well. Hitchcock put it more succinctly: 'A film is its own country.' It has its own rules and practices, necessary for compressing time. The art of the action movie is to bring the hero up against a number of insuperable barriers – and overcome them. At its worst this can be 'With one bound Jack was free'; at its best, much more ingenious. While some critics can accept absurd scenes such as the hero holding the rifle fire of a posse of enemies with a single (inaccurate) revolver, they cannot accept that no one ever puts on a latex mask (which would take more than the film's running time). In *Mission: Impossible* country such things are givens. The film-maker has entered into a conspiracy with the audience that, while in that country, they will suspend their disbelief.

How much money went into Cruise's pocket is hard to estimate. Usually on a movie he might get a twenty-twenty deal: $20 million up front and 20 per cent of the gross. But it was a different matter when the star was the co-producer. He and Paula Wagner would split an initial production fee of $450,000. The deal was that Paramount would pay for the production costs, prints, marketing and distribution. The gross that is quoted is not the rental that comes back from the cinema owners; they hold on to around 50 per cent of the box-office, sometimes more but usually less in the case of blockbusters. But the split between Cruise-Wagner Company and Paramount would be based on the gross, and probably fifty-fifty. But every production contract is different, and secret, although normally a studio writes a window into profit share – say between $86 million and $100 million – where they would take $15 million clear as their undiluted profit. Based on these calculations Tom should have made 17 cents from every gross dollar – a total of more than $70 million dollars.

Nicole, too, had been earning her keep. In late November 1993 she hosted NBC's *Saturday Night Live*, which featured Mike Myers and Christina Ricci. In New York she studied at Lee Strasberg's Actors' Studio to add a knowledge of method acting to her Australian classicism. Withstanding competition from Bridget Fonda, Holly Hunter and Jodie Foster, she prevailed upon Gus van Sant to cast her as the upwardly mobile Suzanne Stone Maretto in *To Die For*, based on the novel by Joyce Maynard and deepened into a black comedy by Buck Henry.

Suzanne luxuriates in her fame when she finally makes it on to TV as a weathergirl in her New Hampshire town and, finding her husband a hindrance to her new celebrity and knowing that divorce might harm her public persona, she gets a younger lover to murder him. The husband, incidentally, was played by Matt Dillon who had had a much larger role than Cruise in *The Outsiders*. Slightly worryingly, Nicole confessed, 'I identified totally with Suzanne because I was pretty naughty when I was growing up. I went through my rebellious teenager turn-my-mother's-hair-grey stage. I stayed out all night. I was a terror.' Tom took Isabella to Toronto, where the film was being shot, and, after lunch with Nicole, they would go off and enjoy the city sights. Canadians proved less intrusive than their southern neighbours.

The film was not a huge success but Nicole was, winning a Best Actress award from the Boston Society of Film Critics, the Broadcast Film Critics and the London Critics' Circle, and the Golden Globe for Best Actress in a Comedy or Musical. She was also nominated Most Desirable Female in the MTV Awards. She was never to equal her husband's parallel achievement in carrying off this award, but she did win MTV's Best Kiss for *Moulin Rouge*. This is, quite legitimately, a shared prize, and the other recipient was Ewan McGregor. Cumulatively, these accolades and her *Saturday Night Live* appearances helped her beat Sandra Bullock to the part of Dr Chase Meridian in Joel Schumacher's *Batman Forever*. Tom's sparring partner from *Top Gun*, Val Kilmer, had taken over the cape from Michael Keaton and now became Nicole's sparring partner as they indulged in fiery boxing matches – something that was not likely to have been taught to young ladies at the Actors' Studio. The film had a captive audience, generated $183 million in the States alone – and if you didn't know who Nicole Kidman was by then, you did now.

She acknowledges this leap forward in her professional fortune. 'The breakthrough was a combination of *To Die For* and *Batman Forever*. It was a good one-two punch. People would come up and compliment me on my work in both films. That was nice – but, of course, they would always get around to asking about Tom.'

One of the reasons Nicole had had something of a movie gap after *My Life* was a tragic one. She had been obliged to audition by the New Zealand director Jane Campion for the leading role of Isabel Archer in Henry James's *The Portrait Of A Lady*. The two women knew each other: Campion had done most of her work in Sydney, and still saw Kidman in part as a television actress in the medical series *A Country Practice* back home. Campion was at the apogee of her career. She became the first woman to win the Palme d'Or at the Cannes Film Festival with *The Piano* and went on to win an Oscar for Best Original Screenplay and an Oscar Nomination as Best Director. But Nicole was not yet in that league. Campion wanted her to audition and also to hang out with her to see if they would get along. 'And then I had to wait two agonising weeks,' Kidman recalls. 'So nerve-racking. But I really felt I'd earned the part. I'd read the book when I was twenty-two and felt quite connected to the character.' Campion eventually offered her Isabel, but then discovered she was pregnant and the movie was delayed. And further delayed when Campion's child tragically died in the first weeks of its life.

Although Tom was in mid-*Mission: Impossible* he and

Nicole thought it was time to adopt another child. The boy was born to a single African-American mother in New York on 17 January 1995 and passed to Nicole three weeks later. He became Connor Kidman Cruise. Nicole took him with her and Isabella to the *MI* location in Prague, where Tom would sometimes attend production meetings wearing Connor in a baby harness around his neck. The Hotel Praha still uses the Cruise presence there as part of its promotion. In fact there had been no establishment in Prague luxurious enough for Hollywood royalty, so an enterprising young Czech, Martin Lukes, took this former Communist Party hotel and dressed Tom and Nicole's suite like a film set with carpets and furniture and paintings borrowed from surrounding castles. The Cruises had brought their own American chef, but Tom would sometimes cook pasta for his entire entourage.

Lukes was also able to advise him on the ways of the Czechs. When Tom wanted to go shopping he was about to set out with his usual retinue of bodyguards, but Martin advised him he would not be bothered if they merely walked along together. People did not expect to see Tom Cruise in Prague. And so it was – although the bodyguards followed stealthily twenty yards behind.

For the Pinewood shoot he rented just about the biggest house in Holland Park in west London – twelve bedrooms, staff quarters, indoor swimming pool, gymnasium, everything that his per diem could buy. Isabella went to the local school, and her parents frequented a pub in Chelsea's King's Road where Tom could play pool. They also rollerbladed in nearby Hyde Park, Tom sometimes pushing

Connor's pram. With the world market for such snaps being worth hundreds of thousands of pounds, paparazzi stalked them like snipers.

Cruise and Wagner were eager to capitalise on the immense success of *Mission: Impossible* with a sequel, even to turn it into a franchise. While Tom turned an honest dollar in *Jerry Maguire* and *Magnolia*, the start date of *Mission: Impossible II* was put back by an everlasting shoot on Kubrick's *Eyes Wide Shut*.

Maybe the wait was beneficial. With Pierce Brosnan in *GoldenEye* the Bond series had been reinvigorated after a six-year gap. The public had an appetite for a superhero without the need to dress him as a bat or spider or wear his underpants on the outside. And the public liked a lone hero – Clint Eastwood rarely had much back-up – so the Impossible Mission Force was diluted to Luther and Richard. William Goldman has always counselled that you should give the best lines to the star – and the best action pieces.

Also another influence had infiltrated the American mainstream action picture. It was not a recent one but came from ancient China. At the time of the Zhou dynasty, which lasted from about 1027 BC to 221 BC – the country's longest-lasting dynasty – the Emperor was, in fable, defended by the Wuxia – 'wu' meaning war, 'xia' meaning chivalrous knight errant. They were flying swordsmen in possession of more conventional martial arts skills. Early silent Chinese cinema realised the visual appeal of such warriors and the first Wuxia film, *The Burning of Red Lotus Monastery*, was filmed in 1928. Martial arts movies were exported to the West through the Hong Kong star Jackie Chan and the Chinese director John Woo, who made *Broken Arrow* with John Travolta. In 1999 the two Wachowski brothers from Chicago translated the powers of the Wuxia into an artificial future with the hugely popular *Matrix*. Cruise knew his action sequences now had to match those of this new generation of movies, so, while not actually assuming the power of flight – although he did reprise his spider-like lowering into enemy territory – he hired John Woo as director of *Mission: Impossible II* and became proficient in kick-boxing, flying scissors and other martial movements.

He was determined to move on from the first film. 'I never looked on *Mission: Impossible II* as a sequel in making it. I never wanted it to hinge on anything. When you look at the style John Woo brought to it, he said: "I want to make this an action love story." Hopefully we've imbued it with a different kind of tone and character. It still embraces the elements of a mission that's impossible. But it's more character-rich and all the colour tones in the picture are earth, wind and fire.' Paradoxically, the critics of *Mission: Impossible* had attacked Cruise's lack of cold-blooded phlegm and unemotional logic that characterised the television serial. Not only did he ignore them, he now shot off in a different direction.

He didn't have any women on his team, so he needed to recruit a love interest caught between the bad guy and himself. Kidman suggested the half-Zimbabwean, half-British actress Thandie Newton, a protégée of John Duigan who had directed Nicole in the mini-series *Vietnam* and cast her with Newton in *Flirting* (1991). Tom was entranced by the Cambridge-educated actress and suggested to Robert Towne that he craft a part for her. Although, for the moment the two meet, the writers came up with well-honed dialogue to show their mutual attraction, Woo managed to convey it silently in a series of glances – something, he says, he borrowed from the film of *West Side Story*.

Equally, the plot needed to be pinioned around the action scenes that John Woo could offer up to Towne and the *Star Trek* writer, Ronald D. Moore. There was another essential, as Tom Cruise recalls: 'When you are making one of these movies you sit down and say: "What do I think is cool?" I love motorcycles.' (True – whenever possible in his movies Cruise conjures up a pair of designer shades and jumps on a motorbike, the James Dean of the eighties and nineties.) Also Cruise reveals an alarming, but perhaps prescient, part of his childhood. 'As a kid, when I got to the edge of a cliff I wanted to jump off. I didn't want to kill myself; I wanted to fly. I never had a problem with heights. I love climbing.' So he did his own mountaineering, climbing up and then hanging from a mountain ledge in Dead Horse Point in Utah 1500 feet above the ground. 'I do it because it's fun. I'm not a great mountain climber but things like that excite me.' Woo filmed him from a helicopter. 'John said: "Just look at the view. Look at the beauty. Look how awesome this world is." So that's what I'm thinking.' But stars do not live by their fingertips alone, so he had a safety wire attached to him which would later be computered out of the finished shots.

With these three factors and the presence of Cruise, the creation of *Mission: Impossible II* was a perfect Hollywood example of the cart leading the horse. Despite the huge success of the first film, Paramount chiefs insisted on $7 million being cut from the budget. Paul Hitchcock, the film's English executive producer, came up with the simple solution of losing the Spanish location and shooting in the Australian outback for Spain. This made sense, but everyone was wary about Tom's reaction. Not only was he looking forward to a sojourn in Spain, but he wanted the prestige of his production shooting on three continents.

So a meeting was arranged at Paramount on Melrose Avenue to try and settle the matter. Unfortunately, when the participants turned up Tom was not there. He was in New York. Although a two-way video conference was arranged it turned out to be one-way: Tom could see the producers and executives but they could not see him – a bit like Charlie in *Charlie's Angels*. It added to the general nervousness. No Tom, and the whole movie could go down the pan.

Before the main business of the meeting could be put to him, Lizzy Gardiner, the chirpy Australian costume designer who had won an Oscar for *Priscilla, Queen of the Desert* and drawn further attention to herself by collecting it in a dress made, apparently, of American Express cards, asked to go first as she had a plane to catch. Tom said he wanted to wear his hair a little longer for the movie and, perhaps inspired by his Eastern director, described a more flowing outfit. Lizzy's reaction was expressed with Australian bluntness.

'If you dress like that, you'll look like a donkey's bollocks,' she said.

An icy hush fell on those assembled. Nobody, but nobody, had spoken to Tom Cruise like that since he had become the world's number one star. The silence seemed eternal.

'Well, how would you like me to look?' came the disembodied voice.

'Like Steve McQueen in *Bullitt*,' she said. 'Designer clothes but not new. They've worn in.'

More silence. Then – 'Yeah, not a bad idea.'

After that exchange, dumping Spain was dealt with expeditiously. The star was probably still envisaging himself as Steve McQueen.

The plot of *Mission: Impossible II* was simple in its explanation, complex in its exposition. Scientists in Sydney have genetically created a disease called Chimera for which there is initially no cure. When one is invented – Bellerophon – the boffin taking it to the States thinks he is being is escorted by Ethan. But no, it is a renegade IMF man, Sean (Dougray Scott), who rips off the serum and then rips off his latex Ethan mask before parachuting away. Ethan, ascending a perpendicular peak, gets his 'mission' statement from Anthony Hopkins through the legs of some missile-launched sunglasses which he prudently pitches away as they self-destruct in five seconds. Now he has to find the Chimera plant, the profitable anti-agent Bellerophon, and Sean, who has brutally injected his ex and Ethan's future girlfriend Nyah (Thandie Newton) with the disease – the latter goes AWOL with just five minutes to live (Hitchcock's ticking clock – a most effective way of building tension).

As Anthony Hopkins, an uncredited mission controller, says: 'It's not Mission: Difficult, Mr Hunt, it's Mission: Impossible. Should be a walk in the park for you.' It proves more a ride in the park as Ethan and Sean have a biker battle on Triumph Speed and Daytona motorbikes like the horseback knight-errants of yore. 'When you see what John Wood does with motorcycles!' Cruise enthuses. 'I want to scare the audience,' he adds. 'I want to thrill them. John Woo watched the way I walked. It's just raw action. Throughout the fight scenes, when things come danger-ously close, that's all real. We had a great stunt coordi-nator. I just dislocated my finger once and that was it. I never really got injured. The exciting part of acting – I don't know how else to explain it – are those moments when you surprise yourself.' Plus the Wuxian mastery of slow-motion action interpolated in the fights with double-cuts to reprise certain takes, and the sense of weightlessness as Ethan and Sean go for each other's throats.

Woo could not have been more different from Brian De Palma. He planned out every scene in models, playing with cars and guns and people like a child. On the set he would sometimes express his satisfaction of a take of a dialogue scene but Tom would countermand him and ask for it be done again. De Palma, on the other hand, would simply walk away when he knew he had it in the can. Woo's command of English was at best hesitant, and this encour-aged Cruise as producer to take more control. He had also grown exponentially in confidence since he entered movies two decades previously. He fired the production designer and brought in Tom Sanders from *Saving Private Ryan*. The director of photography was another Australian victim. Tom didn't like the look Andrew Lesnie was giving the picture and had him fired in favour of Jeffrey Kimball, who had shot *Top Gun*. Lesnie had subsequent reason to be grateful to him. He was now free to do *Lord of the Rings*, for which he won the Oscar as Best Cinematographer.

The love affair with Woo, however, was uninterrupted. Woo brings a connoisseur's camera eye to the city of Sydney, and computer-generated imagery had advanced to the point where Ethan's mask for Sean, a payback trick at the end of the movie, is not latex but a green screen rendering of Sean's real face which Ethan is able to tear off. Not that all the praise should go to Woo. As Paula Wagner says: 'Tom has creative input in everything. I couldn't do it without him. Making a movie is like being in a war zone. You're constantly problem solving. Equipment can break down, the weather will go bad. But you have to stay on schedule because that's how you stay on budget.'

After shooting each day and night, Tom returned to his Sydney home where Nicole and the children lived. There his life was strictly private. His chief of staff, Michael Doven – the 'Dovenator' as Tom calls him when he is in a good mood – had been to the Australian Pinkerton Agency and hand-picked a selection of bodyguards for twenty-four-hour protection.

In post-production Cruise was more hands-on than ever. In *Mission: Impossible* he ordered a remix of the score because he wanted to hear more woodwind. In *Mission: Impossible II* he and composer Hans Zimmer went for a simple guitar score rather than enormous orchestration. It enhanced both the thud of the bullets and the emotional moments between Tom and Thandie.

Does Ethan destroy the Chimera, save the girl and annihilate the baddies? The answer is as predictable as the reactions of the press and the public. 'A preadolescent action orgy' and 'If not the worst movie of the year, the most insulting and infuriating,' were some of the former, although Cruise did have his fans. But A. O. Scott in *The New York Times* clocked the genre: 'If Mr. Cruise peeled off his face and turned out to have been Chow Yon Fat all along, the movie might have been saved.' It *was* saved – it grossed $525 million worldwide, leaving the two *Mission: Impossible* movies just $19 million short of a billion-dollar gross. As pointed out earlier, the gross may be relevant to the star's percentage but nowhere near the studio's take. However, a survey in 2003 would show that the studios were to take almost five times as much revenue from home entertainment – television, VHS and DVDs – as from cinemas.

The *reductio ad absurdum* of literal and pedantic criticism is well exemplified by a colleague who disliked Kevin Costner's *Robin Hood: Prince of Thieves* because, in reality, Robin could not have ridden from Hastings to Sherwood Forest in a single day as he does in the movie. There are a couple of problems in this approach: In Costner country he can; and Robin Hood did not exist. Neither did Ethan Hunt. Nor did James Bond.

Bond had a licence to kill. With the *Mission: Impossible* series Tom Cruise had created, in the words of Lord Thomson of Fleet when he won the franchise for Scottish Television, 'a licence to print money'.

15

SHOW ME THE MONEY

While Tom was flexing his muscles as the all-action hero of the first *Mission: Impossible*, Nicole was flexing her mind as she approached the inscrutable role of Isabel Archer in Henry James's *The Portrait of a Lady* directed by Jane Campion. The combination of Campion and Kidman was irresistible on paper. Campion had always been a favourite of the Director-General of the Cannes Film Festival, Giles Jacob, who brought her to the attention of the international critical community with boldly experimental films like *Sweetie* in which the eponymous young heroine apes the behaviour of one of Jonathan Swift's yahoos as she climbs trees and defecates on people. Jacob's faith in Campion was rewarded in 1993 with her all-conquering film *The Piano*, which won the Palme d'Or. Kidman, too, post *Batman* and *To Die For*, was at the top of her game.

Both women took their collaboration extremely seriously. Kidman was ordered by her director to treat the role as a vocation, not a part, and banned her from frivolous twentieth-century pleasures while she was in the corseted straitjacket of a nineteenth-century gentlewoman. Nicole readily agreed to these restrictions. '*The Portrait of a Lady* is about a woman who makes the wrong choices in life. She has all these opportunities and then chooses the wrong man. It's about her wanting to explore the dark side as far as she can go. I've certainly been there and done that,' she revealed. 'It's the most personal film that I've made' – something she was wont to say of several of her roles.

Sadly, her sacrifices were unappreciated by the audience who did not find the film a twentieth century pleasure, less because of her than because of an unfathomable performance by John Malkovich as a con artist and the fact that Campion appeared to have lost the plot – at least, Henry James's plot. In the next decade she was not to recapture the flourish of her early work. *The Portrait of a Lady's* most enduring contribution to cinema was to enhance the career of Viggo Mortensen, later to find fame and fortune as Aragorn in *The Lord of the Rings*, the trilogy made by Campion's fellow countryman Peter Jackson.

'History,' they say, 'is just one damn thing after another', and so is a film star's career, though it is not damned by the occasional flop. However, Nicole needed a bit of a rest after her Campion ordeal and Cruise had a little loose change from the success of the first *Mission: Impossible* film, so in the spring of 1996 the couple decided to hire a sumptuous yacht and take the children and their entourage down the coast of Italy. It was a relaxing cruise, interrupted only by

Franco Zeffirelli (who had discovered Tom for *Endless Love*) inviting himself on board for drinks when they passed his villa – he was dissuaded – and Tom saving the lives of five people off the island of Capri. He spotted that their yacht was on fire and managed to get them on board his just as theirs sank.

The marriage was going through the best of times although, unknown to Tom and Nicole, it had already run half its course. Earlier in the year they had flown to Sydney for the wedding of Nicole's sister Antonia – a television presenter. Tom got on well with the Kidman family, although her father specialised in psychology which ran counter to the precepts of Scientology. But Tom was less doctrinaire in those days and Nicole tended to honour Scientology in her own fashion. Besides, he put his private jet at the disposal of the wedding party.

They had a caring, beneficial partnership: she would help him with his movies (like finding Thandie Newton) and he would rehearse her at home for *The Portrait of a Lady*, playing the John Malkovich part – rather better than Malkovich, one would imagine. In many ways they were mirror images of each other; literary licence would have them as identical twins, like Sebastian and Viola in *Twelfth Night*. (Shakespeare appeared not to care – or know, even – that you cannot have identical boy and girl twins). They were both beautiful, talented, rich and hungrily ambitious; both enjoyed being film stars and the worldwide fame of being one of the most famous couples of the decade.

That year, 1996, was a good one for Tom saving people. Quite apart from his quick-thinking action in the Mediterranean, at the London premiere of *Mission: Impossible* he lifted out of the Leicester Square crowd two small children who were about to be crushed; and before that, on the rainy night of 4 March, he was driving through Santa Monica when he witnessed a woman being knocked down by a hit-and-run driver on Wilshire Boulevard. He went to her aid and followed the ambulance to UCLA Medical Center, staying with her as she underwent tests that revealed bruised ribs and a broken leg. She was an aspiring actress, a twenty-three-year-old Brazilian, called Heloisa Vinhas, who was working as a waitress and had no money to pay her $7000 bill. So Tom took care of it. At the time she was too traumatised to realise who her Sir Galahad was, but she found out later. 'Of course I know who he is,' she said. 'He's famous everywhere, even in the North Pole. Tom is a very nice man – the best.' Pat Kingsley, Tom's then publicist, observed: 'If ever I was to get into trouble, I hope Tom Cruise is nearby' – which he frequently was, since she shadowed him from about four feet at every premiere and public occasion.

Soon reality had to give way to fantasy and it was back to work. Tom had already committed to the former *Rolling Stone* journalist Cameron Crowe to play a sports agent in *Jerry Maguire*. The thought of mingling with real football players – just as he had in films past with fighter pilots and racing car drivers – was more irresistible to him than money. Nicole, on the other hand, glad to be rid of her Edwardian corset, plunged into Tom territory as the acting head of the White House Nuclear Smuggling Group – not a widely known post – in *The Peacemaker*.

For some years producers had been trying to come up with the right big screen role that would turn George Clooney, aka Dr Doug Ross of television's *ER*, into a movie star. Early attempts had misfired. *One Fine Day*, a romance with Michelle Pfeiffer, had been hampered by the lacklustre direction of Michael Hoffman. The actor had been ill advised to don the cape for *Batman and Robin*, by some measure the worst of the Warner's series and which attracted reviews that might have sent other mortals scampering back into the emergency room ('George Clooney is the big zero of the film, and should go down in history as the George Lazenby of the series', and 'It *is* as bad as you think').

Nothing daunted, Steven Spielberg and his company, DreamWorks, had faith in the leading man of their internationally successful television series, and offered him the chance to play an action hero without the rubber-ware. Spielberg entrusted the producing to his main lieutenant, Walter Parkes, and Branko Lustig, who had co-produced *Schindler's List*, and gave Mimi Leder, one of the groundbreaking directors of *ER*, her first chance to direct a feature. The story was based on a book entitled *One Point Safe* by the Irish investigative reporter Andrew Cockburn (father of Olivia Wilde – Alex in *The O.C.*) and his wife, Leslie, which revealed the fact that, despite the end of the Cold War, Russia had never itemised its nuclear weapons and there was always a danger that some fanatic might pinch one.

It happens. And Clooney, as a military agent, and Kidman, as the aforementioned scientist, are sent to stop him.

After the traditional 'meet-cute' – the scriptwriting device by which the couple start out mistrustful of each other while we, the audience, know that they will end up an item (Jane Austen pioneered this in *Pride and Prejudice*), Leder and her writer, Michael Schiffer, took on the challenging task of marrying complex details of the realpolitik of the chaotic post-Communist East with a red-blooded action movie. Commendable though this is, it builds obstacles into the flow of the film. If the audience, having temporarily suspended their disbelief, have to deal with rational thoughts about the real world – would an atomic bomb in the UN truly help the cause of Bosnia? – then it takes artful legerdemain to lure them back into the world of the movie. There, Clooney and Kidman hurtle via unpronounceable places from Emamshahr to Azerbaijan through gunfire and flame, on foot, by helicopter and plane until it is Mission Accomplished.

It is a well-made, complex yet predictable film, and Clooney moves through it with pace and grace. Kidman is pertly alert, a little older than she was as a surgeon in *Days of Thunder* but still very young for the head of the White House Nuclear Smuggling Group, acting or not. Why then did it gross $41 million in the United States box-office to *Mission: Impossible's* $181 million – less than a quarter of the take?

There is little doubt, especially today, about who would be the winner if Clooney and Cruise were to go head-to-head in a charisma competition. The two men know each other – indeed, Tom flew over with the children to Bratislava in Slovakia to reunite them with Nicole and play some basketball with Clooney. 'They wouldn't let me play,' Kidman recalls stroppily. But what Tom didn't do was to impart to Clooney what really makes an action hero. It is insufficient for him to be *in* danger; he must *be* danger. There has to be a continual sense of suspense that he himself might explode in anger or madness or both, such is the nerve-racking intensity that never leaves him. Gorgeous George on occasion gives the impression that he has just stepped out of his trailer before the scene begins, or that he has a first-class return ticket to JFK safely in his inside pocket. Tortured Tom is living in a two-hour world of strife and evil and constant jeopardy. He has no other place to go.

The fact that *The Peacemaker* had its origins in well-researched journalism may have hampered the film's chance of being a more unfettered popular thriller. Paradoxically, the popularity of Tom Cruise's next film was due largely to the fact that it was based in well-researched journalism. Cameron Crowe is one of a rare breed in Hollywood – a journalist turned film-maker. It seems strange that, when one of the most innovative and original periods of post-war film making was driven by the French New Wave in the fifties and sixties no one attempted to replicate the phenomenon in America or England. Film writers from *Cahiers du Cinéma* turned their talents from comment to creation. Men like Jacques Rivette, Eric Rohmer, François Truffaut, Jean-Luc Godard and Claude Chabrol laid down a body of work that was vital and provocative. Films like *Ma Nuit Chez Maude, Claire's Knee, Fahrenheit 451, Jules et Jim* and *Weekend* didn't remain in the cinema when you left; they remained in your head. 'Film is truth twenty-four times a second,' Godard somewhat pretentiously declared – but the work of him and his colleagues certainly stimulated the mind and provoked discussion.

Cameron Crowe grew up in San Diego, California, a precocious, talented and sickly child – he had nephritis, a kidney disease. At fifteen he was writing for local papers and later contributed to *Rolling Stone*. Because he looked so young he was able to enrol in high school at the age of twenty-two and find out what life was really like there in the early eighties. The resulting book and movie, *Fast Times at Ridgemont High* (1982), painted a true portrait of the prevalent teenage lifestyle centring round malls and fuelled by sex, drugs and rock-and-roll, every bit as eye-opening as *400 Blows*, Truffaut's film about disillusioned Parisian teenagers twenty-three years previously, and much funnier.

Truffaut and Jean Renoir were prominent among the film-makers whom Crowe studied as he was preparing to direct *Jerry Maguire*. The film had begun as an attempt to portray contemporary American man – 'that faceless guy who puts on a suit and tie every day.' After a year of research, visiting unsuspecting businessmen in their offices and making notes of their behaviour patterns, a friend pointed out to Crowe a picture in the *Los Angeles Times*. It was of two stern-looking men in loud shirts and sunglasses. One was a sports agent and the other his client. So Crowe – never a jock himself at school, due to his illness – switched to an examination of the business of sport, where the big deals ran in tandem with the flourishing of talent and top players were sold like slaves of yore.

'I thought the world of sports agents was something that hadn't been written about,' says Crowe. 'Where can you get a more highly concentrated pursuit of pure money? I wondered: what if love and honour attempted to flourish in that world? And so I embarked on a little wild journey of research. I watched a lot of football and travelled with the teams. I just clanged around the NFL for a few years and picked up conversations, went to people's homes and saw what their world was like.'

His guide was a sports attorney called Leigh Steinberg, whom he rewarded with a small speaking part in the movie. After meeting innumerable sports agents and their clients, he began to formulate the character of Jerry Maguire. The idea was that he would be a man of ideals. He is a top agent at the fictional Sports Management International, but the film begins with him quitting this firm, which he regards as cynical, and giving the office floor a farewell sermon in the form of a Mission Statement about downsizing. He then does precisely that himself as only one client, footballer Rod Tidwell, and one secretary, Dorothy Boyd, are prepared to accompany him on this individual journey towards what he perceives as decent success. The part was created with Tom Hanks in mind, but Hanks turned it down as he wanted to direct his own film *That Thing You Do!* But Creative Artists had another client on their books who might take a look at it.

Tom Cruise was in London where Nicole was still filming *The Portrait of a Lady*. He read *Jerry Maguire* and called Crowe. 'I liked your script. I relate to this character. I cried when I read it.' They already knew each other socially. Sean Penn, who had been with Tom in *Taps*, had played Jeff Spicoli in *Fast Times at Ridgemont High*. Tom had graduated to *Risky Business*, and the two of them and their friends sometimes partied together.

Crowe was delighted: the presence of Cruise would multiply the box-office. But it was not a done deal. The star flew to Los Angeles to meet Crowe and his collaborative producer, James L. Brooks, who was something of legend in the business – he had learnt his craft writing *The Mary Tyler Moore Show*, won his Emmies for *The Simpsons* and his Oscar for *Terms of Endearment*. Both men had been counselled that Cruise would not play a 'loser', which Jerry is for most of the movie, but the star seemed unconcerned. 'Who knows if I'm right for this part?' he told them. 'How about if I just read it for you?'

They were happy with him – surprised, even, that such a major star would read – but he was not yet happy with himself. He needed to get deeper into the part, and it was only after two months of research and studying of videos of sports agents that he felt he had cracked the character.

His gain was Winona Ryder's loss. She had been scheduled to play Dorothy, the loving secretary, opposite Hanks – but when she tested with Cruise they looked too like brother and sister. The producers rounded up other candidates – Cameron Diaz, Marisa Tomei, Bridget Fonda, Posey Parker, Mia Sorvino, Courtney Love etc. – but timing is everything in a movie career. At the time the scouts and agents were returning to Hollywood from Robert Redford's Sundance Film Festival. The toast of the mountain had been Renée Zellweger, who had played a nineteenth-century pulp fiction writer in a small independent film called *The Whole Wide World*. Renée had a distinct advantage over her competitors when she came to test for the impoverished young widow struggling to bring up a son. No Method acting was required. That morning she put her card into an ATM machine to withdraw some money and found she had none. Crowe looked at those bee-sting lips, and knew he had found his Dorothy.

Jamie Foxx, a high school quarterback who would later win the Best Actor Oscar for *Ray*, tested for Rod – the footballer client – but was beaten to the part by Cuba Gooding Jr who had had a small part in *A Few Good Men*. When summoned to audition for the role he informed Crowe, 'I'm going to pee all over this part' and on arriving to test with Tom yelled, 'Let's do it. I'm going to knock this motherfucker out of the park!' Rubbing Cruise and Cuba together was like a skilled boy scout with two sticks: they were combustible. The double-charged electricity they brought to the screen reached its apogee in Cuba's memorable ad-lib, 'Show me the money!'

Cruise was more considered in his approach to the part of Jerry. 'It was a great role, a difficult role and I knew I'd go places I hadn't been before as an actor. The structure of the script defies, really, what people think works in a movie because you never knew where the story was going to. Cameron's got so many stories being told.'

The central story was Jerry's determination, after being double-crossed by a valuable client and dumped by his girlfriend, to keep the faith in Rod where others have little. At the same time he makes a curiously sacrificial marriage to Dorothy, who loves him but whom he does not love in return. Do things turn out all right in the end? Does the box-office dollar wave its magic wand over the laws of probability?

The film has nice touches, not least Jerry's artfully ad-libbed scenes with six-year-old Jonathan Lipnicki (Dorothy's son) who himself provided the information that 'the human head weighs eight pounds' and his reconciliation with Dorothy in the middle of a divorced women's support group (providing a part for Crowe's mum) where Dorothy calmly tells him: 'You had me from hello.' This matrimonial reconciliation had its repercussions on some cinema-goers. 'People come up to me and say, "This is the movie I showed to my boyfriend and he proposed,"' Tom reveals.

Once again Tom Cruise played foil to an Oscar winner – Cuba won Best Supporting Actor – and once again he was denied one himself. Although he was nominated for a compelling performance, disability once again ruled the day and Geoffrey Rush, as the mentally impaired pianist David Helfgott in *Shine*, was the winner.

It was, however, the fifth Tom Cruise picture in a row to gross more than a hundred million dollars. Much more.

16

CAPTURED BY KUBRICK

In the summer of 1996 Tom Cruise's star was more than in the ascendant; it was higher than any other in Hollywood. This was the United States box-office gross of his last five films: *Interview with the Vampire* $105 million; *A Few Good Men* $141 million; *Jerry Maguire* $154 million; *The Firm* $158 million; *Mission: Impossible* $181 million. By the time foreign rentals, TV, VHS and DVD profits had been accumulated this total would exceed half a billion dollars, of which Tom would get a substantial bite. He insists: 'I've never done work for money, ever. If your choices are based on grosses and the film doesn't do well, what does that mean? It leaves you with nothing.' But now that he had earned substantial money he had time to think about what he would do next, always knowing that he was committed to producing and starring in another *Mission: Impossible* for Paramount.

'Chance', as Louis Pasteur famously observed, 'favours the prepared mind', and seemingly out of the blue a fax arrived from Stanley Kubrick asking him if he would mind looking at *Eyes Wide Shut*, a script the director was thinking of shooting, with a view to playing the leading role. Would he mind? Cruise venerated Kubrick above any other director then working in the cinema.

Nicole was still in London at the time, filming *The Portrait of a Lady*. She, too, was asked if she would read a script from Stanley Kubrick. 'I was stunned,' she recalls. 'There was a letter from Stanley saying he would love me to play Alice Harford [Tom's wife in the film]. He asked me to sit down, make sure I was well rested and not distracted, and to read the script right through.' Flattered, she agreed, and was then told to make sure that she was in her London house at a fixed time at the weekend when the top-secret document would be delivered by messenger. She shared the news with her agent, to whom it came as no surprise. 'He told me Stanley had been looking at different takes of my work for the past nine months.'

Tom had barely finished reading the script – actually it was more of an eighty-five page short story with dialogue – before he contacted his co-pilot to file a flight plan for a trip to London at the earliest opportunity. Were they going to agree to do the film? The truth of the matter was that if Stanley had asked them to film a map of the homes of Hollywood stars they would have agreed. Tom recalls: 'Once in your life you get the chance to work with someone like Stanley Kubrick. It could be two years of your life, but it would be worth it.'

Nicole's time was tight as she was filming nearly every day, so they hired a helicopter to fly from London to Kubrick's home in St Albans. Stanley was himself a trained pilot and eagerly gave Tom the coordinates to enter into the helicopter's Global Positioning System so that he could land in Kubrick's back yard. Well, not quite yard. Stanley and Christiane Kubrick lived on a sprawling estate with several gabled houses scattered about a winding drive and the main house, a vast but low Victorian building with stuccoed pillars. It was home and workplace for them both: Christiane painted there, and Stanley did all his pre-production and most of his post-production as well as controlling the worldwide distribution of his twelve movies there.

Stanley was waiting for them, dressed in his favourite home gear of a one-piece dark blue boiler suit with black buttons. His *Eyes Wide Shut* co-writer, Frederic Raphael, recalls: 'He might have been a minor employee of the French railways.' Even Nicole was a little shocked. 'He looked kind of stuffy. But he had the most extraordinary eyes you have ever seen. Hooded, mischievous, a great sense of having lived.' She was terrified of him; Tom, too: 'I was so nervous.'

Kubrick put them at ease with small talk about the helicopter they had just planted on his lawn and his own complex attitude to planes. Although he was a pilot he didn't fly, not even as a passenger. Inside the house he had a short-wave radio that picked up all the conversations between pilots and Air Traffic Control at Heathrow Airport, which was not far away. Stanley's theory was

that, although the international language of air communication was English, pilots thought in their own languages and the moment they panicked they spoke in them
as well. This very often explained a near-miss – or worse.
He cited the KLM plane that had ploughed into a Pan Am
jumbo in Tenerife. 'Communications difficulties' were the
main problem – people were shouting in French/Spanish/
English; 578 people had died.

On a much lighter note, he and Tom found a passionate
common interest in sport: Stanley had grown up in Brooklyn and followed his American teams intensely. And the
younger couple were introduced to the delights of the
Kubrick kitchen table, always groaning with food and
wine and open to anyone who happened to be working
in the house, which included two of his daughters, Katharina and Anya, and, of course, Christiane, his wife.

Paradoxically, Tom and Nic would not have been sitting
there if it were not for Christiane. Stanley had first read and
optioned Arthur Schnitzler's *Dream Story* (which is the
basis of *Eyes Wide Shut*) in the fifties and wanted to make it
then. But Christiane, who is German (they met when she
was cast as the German girl who sings in the café at the end
of *Paths of Glory*), recalls: 'There was in the fifties a
reaction in Europe against the American preoccupation
with psychoanalysis. I thought many guilt-free people
who walked out of an analyst's office could have done
with a bit more guilt. "Use your conscience to good
purpose, don't whinge over everything." Then Terry
Southern gave Stanley *A Clockwork Orange*. I read it
and said: "Forget Schnitzler, read this." He jumped to

that one immediately and Schnitzler was forgotten for a while. But he kept coming back to it.'

Schnitzler, a doctor who practised psychiatry, had been a friend of Freud's in Vienna. The interpretation of dreams was their not always similar voyage of discovery into the human mind through the unconscious. Billy Wilder, who had been a journalist in Vienna, had wanted to film the story but was unable to crack it. Indeed, when Louis Malle told him that he had made another dream-within-a-dream film, *Black Moon*, for just $2 million Wilder quipped, presciently: 'You've just lost two million dollars.'

Kubrick had given *Dream Story* to several writers over the years, but none had come up with a script he felt he could film. Frederic Raphael was, in some ways, a curious choice for a collaborator since his best work had been done thirty years previously. Kubrick made the going, though. He wanted the story to take place in modern Manhattan and he didn't want the married couple to be Jewish: they were called Harford (Bill and Alice) after the all-American Harrison Ford.

Raphael was publicly miffed about Stanley's changing of his formal script to a looser treatment, but had he consulted any of those close to the director he would have realised that Kubrick didn't want any scene or character to be nailed down. Leon Vitali, Stanley's right-hand man for a quarter of a century, told me how Kubrick required the basic document from which he worked to be as fluid as a river. Leon would do a lot of the casting, and when Stanley saw the video of the audition he would frequently amend the character to fit the actor. On occasion he would create a

With Nicole Kidman in *Eyes Wide Shut*, 1999

In the park with Nic and Isabella.

Tom and Nicole. Mr and Mrs Cruise (December 1990 – August 2001.) Nicole became Mrs Keith Urban in June 2006.

With Antonia Kidman, Nicole's sister, at the Golden Globes awards, 2000

Paula Wagner, his agent and then partner – the most significant woman in his working life.

With Penelope Cruz in *Vanilla Sky*, 2001.

With mentor
Steven Spielberg.

The Last Samurai

Two significant others: his mother, Mary, and former press agent, Pat Kingsley (in sunglasses).

The Scientologist – Tom Cruise speaking at the opening of a Scientology church in Madrid, 2004

With mentor David Miscavige.

Tom and Katie putting on a performance in Madrid, 2005

To the 'TV reporter' who fired a water pistol at him in Leicester Square: 'You're a jerk . . . jerk . . . you're a jerk.'

Mission Impossible III, 2006. Auditioning for Spiderman?

new character if he saw an actor he wanted. He never stopped writing and rewriting, something Tom was to testify to when he began to receive faxed pages in the middle of the night. And Kubrick liked, where possible, to shoot in sequence, so that he was free to let a finished scene have an influence on the one that followed it, causing alterations where they arose organically.

One passage in Raphael's memoir, *Eyes Wide Open*, published just three months after Stanley died, indicates that he may finally have reached this conclusion. 'Kubrick never explains why he doesn't like a scene, especially when he has to concede that it is pretty funny. I have come to see that he distrusts my jokes – any jokes – probably because a well-scripted passage of dialogue which presages a climactic laugh demands that the scene be shot precisely to that end. Joe "*All about Eve*" Mankiewicz used to say that a good script had, in some sense, been directed already. That is not the kind of script Kubrick will ever want. Anything too finished leaves him with an obligation to obedience. He did not want the scenes to carry any authorial mark but his. If I was preparing the way for him to do his stuff, anything that was markedly mine was never the stuff he was going to do.'

Kubrick knew who his leading actors were from their films. He had studied Nicole, as her agent informed her, and he had earmarked Tom for the top ever since *Risky Business*. He had thought his performances in *Born on the Fourth of July* and *Rain Man* quite brilliant, according to Leon Vitali. Before the couple left, Stanley, Tom and Nicole sat down and worked their way through the story. Stanley was emphatic to both of them: 'This film is about sexual obsession and jealousy. It is not about sex.'

Eyes Wide Shut – presumably Stanley's title came from Tiresias, the Ancient Greek prophet who was blind and warned: 'Your eyes are open and you see not a thing' – remains fairly faithful to Schnitzler's book, not surprisingly since Kubrick wanted to examine its essential theme of jealousy. To be more precise, Dr Bill Harford's jealousy of his wife's mental infidelity. Like President Jimmy Carter, one evening after they have shared a joint she confesses to her husband that she has lust in her heart. This is normally a prelude to sex, but she chooses to tell him about a holiday when she set eyes on a naval officer and realised that if he had asked she would have left Bill and their daughter for him.

This confession launches the entire movie, which consists of Bill's impassioned, ambivalent response to it. Is he looking for revenge? He certainly punishes himself with images of his wife coupling with the officer – although that never actually happened. These images are the most passionate in the film.

Dr Bill is called away to confirm the death of a patient, and his odyssey that night is imbued with sex. The dead patient's daughter makes a passionate lunge for him – but she is interrupted by the arrival of her fiancé. Bill picks up a hooker, Domino, in the street. Back in her apartment potential sex is interrupted by a mobile call from Alice. An old friend, Nick, gives him the password to an orgy, and Bill hires a cloak and mask (later the shopkeeper will apparently offer him his under-age daughter). The orgy, the main set-piece of the movie, is a black Mass, an almost religious ritual with a priest singing an Orthodox Romanian mass – backwards. Full-breasted naked women choose from the circle of men dressed as masked monks. And people fuck throughout the house, in all positions, in some rooms women having sex with other women. One woman selects Bill but warns him his life is in danger. He is unable to give the second password (not surprisingly, we later learn that there isn't one). He is unmasked and exposed. His life *does* seem in danger. But the woman sacrificially offers to take his place.

Alice is asleep when he gets home. When he wakes her she tells him she has been having a dream that they were both naked in a strange city, and that when she sent him away to get their coats she fucked many men.

The following day he retraces his steps to try and validate the previous night. A bruised Nick has been taken from his hotel by two men; he learns from his room-mate that Domino, the hooker, has been diagnosed with AIDS; he finds the orgy house but is given a note telling him to give up; a newspaper story reveals that the woman who saved him there is dead – he goes to the morgue to confirm this. Victor Ziegler, at whose party this strange sequence began, suggests to him the whole orgy was a charade to scare him. Back home, his missing mask is on the pillow beside Alice. He tells her all.

Did it happen? Was it a nightmare? Or a waking dream? Certainly, it had the heightened reality of a dream. Alice forgives him: 'One night is not the whole life.' But Bill knows he has been changed for life: 'No dream is just a dream.'

It is a mature and subtle movie. Kubrick does not spoon-feed you stories; he tries to infiltrate your mind and disturb it. Tom and Nicole entered this wholeheartedly. Their characters must have been married for at least eight years and while he undoubtedly loves her, like many men that long into marriage he doesn't really notice her. She is on the lavatory sniffing her armpit when she asks him: 'How do I look?'

'Perfect,' comes the answer.

'Is my hair okay?'

'It's great.'

'You're not even looking at it.'

No wonder, when they go to a ball and an elegant Hungarian dances seductively with her, she is intrigued when he dismisses the protective armour of her marriage with slick lines such as: 'One of the charms of marriage is that it makes deception a necessity for both parties', and, absurdly, 'It was the only way women could lose their virginity and be free to do what they wanted.' Nicole may float on the raft of his seduction, but she raises her finger with her wedding ring to ward off his evil intent. It was a spontaneous, unscripted gesture. 'Just that moment early in the film when she raises her finger and says, "I'm married" ', Tom remembers. 'Stanley loved that about her. He called her his thoroughbred.'

But the experience of this flirtation in comparison with everyday life is part of the prompt that makes her character reveal her infatuation with the sailor. 'Subconsciously she wanted something more from her husband,' Nicole explains. 'It triggers all sorts of reactions. It is dangerous territory. I am saying things I have held back for so long. Fascinating but so real.'

She, more than Tom, had real worries about being good enough for Kubrick. 'I was so in awe. Terrified, I had fear for a month. I had these two big monologues but over time he gave me such confidence and gave me such freedom. He would say: "Do what you want to do. Get lost in Alice". And over a year and a half I became that woman.'

Tom, too, was aware that their relationship would not emerge from this unchanged. 'I'm glad it didn't happen in the first years of our marriage. It could be very difficult during the making of the film. The characters are at odds, they have to confront their issues, there are raw emotions. It was pervasive, it does invade your life. I worked nearly every single day and Stanley knew what I was going through.'

One thing that is known in the cinema community and beyond is that Kubrick liked to do an incredible number of takes of each scene. Well, this wasn't invariably true: sometimes he would buy the first. And, on occasion, he would do seventy and then use the first. Nicole enjoyed this method. 'You've reached his interest. You never walk away thinking, "If only." ' Kidman had an instinct for Kubrick's methodology. 'He did an unpredictable number of takes. Stanley was always waiting for something to happen. As long as you relaxed into the situation, it was the most wonderful experience.'

The one person I know to have cracked the Kubrick Code is the English actor Murray Melvin, who played the Reverend Samuel Runt in *Barry Lyndon*. 'Kubrick watches the actor get into the character's emotions in the first few takes and then he sees a gesture or a reaction, a piece of timing or tone of delivery that he really likes. But they are not all in the same take. And he knows that if he tells the actor what it is he likes, there is a danger of the person becoming self-conscious about it. So he waits for them to come together.'

17

EXIT STANLEY

For their Kubrick odyssey, the Cruises lived at first in Holland Park in west London, managing to retain a degree of anonymity in Hyde Park or at their favourite pub in Chelsea. But they found it more convenient to be nearer the studios and with Isabella, who was nearly four, and Connor, not quite two, and an attendant court of bodyguards, personal trainers, nannies and a French chef, moved to a twenty-room Georgian mansion near Shenley in Hertfordshire. There Isabella was able to go to the local school and attend mother-and-daughter riding lessons at the local equestrian centre.

Luxury was never far away and Tom's private jet, stationed at nearby Elstree airport, took them for a brief break in the Scottish Highlands. Nicole's romanticism was fed by a trip to the home of the Brontë sisters on the windswept Yorkshire Moors – 'There's something about the place that you know inspired great writers.' She even took a poetry course in the Lake District, visiting Words-worth's house. After filming finished, she returned there with Tom and they stayed in a local guest house.

All this was possible because Nicole was on call for many fewer days than her husband. She is only on the screen for forty minutes out of the film's two hours forty minutes' running time. Nevertheless she is powerfully present throughout as he visualises her passionate lovemaking with the naval officer, something Nicole shot herself, declining a double. 'Stanley wanted it to be harsh and gritty, almost pornographic,' she confessed. 'He didn't exploit me. I did it because I thought it was important to the film. The film deals with sex and sexual obsession, and the scenes could not have been of me in a bra and panties pretending to have sex with someone. It had to have a graphic quality to it. I certainly wouldn't have done it for any other director and, yes, it was a little difficult to go home to my husband afterwards.' These were the only three days during the prolonged shoot that Tom did not come to the studio.

When Stanley was named a recipient of the Golden Lion of Venice as a Lifetime Achievement Award, to be pre-sented on 6 September 1997, he naturally declined to fly there, but it was agreed that Nicole would pick it up for him. Sadly the date coincided with the funeral of Diana, Princess of Wales – a friend of Tom's and certainly an acquaintance of his wife. It was agreed that their atten-dance at this solemn event should take precedence but Stanley, ever the minute planner, got out a map of London and found that Westminster undergound station was only a short walk from the Abbey. Nicole could get a train, and a car would then pick her up at Hillingdon station to take her to a private plane. He telephoned Julian Senior with the plan. Julian politely pointed out that it was unlikely Nicole would wish to be seen on the tube in her mourning outfit and, besides, there would be about a million people in the area. Stanley reluctantly agreed, but Tom then called suggesting that Julian contact the coastguard who could take Nic by river down to the City airport. Julian duly did, but was informed that there would be more mud than water at the landing stage on the tidal Thames. In the event Jane Campion, Nicole's director on *The Portrait of the Lady* and, fortuitously, chairman of the Venice jury, picked up the award.

Tom, spending more time in the Kubrick household, was not unaware of Stanley's eccentricities. One day the director had come to work extremely depressed. Priscilla, one of his cats, was dead. Stanley had seven cats and several dogs and, on occasion as is their wont, the dogs would chase the cats. Stanley got a studio chippie to cut holes in the three-inch mahogany doors of the house so that they could escape. Priscilla was being chased but missed the hole, hurtled into the door and was killed. But then Stanley brightened slightly. 'I think I've solved the problem. I'm going to cut bigger holes and line them with foam rubber.' Stanley was particularly concerned with the welfare of cats. He warned Tom that when loading cutlery into the lower layer of a dishwasher, he should make sure that all the knives and forks were put in sharp end down in case the cats should jump on them.

Although Stanley did not choose to analyse the film, he had already expressed some general thoughts on what he believed. 'The perfect novel from which to make a movie is, I think, not the novel of action but, on the contrary, the novel which is mainly concerned with the inner life of its characters. It will give the adaptor an absolute compass bearing, as it were, on what a character is thinking or feeling at any given moment of the story. And from this he can invent action which will be an objective correlative of the book's psychological content, will accurately dramatise this in an implicit, off-the-nose way without resorting to having the actors deliver literal statements of meaning.

'I think that for a movie or a play to say anything really truthful about life, it has to do so very obliquely, so as to avoid all pat conclusions and neatly tied-up ideas. The point of view it is conveying has to be completely entwined with a sense of life as it is, and has to be got across through a subtle injection into the audience's consciousness. Ideas which are valid and truthful are so multi-faceted that they don't yield themselves to frontal assault. The ideas have to be discovered by the audience, and their thrill in making the discovery makes those ideas all the more powerful. You use the audience's thrill of surprise and discovery to reinforce your ideas, rather than reinforce them artificially through plot points or phoney drama or phoney stage dynamics put in to power them across.'

The outside world was not privy to what had been happening in this strictly secret film and some journalists smelt trouble. 'WHERE IN THE WORLD IS TOM CRUISE?' demanded *US* magazine in November 1998.

'Risqué business: Working on Stanley Kubrick's sex thriller *Eyes Wide Shut* may have cost the actor two years at the peak of his career.' It seemed mad for a 36-year-old actor, who had 'spent the '90s crafting one of the most critically and financially successful careers in Hollywood' to have been entangled, with his wife, Nicole Kidman, 'in the seemingly endless shoot of *Eyes Wide Shut*.'

Tom had given some indication of what he had been up to at the Toronto Film Festival where he was promoting *Without Limits*, a film he and Paula Wagner had produced with his favourite writer, Robert Towne, directing. It was the story of the famed athlete Steve Prefontaine, who had died at the age of twenty-four. The film found favour with the critics but not with the public. Costing nearly $25 million to make, it grossed less than a million at the US box-office. If, as had originally been the plan, Tom had played Steve (instead of Billy Crudup) and Tommy Lee Jones had played his coach, Bill Bowerman (instead of Donald Sutherland), it would have been a great deal more commercial.

At Toronto Tom defended his career decisions. 'It's a finite period of time for anyone in the movie business and not just actors. How many movies can you make? How many years do you have the energy, the power, the time to produce movies? I know I've got to do it now. I want to use time in a way that's constructive. I don't want to sit down when I'm seventy and say I've wasted my time away and not made the films I wanted to make.' Regarding the millions of dollars *Eyes Wide Shut* cost him in lost fees, he was very sure of himself. 'People say: "You've lost 40,

60, 80 million dollars. You've lost all this money. You've lost all this time." I don't understand that kind of thinking. I've been doing this for eighteen years. Yeah, I make money. I make a lot of money. And money's wonderful and nice. But that does not enter into why I make movies. There are some things you don't do for the money. I know that's hard to believe. To have a chance to work with a genius is one of them.'

It seemed Hansel and Gretel had been kidnapped by the wicked witch – or, in this instance, eccentric wizard. Matters were made worse by the film's over-run, and Warner's decision to postpone the release from Christmas 1998 to summer 1999. There were rumours of troubles on the set, that Harvey Keitel had been replaced by Sydney Pollack as Ziegler. This was true: Stanley never really got round to the part of Ziegler until Keitel had to leave for another movie, and Pollack was a friend of the film, having assured Stanley of Tom's dedication after directing him in *The Firm*. It was rumoured that there had had to be reshoots and Jennifer Jason Leigh would not return for them. Also true. She had the lead in a new film, David Cronenberg's *eXistenZ*, and Stanley had wanted to give a completely different emphasis to her small cameo – she was the dead patient's daughter who embraced Bill while declaring her love.

There was trouble with the rating. The orgy with its sex and nudity was unacceptable to the MPAA and Kubrick had promised Warner's he would deliver an R-rated film. Computer-generated people and images were added to hide the offending parts from the American audience so to get the contractual certificate. Elsewhere in the world, apparently, the nudity didn't give as much offence and was left in, save in Japan for which country Stanley had already shot the relevant scene with a view to avoiding what the Japanese consider improper – genitalia, and especially pubic hair, are off the menu there.

Tom recalls the conclusion of shooting in August 1998. 'I was looking forward to and dreaded the last day. I didn't want the experience with Stanley to end. I gave him a kiss and a hug and I said: "I love you, Stanley, you know that.' He said: "I love you, too."'

Nicole, meanwhile, was extending her love affair with Arthur Schnitzler. She was already in rehearsal for his most famous play, *La Ronde*. It had been updated by the British playwright David Hare for the two leading actors, Nicole and Iain Glen, to play all ten parts – most of them in bed. Glen was to make a naked appearance and Nicole too, from behind, thereby ensuring a sell-out at London's Donmar Warehouse. Or was that due to whiz-kid Sam Mendes's direction?

The Cruises had moved back into London while she was doing the play, renting a £4 million Nash house in Cumberland Terrace overlooking Regent's Park. There Tom experienced some drama of his own. On the afternoon of 23 September one of his neighbours, Mrs Rita Simmonds, was getting out of her Porsche when she was set upon by two muggers. She screamed loudly, fearing for the safety of her two-year-old daughter Sophie, who was with her. Cruise, accompanied by his bodyguard, came racing out of his house. 'Tom was brilliant,' Mrs Simmonds said later. 'He rushed down the road and chased the attackers away.' Unfortunately they were unable to catch the men, who made off in a Ford with £87,000 worth of Mrs Simmonds' jewellery. But Tom came back and comforted the shaken woman.

Before *Eyes Wide Shut* wrapped, Nicole had already squeezed in a leading role in Griffin Dunne's *Practical Magic* as Sandra Bullock's weird sister. The actress liked to keep busy. When she was promoting *Eyes Wide Shut* in Venice, a Warner's executive observed her attending two meetings and accepting two parts in the short period between the lunchtime press conference and the early evening premiere.

Tom was already in pre-production for *Mission: Impossible II* which he was producing for Paramount with his partner, Paula Wagner. They had taken the bold step of hiring the Hong Kong action director John Woo to make this one while at the same time ensuring the plot was powerful thanks to a final polish from Robert Towne.

Stanley was deeply into post-production with the movie. He worked at the house and now *was* in contact with Warner's. Most days Julian Senior would come in to work on the marketing campaign: Stanley had already researched the optimum dates to open in territories throughout the world. Leon Vitali looked through the selected frames that would be released to the press as stills: although he had started his career as a photographer, Stanley didn't like the idea of having stills shot on the set. Both men had worked with him for thirty years and knew his ways well. Julian once ensured that 286 French cinemas got masks for their projectors so that they could show *Barry Lyndon* correctly in 1:66 ratio. Leon had helped Stanley have a New York theatre painted matt black so that nothing would distract from the press screening of *Full Metal Jacket*.

The thirty-second teaser trailer for *Eyes Wide Shut* had Tom and Nicole evidently making love to the strains of Chris Isaak's 'It's a Bad, Bad World.' The poster had them in a similar embrace, but with Nicole's right eye glancing away from her husband at something – or someone – else. The question of whether this soul-searching story had put a strain on their relationship was still alive. Christiane Kubrick had been adamant that Stanley should not embark on the film in the early years of theirs: 'Let's not go there at this stage of our marriage,' she told him. Tom was publicly untroubled. 'Our marriage is stronger because of it. And our friendship is deeper because of it. And that's the way it is.' Nicole observed, 'The lines of reality and pretend get crossed. It was exciting and dangerous, so much more than just making a film. All of the things that you would not want to explore in a relationship or reveal came out at different times. So that was tough.' Stanley vouchsafed to Julian Senior: 'There are things you just don't talk about in a marriage. I worry about Tom and Nicole.'

By the end of February 1999 he had completed a cut of the film to his satisfaction and, with some music tracks still to be dubbed, let go of his precious project so that others could see it. On 2 March at 10.45 p.m. Tom and Nicole went to a private screening room in New York to view the film for the first time. 'It was just surreal,' said Nicole. 'We

watched it again immediately.' They loved it. And telephoned Stanley in St Albans to tell him so.

Nicole had been playing to another sell-out season of
The Blue Room on Broadway, although she had been
obliged to drop out temporarily with a viral infection.
Tom needed to get back to Sydney to continue production
on *Mission: Impossible II*. Stanley continued to work with
Julian and Leon on the minute details of international
release dates and marketing.

At 7.30 a.m. on 7 March Julian was driving to Stanley's
house as usual. His mobile phone rang. It was Stanley's
assistant editor. 'Something has happened,' was all he said.
'I don't think we'll be working today.

Julian stepped on the gas. When he entered the house 'it
was like something out of a Russian movie. Christiane
was moaning, her two daughters were in the kitchen
crying, her brother, Jan, was wandering around, bewil-
dered and lost.'

Stanley had died of a massive heart attack during the
night. 'He wasn't feeling ill, he was just very tired. Many
heart attack victims are like that,' Christiane later concluded. 'He was very careless with his health. He was afraid
of doctors. That comes from being a doctor's son. He was
very much an optimist.'

It fell to Leon to call Tom in Sydney. 'I broke down when
I heard,' the actor later recalled. 'I was in absolute shock
and disbelief. We had shared two years of our lives
together.'

Julian telephoned Nicole in New York. 'I was in total
shock,' she remembered. 'I didn't want to believe it. It just

seemed wrong. He had too many other things to do and say.'

Curiously, the next priority was to feed the dogs. The problem was that there was no dog food left and only Stanley knew where he got the tins that he fed them. Thanks to his aversion to personal publicity, he was able to potter around the shops in St Albans unrecognised – in sharp contrast to Tom. His daughter Katharina Kubrick recalls: 'There's a scene in *Eyes Wide Shut* where Tom had to walk to a hospital – this was in London. Word got round and, within half an hour, the police were having to put up cordons and people kept ruining the shot by shouting: "Tom, I love you!"' Her mother added: 'Stanley watched from the car and said it was just terrifying. Tom Cruise is literally a prisoner of the Midas touch. He cannot go anywhere.'

The funeral was held on 12 March. It was Stanley's wish to be buried beside his dogs in his garden. As executive jets from round the world landed at Elstree airport Jan Harlan, Christiane's brother who worked for the director, discovered to his horror that a special licence from the local council was needed to do that and they didn't have one. A registrar was woken late that night.

Tom and Nicole came from Sydney. 'I was not in a good way at that funeral,' he said. 'Somewhere, deep down, however illogical, I just didn't believe it was true. I saw the kitchen where we ate and drank and the main room with the fire in the fireplace. And there was the coffin. It was absurd.'

Steven Spielberg, who had agreed to take on the mantle

of Stanley's next project, *AI: Artificial Intelligence*, told how he and his wife, Kate, were having people to dinner the night they learned Stanley had died. The meal went ahead anyway, but afterwards Spielberg projected the last reels of Kubrick's *Paths of Glory* to his guests. 'When we reached the part with the captured German girl [Christiane] singing, even those who had never seen it before were crying.'

Tom was one of the pall-bearers. After the interment he spoke admiringly of Stanley's rare talent and how he had been both a friend and father-figure to him. Nicole shared those sentiments. 'Stanley dedicated his life to making films. The great storytellers of our time are so important to our future, and he used film to tell stories. Getting lost in that world is exquisite when it happens.'

Terry Semel, Chairman of Warner Bros, took Tom and Leon Vitali aside afterwards and asked them if they would take charge of the film now. Leon knew how Stanley worked but he was amazed at the way Tom threw himself into the task, using his immense clout to make sure that there was no cutting of the film, no undue censorship, that the marketing and international distribution would be just as Stanley would have wished. Tom had learnt from the master how important it was not just to give the movie over to dubbing agents for foreign versions (where, tradition-ally, he had his widest audience) but to seek out the right actors and voices for the leads. He did this religiously. Sky Dumont, who breathed seductive notions into Alice's ear at the party, was born in Argentina but had worked as the station voice of the German TV network Kabel 1, so he dubbed himself into German. Rade Serbedzija, the dodgy owner of the fancy dress shop, revoiced himself in Italian to ensure it was Italian with a Croatian accent.

Eyes Wide Shut had its American premiere in Los Angeles on 13 July 1999. Tom and Nicole were there. Tom said that when he had shown the film to his mother she had hugged him and said how incredible it was, what a moving piece of work. Unfortunately not all the critics shared her sentiments. It got mixed reviews, despite being the only Kubrick film to open at number one in the box-office charts and enjoying the highest US gross ($56 million) of any of his films.

Kubrick did not make blockbusters, and it was very hard for anyone to take in at a single press viewing everything that he had put into a film. As the critic Jeremy Hellman wrote: 'It's one of the true masterpieces of the nineties, even if it took me a third viewing to realize just how phenomenal it was.' Molly Haskell in *The New York Times* thought Cruise was a square peg in a round hole. 'You have to admire the actor for taking virtually three years out of his career at his bankable prime to offer himself up to the erratic genius of Kubrick,' she wrote. 'If the movie proved to be a disaster of overreaching, it was not Mr. Cruise's but Kubrick's fault, inasmuch as the director wanted to have it both ways: a moody art film with a Hollywood marquee star to boost the budget and bring in the crowds. The sexual insecurity and introspective bent of the protagonist in the Arthur Schnitzler novel Kubrick chose to adapt is something Cruise simply can't project. The reflective spirit of an intellectual, self-doubting man, anxious about middle age, is not in his repertory.'

But when Puccini's *Madame Butterfly* opened at La Scala, Milan, in 1904 it had a totally hostile reception with vicious reviews, one critic calling it an 'automobile accident.' It went on to become one of the world's most popular operas. *Eyes Wide Shut* certainly seems a little too pensive and protracted in its execution, but whether it or that year's Best Picture and Best Director Oscar winner, *American Beauty* (directed, paradoxically, by Nicole's *Blue Room* director, Sam Mendes), will be the movie that stands the test of time is hardly a fair competition.

Tom and Nicole duly continued to bang the drum for the movie, attracting a crowd of nearly ten thousand at the London premiere in Leicester Square in September. In what was to become his trade-mark, Tom got out of their limo and, instead of walking up the red carpet, began to work the crowd. A little less confidently, so did Nicole. But she paid Kubrick what was probably the most heartfelt compliment of all. 'It changed the way I view film-making and it gave me belief in the purity of the art form.'

18

EXIT NIC

Although throughout the prolonged shoot and publicity the Cruises had remained commendably championing of Kubrick and his genius, maybe somewhere in their subconscious minds lay a feeling that the film was not without problems and possibly not wholly career-advancing. It moved at too stately a pace for multiplex man; the Freudian opportunity that Schnitzler had given the reader to feel that these temptations were not just one man's dream was not offered on the screen; and the orgy scene was neither serious nor sensuous, more of an old man's reverie. Whether they had such thoughts or not, both Nicole and Tom now made brilliant choices to remind the public of their versatility and, equally important, that they marched to the beat of the modern world. Both these choices relied heavily on sex.

Tom, somewhat surprisingly, agreed to appear in Paul

Thomas Anderson's *Magnolia* as the oleaginous Frank T. J. Mackey, a television and video guru who gives men self-help lessons on how to pick up and fuck women under the banner 'Seduce and Destroy' – hardly the mantra for a loving relationship. Anderson's previous contribution to American culture had been *Boogie Nights*, a movie about the porn industry. By coincidence – or, perhaps, not by coincidence – Nicole's choice centred on one of the most direct plays ever written about sex, *Reigen*. By coincidence – or, perhaps, not by coincidence – it had been written by Arthur Schnitzler, whose *Traumnovelle* had been the source of *Eyes Wide Shut*. Tom endorsed Nicole's decision to take on a part that would have his wife naked before a very close audience in the small Donmar Warehouse theatre in London, and became a house husband. He even bought a house next to Nicole's co-star Iain Glen and his then wife, the actress Susannah Harker, in Dulwich in south London.

Schnitzler's *Reigen* had precisely one performance in Vienna in 1926 before the police closed it down as being obscene. Indeed it was, according to the Oxford English dictionary definition of obscenity as 'the portrayal of sexual matters offensive according to accepted standards of morality'. The German word *Reigen* literally means 'round dance', but the play consisted of a daisy chain of sexual intercourse between ten characters – after each coupling one moves on to a new partner. His purpose was to show that we are all, regardless of class, similarly driven by sexual desire and fulfilment. Later interpretations would see it as a lethal dose of syphilis being passed from partner to partner. Two French films, both called *La Ronde*, were based on it. The female lead was played by Simone Signoret in a classy 1950 production directed by Max Ophüls and by Jane Fonda in a less classy 1964 version directed by her then husband, Roger Vadim.

The bait with which the director, Sam Mendes, managed to catch Kidman for *The Blue Room*, as the adaptation by David Hare was called, was to offer her the chance of playing all five female roles, just as Iain Glen would play all the men. Kidman says, in retrospect: 'I wanted to do theatre again. I'm glad I jumped and did it. Everyone said to me, "Why are you doing this in a little theatre in London?" and I said, "I want to play five different characters. I want to risk it."'

She felt less bold when she first met Glen at Mendes' apartment in Primrose Hill. 'I was so shy I could hardly speak. I kept feeling like I was going to vomit. I had heard how brilliant Iain was on stage and he was formidable just as a person. I thought, "I'm out of my league." But he really was so gentle. He said: "Don't worry. I'm not going to let you fail."' Her fear and worry continued throughout rehearsals, somewhat allayed by group massage that Mendes introduced and lunchtime sushi provided by Nicole from the expensive restaurant Nobu, made famous by Boris Becker in a well-chronicled episode of cupboard love.

The challenge was to mutate into five entirely different characters, from Cockney harlot to politician's fancy and faithless wife. There was also a crucial moment in scene seven which ensured the show never played to an empty seat either in London or Broadway. A model who has just made love to a playwright (Schnitzler had actually written himself into the original) stands up, naked, and puts her underwear on. Nicole suggested this might be done under a sheet. Mendes persuaded her otherwise: 'I think it's very important. I don't think it's exploitative. I think it's totally character-driven.'

And so she did it, night after night, with the front row of the audience a few feet away. She stood with her back to the house and pulled on a pair of black knickers while Glen fastens her bra and they exchange philosophies on the nature of happiness. That moment, and Charles Spencer's description of the play as 'pure theatrical Viagra' in the *Daily Telegraph*, ensured that it became an event of international note.

'Something happened that was not to do with theatre,' Mendes now notes. 'Like the Alien in the Ridley Scott movie, the play kind of lived inside the Donmar for a while, exploded out of its chest, left the theatre bleeding on a table somewhere, gasping for breath, and was gone.'

Sensation apart, Kidman earned reviews for the seductive versatility that put her acting career on a whole new footing. David Benedict in the *Independent* referred to 'Kidman's superbly differentiated gallery of women – from skittish, deer-like prostitute to an hilariously grand, throaty actress.' 'Kidman switches personae with consummate ease, endowing the prostitute of the opening and closing scenes with a bruised loneliness. She is not just a star: she genuinely delivers the goods,' enthused Michael Billington in the *Guardian*. And Charles Spencer simply fell in love. 'She's drop dead gorgeous and bewitchingly adorable. The vision of her wafting round the stage with a fag in one hand

and her knickers in the other as a delicious French au pair will haunt my fantasies for months.' And he may not be alone. Her performance conquered both Broadway and her husband. Tom went to see it more than twenty times, sneaking into his seat just after the lights went down. 'I feel for Nicole it was a very special time. It was the moment she became a quite separate entity from Tom Cruise. And I'm sure she was aware that was happening,' Mendes adroitly observed.

The transfer of *The Blue Room* to the Cort Theatre on Broadway brought the family back to the States, and it was time for Tom to give up his role as house husband and father and earn some money. Curiously, the author and director of his next film was a sort of Schnitzler of the San Fernando Valley. That is where Paul Thomas Anderson grew up and that is where America's most financially successful films are made – porn films. The industry dwarfs Hollywood. There are more video stores renting and selling so-called 'adult' videos than there are branches of McDonald's.

Anderson was born in 1970 and grew up in an era where sex had become as free as it was in Vienna at the beginning of the twentieth century. Except for porn films; you had to pay for those. At the gentle age of ten he used to rummage through his father's videos and got his first exposure to porn. Ernie Anderson had been something of an unusual character. He hosted a late night horror show on television going under the name of Ghoulardi. He was very much a madcap hippy with long hair, a moustache and a goatee beard, who not only dumped on many of the movies he introduced but also edited himself into them from time to time so that he could escape from monsters or emit inscrutable phrases such as 'cool it with the boom-boom.'

Not unsurprisingly, Paul was increasingly aware of the decadence that surrounded him and, at the early age of eighteen, with the new-found freedom of the video camera made his first amateur film, *The Dirk Diggler Story*, a semi-satire about a famous porn star whose life on top was coming to an end. It was a subject to which he was to return eight years later when he had established professional credentials as a film director: New Line Pictures bankrolled him to the tune of $15 million and he expanded his story to chronicle the rise and fall of Mr Diggler. Leonardo DiCaprio would have played the part, so we are told, but he had an appointment with destiny in the shape of *Titanic* and suggested Mark Wahlberg. Burt Reynolds, whose career was in free-fall at the time, took the part of the porno-impresario who transformed Dirk from nightclub host to a man with a prosthetic penis. The American critics made this film a *succès d'estime* and Burt, Julianne Moore (with her innocent porcelain features cleverly counter-cast as a coke-addicted porn star, Amber Waves) and Anderson himself were all nominated for Oscars. Enough people went to see it for it to turn a profit for New Line, considerably enhanced by the nine deleted scenes that appeared on the subsequent DVD.

Two years later Anderson made another examination of life in the Valley, this time compressing into twenty-four hours the lives (and several deaths) of nine people in *Magnolia* (1990), so called because of the boulevard of that name which runs through the area. Their lives are tangentially linked by a television show, *What Do Kids Know?*, in which gifted children compete with less-gifted adults, and followed the lives of the owner, producer, presenter, participant and their various partners. Anderson used his dependable repertory company from *Boogie Nights*: Julianne Moore, William H. Macy, Ricky Jay (the sinister magician), Philip Baker Hall and Philip Seymour Hoffman. The last was to be a fortuitous encounter for Cruise, who cast him as the villain in *Mission: Impossible III* which opened just three months after Hoffman had been ennobled with an Oscar for *Capote*.

To some observers it seemed strange that Cruise would forfeit his status as a leading man to join this group, especially as the foul-mouthed misogynist who makes a living lecturing men on how to meet and persuade the fair sex to, as he so delicately puts it, 'suck my big fat fucking sausage'. Others assumed that he had been persuaded by the prospect of playing the reconciliation scene with his father, Jason Robards, the patriarch of the TV company, who is dying of cancer. Robards had come to the movie after having gone through nine weeks of a true life-or-death coma, and was himself to die of cancer a year later. It was known that Tom had had a deathbed reconciliation with his own estranged father but he denies that this was why he took the role.

'No, it isn't the reason. When I read the script I thought, "When do you get to have a chance to go to seminars like that?" I'm an actor. I'd never played a character like that. I like humour. I thought it was dark and funny. And that's what I focused on, working on the humour. In the script it says, "When he gets to his father's door he breaks down." I said, "Look, I don't feel that." I was looking for a way to make this guy human. I thought it was funny that he was afraid of his father's dogs. I didn't know what was going to happen when I got to the house. The whole time with the character I was skating on the edge.'

The part certainly gave Cruise the chance to travel the descending steps of arrogance. At first, as this sex guru, unshaven with long greasy hair and a waistcoat to match, he almost apes the madness of Peter Finch in *Network* as he howls, 'I will not take it any more' when he hears of a young man's rejection by a woman. 'You think she's going to be there when things go wrong?' he sneers cynically. Offensively, he dismisses the opposite sex as mere 'bushes', a phrase he delights in when he meets a black female television interviewer. He salivates like a dog with his tongue hanging out, but is reduced by this artful woman to a stunned silence when she proves that he is mythomaniac. No wonder he tells his audience to dismiss the past – his own is a tissue of lies, even denying the death of his mother. When he watches over his father dying – a man he has previously claimed was already dead – he needs no words, just eyes that telegraph his true fear of reality. It is a triumphant performance.

The rest of the film is well played but too ambitious. 'We may be through with the past but the past ain't through with us,' says the epilogue. For three hours Anderson manoeuvres these largely tragic people to illustrate the inevitability of fate, chance and mere happenstance in human life. It ends with a plague of frogs, a metaphor that is a little unsteady. God and Moses failed to liberate the Israelites by this ruse since, according to Exodus, Pharaoh reneged on his promise the following day as soon as it stopped. But it did provide the director with some arresting amphibian imagery.

Cruise can have no complaints about the hand he was dealt. He was given various critics' awards, a Golden Globe and another Oscar nomination. Like his wife before him, he had taken a bold risk and won widespread admiration for it.

They were both in their prime. Not just Hollywood's golden couple, famous for their exceptional beauty, wealth and celebrity, but demonstrably gifted and powerful actors, the Burton and Taylor of the late twentieth century. When interviewed, they would pour out their love and admiration for each other and their plans for a harmonious life ahead. But, as we know, it was not to be. Why? Well, a film critic is ill qualified to play marriage guidance counsellor and, were Cruise the sort who chooses to keep his romantic life a guarded secret, it might not be relevant to any assessment of him as a man. But he doesn't. He jumps on sofas to tell the world about it. So maybe, if presented with a brief chronicle of the events leading up to the announcement on 5 February 2001 that they were to break up, the reader might deduce more than the writer.

After the obsequies for Stanley Kubrick were concluded, both Tom and Nicole turned their thoughts to major movies in Australia. He was going back to produce and star in *Mission: Impossible II*; she was going to sing and star in

Moulin Rouge, an original musical by Baz Luhrmann, a Sydney writer-director who made his mark with the dead-pan comedy *Strictly Ballroom* and the bold, hip reinterpretation of *Romeo and Juliet* with Leonardo DiCaprio.

But stars of this magnitude plan well ahead, and after these long shoots, needed to have future projects on their respective horizons. It could be said, at that time, that Cruise was the most powerful man in Hollywood and what he wanted he got. A surreal Spanish love story, *Abre los ojos* (*Open Your Eyes*) by the young director Alejandro Amenabar, had caught his eye. It had done very well in Spain, but there was little market for foreign language films in the States. So Tom decided to remake it in English with a New York setting. Having acquired the rights, he handsomely paid his friend Cameron Crowe to rewrite it.

Amenabar too was well rewarded, even to the extent of Cruise asking to see his next script. This was a ghost story called *The Others*, set in Santander, a town on the Bay of Biscay. Tom liked it and Amenabar was flown to New York for talks with Cruise, Kidman and the Miramax producers Harvey and Bob Weinstein. 'At first you couldn't help but be impressed,' the Colombian-Spaniard recalls. 'But they are so obsessed with the work and quality, you quickly forget to be star-struck – you have to work hard.' To Amenabar's delight Cruise agreed to co-produce *The Others* with the Weinsteins, and Nicole was cast in the leading role. The film would have to be made in English to stand any chance of recouping its costs. They agreed it would still be filmed in Spain but set in the Channel Islands.

Down under, Tom endeared himself to the natives by

giving money to the Aboriginals after they claimed a *Mission: Impossible* helicopter had landed on a sacred burial site. And Nicole endeared herself to Baz by four months' hard training on her singing and dancing and even taking lessons from circus performers to swing on a trapeze seventy feet in the air. The plot consisted of the Scot from *Star Wars*, Ewan McGregor, an impoverished poet, falling in love with Satine (Kidman) the star of the Moulin Rouge who is both a courtesan and a consumptive. The period was turn-of-the-century but the songs more recent, ranging from Jule Styne's 'Diamonds Are a Girl's Best Friend' to Lennon and McCartney's 'All You Need Is Love.'

At one stage the Cruises were shooting side by side in Fox Studios in Sydney. Although the whole of Nicole's film was being made there, *Mission: Impossible II* only needed to build the laboratory set and the interior of the Spanish house where the diamond burglary takes place. Both Tom and Nicole had extensive caravans on the lot but did not visit each other at work. Their children did, and were able to see their mother twirling on her trapeze in the morning and their father twirling his guns in the afternoon.

The Cruises lived in their house in Sydney and were able to make use of the harbour. Tom took the children, Isabella, now seven, and Connor, five, on a fishing expedition but unfortunately the engine of their converted smack, *Alibi*, gave up and the barbecue Tom was cooking caught fire. He threw it overboard but then, typically, dived in to retrieve it. Without the children he teamed up with Australian actor Russell Crowe and jumped into his Gulfstream jet to fly 300 miles north of Sydney to Coff's

Harbour, home of Australia's motorbike enthusiasts, where they hired and raced Harley Davidsons.

The millennium came to Sydney sooner than to most of the rest of the world, and was celebrated with a firework display on the Harbour Bridge which was bigger and brighter and more spectacular than any that had gone before. Tom booked part of Café Sydney, high in the Old Customs Building overlooking the harbour, so that his guests and retainers could have the best view in town. Nicole's family were there, as were Iain and Susannah Glen who had remained firm friends of the Cruises since *The Blue Room*.

The new millennium dawned auspiciously for Cruise on the work front, too. With Nicole back at work on *Moulin Rouge* he invited her sister, Antonia, for a trip on his jet to Los Angeles. On 23 January 2000 she accompanied him to the Beverly Hilton for the annual Golden Globes ceremony. He had been invited as a presenter but, to his evident surprise, was named Best Actor in a Supporting Role for *Magnolia*, beating a strong field of nominees: Michael Caine for *The Cider House Rules*, Michael Clark Duncan for *The Green Mile*, Haley Joel Osment for *The Sixth Sense* and Jude Law for *The Talented Mr Ripley*. 'Wow! God, I didn't expect this,' Cruise said when he grasped the Globe. He gained renewed respect in the Hollywood community for a heartfelt tribute to Jason Robards, who was to die some months later, and then sang the praises of his absent wife: 'Her generosity, her support, her sacrifices, her talent – she inspires me.'

Nicole, meanwhile, was having her ups and downs on

Moulin Rouge. Baz Luhrmann had organized weekend parties to keep the performers in the spirit of the nightclub, with bottles of absinthe, dancing on tables and attendant hangovers on Monday mornings. Unfortunately, on set Kidman was going through one of her acrobatic routines, being thrown from person to person, when she cracked a rib and production was closed down for two weeks. But she was fit enough to attend her mother's sixtieth birthday party in March, accompanied by her bodyguard, Peter Crone.

Tom was intensely busy on post-production for *Mission: Impossible II* and pre-production for *Open Your Eyes*. He liked Cameron Crowe's script and his new title, *Vanilla Sky*, which had little to do with the story but was an alternative name for Monet's wonderful 1873 painting *The Seine at Argenteuil* – which was to hang in Cruise's bedroom in the film, evidence of the character's extreme wealth.

Vanilla Sky is a complex, not to say convoluted, story of a handsome, rich publishing tycoon who falls in love with a Spanish dancer, has a car crash, is grotesquely disfigured, dies but manages to continue on earth courtesy of the Life Extension Corporation who put him into a 'lucid dream' so that he can hallucinate a fictional existence. Cruise and Crowe were determined to put together a top cast for the project: Kurt Russell, hot from *Backdraft*, and Cameron Diaz, who had come to the fore with *There's Something about Mary*. Crowe was finishing the autobiographical *Almost Famous* and brought in his top two players from that: Jason Lee and Noah Taylor.

But who should play the exotic Spanish dancer? Why not the girl who had played her in Amenabar's film? She had already made the leap to American cinema, having starred with Billy Crudup (the lead in Crowe's *Almost Famous*) in *The Hi-Lo Country*. Penelope Cruz came from a humble family but, at the age of fifteen, danced her way from the working-class suburbs of Madrid and into a music video for the famous Spanish pop star Nacho Cano – and into his arms, as well, for the next seven years. By sixteen she was a national personality on children's television and, with her liquid ebony eyes, siren smile and traffic-stopping figure it was not long before she made her way into films – or films made their way to her. A propensity to disrobe in most of her movies did nothing to inhibit her career; indeed, her prolonged naked table-top writhing in Bigas Luna's *Jamon, Jamon* was the main talking point among critics at the 1992 Venice Film Festival.

Wives and girlfriends were rarely overjoyed when their partners starred with Penelope: Matt Damon split with Winona Ryder when he worked with her in *All the Pretty Horses*, and Nicolas Cage's marriage to Patricia Arquette foundered when he romanced Cruz in *Captain Corelli's Mandolin*. Such mishaps did not dissuade the producers from thinking she would be an asset to *Vanilla Sky*. Crowe was despatched to the island of Kephallonia in Greece, where she was filming Corelli, to see if she was interested. She was, and after the shoot she came to New York where Cruz met Cruise and the deal was done.

Nicole's chapter of accidents had not come to an end. Wearing a pair of high heels, she fell down a stairway and tore the cartilage behind her kneecap in the last weeks of shooting. She had to dance through the pain and recuperate in a wheelchair between shots. Despite having an operation, when Tom flew her to Spain to start work on *The Others* she was still on crutches. Bravely she adhered to the thespian motto: 'The show must go on.'

But as rehearsals approached for this eerie story about a neurotic mother in an echoing mansion with two children who are allergic to light, and who discovers that the three servants who come to work for her are revenants who have stepped out of their graves, she got cold feet and wanted to quit. She was to tell *BBC Breakfast* at the time of the film's release in the UK: 'When I got there and was just about to start rehearsals I really didn't want to do it. My whole being, my whole psyche was rejecting it, and I was desperate to try to get out of it. I begged them to let me out. I was so involved in *Moulin Rouge*, with stars in my eyes, and all I wanted to do was make love stories and musicals and be happy.'

But her husband (and producer) stood by her and she was coaxed into continuing. The shoot was to last from October until mid-December, but Tom was obliged to leave her and the children and return at the beginning of November to New York where he had to start work on *Vanilla Sky* – ironically yet another story of the confusion between reality and illusion.

Filming in New York went fine. They were due to move to the Paramount Studios in Los Angeles after Christmas to shoot the interiors. Cameron Crowe expressed delight with his work – and Tom's. 'We really have an intense love story. So Penelope had to appear to fall truly in love. And Tom's character falls in love with her. You watch them going through that hideous, great, awful, intoxicating moment. Without it we couldn't have a movie. The first time we screened the movie – just in-house – it was the kind of situation where at the end you get a reaction of "Wow! They really were in love." '

Nicole finished in time to return to their Pacific Palisades home for Christmas. There, on their tenth wedding anniversary – 24 December 2000 – they held a party for family and friends and renewed their wedding vows before them. After Christmas the Cruise family went to Las Vegas where, on 28 December, Tom used his clout and cash to have the Big Shot Ride at the Stratosphere Hotel kept open late, so that he and his wife could soar through the skies.

On 1 January 2001 Tom returned to work on *Vanilla Sky* at Paramount and Nicole began a new movie, *Panic Room*, again playing a mother with two children in a mansion who hide in the location of the title when burglars invade the house. But on 19 January she dropped out of the movie, the reason being her continuing leg injury. The director, David Fincher, wanted to close down the production and claim the insurance; however, Jodie Foster stepped in to fill the breach.

On 23 January Nicole honoured her commitment to present the Golden Globe for Best Actor in a Comedy or Musical to her co-star in *The Peacemaker*, George Clooney, for *O Brother, Where Art Thou?* Her parents must have remained in Los Angeles as her father accompanied her to the Beverly Hilton. Tom presented the Globe for Best Supporting Actress to Kurt Russell's stepdaughter Kate Hudson – daughter of his wife, Goldie Hawn – for her role in Cameron Crowe's *Almost Famous*.

Hollywood can be a small town, and that night it was observed by many that relations between Tom and Nicole were not at their best. This was confirmed on 5 February, when Cruise's publicity agent, Pat Kingsley, issued a terse press release: 'Tom Cruise and Nicole Kidman announced today that they have regretfully decided to separate. The couple, who married in 1990, stressed their great respect for each other both personally and professionally. Citing the difficulties inherent in divergent careers which constantly keep them apart, they concluded that an amicable separation seemed best for both of them at this time.'

19

CRUISE AND CRUZ

Matters moved on from there with barely decent haste. Eschewing the etiquette that normally allows the wife to sue for divorce, Tom's lawyers served papers on Nicole just forty-eight hours later. Why? the public wanted to know.

'Nicole knows why,' Tom replied.

But apparently she didn't. And said so. And appears not to know why to this day. Her immediate response was to call her Australian chums, Baz Luhrmann and John Duigan, to express her shock and bewilderment. The Pacific Palisades house was besieged by journalists and photographers as TV news helicopters hovered overhead. Her sister Antonia took leave from her TV job in Sydney and within four days arrived with her children, Antonia and Lucia, to comfort her.

Tom moved out to the Bel Air Hotel where he and his entourage rented five bungalows at £10,000 a night. He went back to finish *Vanilla Sky* and was seen at a Spielberg party, joking and relaxed. The two men were to work together in *Minority Report*, a short story by Philip K. Dick that Tom brought to the director. It was set fifty years in the future and, in order to achieve a certain plausibility, a weekend think-tank was assembled at the trendy Shutters Hotel by the beach at Santa Monica. Politicians, professors, futurologists, architects and a wide sweep of other professionals debated how 2054 might look and what technological advances seemed likely.

Five weeks after receiving the divorce petition, on 16 March 2001, Nicole suffered a miscarriage. In a deposition to the court her lawyers stated: 'During December 2000 the parties were intimate, in fact Kidman became pregnant but lost the baby through a miscarriage.' Tom sent her flowers, but did not visit her in hospital.

Six days later she had recovered sufficiently to give a small party at Ago restaurant – a trendy trattoria on Melrose Avenue named after the chef, Agostino Sciandri, and owned by, amongst others, the Weinstein brothers and the Scott brothers (Tony had directed Nicole in *Days of Thunder*). It was for fellow Aussie Russell Crowe, who, the following Sunday, won the Best Actor Oscar for *Gladiator*. Not that Nicole was there to see him, although she did grace the cover of the new issue of *Vanity Fair*, along with Meryl Streep and Gwyneth Paltrow. Penelope Cruz also appeared in the Annie Leibovitz montage but, in a separate panel.

Nicole watched the ceremony at home with her sister. Although not in the programme, Tom attended and gave the Best Director Oscar to Steven Soderbergh for *Traffic*. Penelope Cruz gave away the Oscar for Best Costume Design. Shortly after the Oscars, Cruise took off for Washington DC to start filming *Minority Report*.

Nicole did not want the marriage to end, and suggested marriage counselling. But she should have known that the Church of Scientology would hardly endorse such a route and Tom, in a court declaration (BD339413), stated: 'Irreconcilable differences have arisen between Nicole and me. These differences have led to an irremediable breakdown of our marriage. I do not believe professional counselling or the assistance of any mental health professional, lapse of time or any other factor will change this breakdown.'

Nicole was, reportedly, devastated and depressed. She had no immediate desire to do another movie. She wanted a rest and to spend time with the children. But she did emerge from her self-imposed professional exile to attend the New York premiere of *Moulin Rouge*, and three weeks later flew to the Cannes Film Festival where the movie was in competition and opened the event on 6 May. It didn't win any prizes – the film that did, the Italian *My Son's Room*, was barely seen again. There is an obligatory press conference in the vast Palais du Cinema on the day of every film, but Nicole confided to Baz Luhrmann that she just couldn't face the press. 'I told her she had to,' he says. 'Get back up on that horse and be Nicole Kidman, not a member of the royal family.'

She did, and later emerged as a swinging single at the opening party, dancing with Baz, Ewan McGregor and the quaintly named British disc jockey Fatboy Slim. But she didn't want to do any individual promotional interviews, publicly confiding: 'I'm not coming out until I am completely healed.'

When, prevailed upon to do some interviews later in the month, she was asked about her marriage, she said: 'It is better to have loved and lost than never to have loved at all' – Alfred, Lord Tennyson's lament for his friend Arthur Henry Hallam. On the Oprah Winfrey show she revealed her continuing pain: 'All I will say is that it has been awful, one of those things where you just say, "I cannot believe this is happening to me".'

Tom, on the other hand, seemed to be feeling no such pain. On location in Virginia for *Minority Report*, he and Colin Farrell were running round their hotel at night enjoying themselves. After returning from that location he confirmed the rumours that had long been in the air about him and Penelope Cruz by taking her on a July holiday to the $1500 a night Wakaya Club resort in Fiji. The day following their arrival Tom's PR spokeswoman, Pat Kingsley, announced that the couple had been 'going on dates' in the days preceding the trip. Cameron Crowe revealed that one of the things that endeared Cruz to Cruise was that she had perfected an imitation of him in *Mission: Impossible* which involved her making a gun with two fingers and holding it to the side of her head. 'Tom loves it,' said the director. 'He makes her do it all the time.'

The two-week holiday had, in fact, been planned a year earlier for Tom and Nicole and their children. So Nicole had taken the first week with Isabella, now eight, and Connor, six, as well as Russell Crowe and friends. Nicole then departed for Sydney without seeing her ex but leaving the children for him. It evidently came as a surprise to her that he arrived with the Spaniard since she later expostulated: 'He flat out swore to me up and down that there was nothing going on.'

But reality loomed in the shape of their divorce. Tom further stated: 'Nicole and I were married on 24th December 1990. We separated in December 2000 . . . I have personal knowledge of the facts. If called to testify to them, I could and would competently and truthfully do so.' It looked as if the truth was about to come out. Had the couple separated before or after they renewed their marriage vows? The mystery deepened. There had been no prenuptial agreement. Legally, in California, if they had been married for more than ten years Tom would have been obliged to support his wife for the rest of her life or until she remarried. Was this the reason for his claim that they separated in December? The case would make headlines around the world as all the details of their extraordinary wealth were revealed.

In 1989, when Clint Eastwood fought Sondra Locke's palimony case, he told the court she occupied his house on a 'non-exclusive basis' and was a little taken aback when her lawyer subpoenaed both an early will to show that he had left it to her and many more details of his financial affairs.

Perhaps mindful of this, there was an outbreak of common sense among the lawyers and litigants and the Cruises settled their differences in private. Whether Nicole walked away with $75 million or $175 million was not a problem most mortals have to wrestle with. The couple had always agreed on joint custody of the children. What is public knowledge is that Cruise changed the name of his plane from *Sweet Nic* to *Sweet Bella*.

On 7 August 2001 they both attended the Los Angeles premiere of *The Others* – Tom, of course, was a producer – but separately. The following day they were divorced. Cruise then took the children to his estate in Telluride for the rest of the month. 'My kids are the most important thing in the world to me,' he told *People* magazine. 'They always have been and they always will. There is nothing else in the world that matters to me right now.'

In the autumn Nicole flew east to England – to appear as a suicidal Virginia Woolf opposite Meryl Streep and Julianne Moore in Michael Cunningham's *The Hours*. Her marital troubles did not appear to have had any ill effect on her acting prowes; in fact, the contrary. She was to win the Best Actress Oscar for her performance.

Vanilla Sky opened to relatively poor reviews in December but the American public, possibly intrigued by the prospect of seeing Cruise and Cruz together, again pushed his box-office over the $100 million mark. Tom went on *Larry King* who, after showing a clip of the two of them, provocatively suggested: 'Are you in love with this beautiful woman? You are either the greatest actor in the history of mankind or you like this lady.'

Cruise was cautious. 'I was going through a lot of things at that time. People say that there is chemistry on the screen. There are many elements that go into that.' He insisted: 'Things that evolved for Penelope and I were not until later.'

King persisted: 'Oh, they weren't happening when making—'

Tom did not let him finish. 'No, no, no, no, no, no.'

He was more positive about his current relationship with Nicole. 'When you're going through stuff it was difficult at times. But I have to say that where we are now is a beautiful, beautiful place. I love Nicole. I've always loved her.'

What he didn't love was the use of the drug Ritalin in treating attention-deficit hyperactivity disorders in children. The teachings of L. Ron Hubbard with regard to such medication were, to him, more accurate than the studies done by many universities which claimed not only that the drug was effective but that it actually reduced the probability of the child abusing alcohol and drugs in later life. Some four years before Brooke Shields and Matt Lauer were on the receiving end of his criticism he preached the gospel of Scientology to King, assuring the audience that 'If you pick up a book and read about it, there's so many tools that people can apply to their lives to make them better instantly.'

Having abandoned conventional education, Cruise had a voracious appetite for self-improvement and clearly Scientology fed that need. In his work, too, he was looking for characters who had this same urge and lived by a strict code. He had long been interested in a famous American mercenary, Frederick Townsend Ward, who had served with William Walker in Nicaragua and with the French forces in the Crimean War. In 1859 he headed for Shanghai in southern China where the Taiping Rebellion against the

Manchu Dynasty had entered its tenth year. The authorities hired Ward to instil Western discipline into their troops and he became something of a local hero. The West was concerned that a victory for the insurgents would disrupt valuable European trade. Ward met with considerable success but, unfortunately, was killed in battle and the English General Charles George Gordon seems to have been accorded most of his glory. (Gordon was to obtain lasting fame through his noble death during the siege of Khartoum – failure or death or, better still, both are much more likely to ensure immortality in British history books.)

There had been various attempts by Ward's contemporaries and biographers to grant him the credit he so sought. Several books on Ward and the 'Ever Victorious Army' were published, culminating in the bestselling *The Devil Soldier* in 1992 by the historian Caleb Carr. Tom saw a great part for himself and optioned the book for Cruise-Wagner Productions. He and John Woo tried to develop a movie, working from a script by Carr, but they couldn't crack it.

Possibly armed with this knowledge, the producer and director Edward Zwick later approached Tom with a screenplay by himself and John Logan that was partially inspired by Ward's adventures, only set in Japan. This gave Captain Nathan Algren, the part on offer to Cruise, an appetising career arc from disillusioned Civil War officer to someone who trains government troops but then is captured and embraces the knightly bushido code of the Samurai. All that, plus plenty of heroic action. As Zwick outlined the movie with expansive gestures in the screening room of Cruise's house, he knew he had a spellbound audience.

'We talked about honor, integrity, loyalty and compassion,' Cruise recalls. 'Virtues that Ed held true and that were very important in my life.'

Zwick agrees. 'We both had sons, and this movie would deal with what we hope to teach them.'

Indeed, filial piety was high among the virtues required by bushido, as well as frugal living, kindness and honesty. But the supreme requirement was martial spirit, honed by athletic training, and a total fearlessness towards the enemy in battle. Cruise not only agreed to play the part – he and Wagner came in as co-producers of the project. Knowing that it was questionably commercial, since most of the leading players apart from Tom were Japanese and the story was a step into new territory, Cruise agreed to forego his fee in return for a back-end deal. They worked together on the script. Zwick was of the opinion that ideas and action do not have to be mutually exclusive – as was the case in most Hollywood product – citing films by David Lean such as *Lawrence of Arabia* and *The Bridge on the River Kwai*.

'I like a movie that operates on various levels,' Cruise declared. 'Both action and a deeper message that embraces life fully. Algren had integrity at one point but he became dishonored. I read how some Civil War officers felt about the Indian atrocities. So he is someone who is tortured about where he is, an explosion waiting to happen.'

In the movie, Captain Algren is recruited to train the Japanese government army but it is ill prepared for a battle with the Samurai and Algren is taken prisoner by Katsu-moto (Ken Watanabe, Japan's leading actor in his first English-speaking role). There he is slowly converted to bushido and learns the swordplay of the Samurai. Ulti-mately he joins their side against the imperial army but, despite their noble bravery, swords are no match for Gatling guns. Katsumoto is mortally wounded and com-mits seppuku – ritual disembowelling. But, in a Hollywood happy ending, the injured Algren is able to convince the Emperor that the dead Samurai and his ancestors were true patriots. The Emperor is thus dissuaded from signing a treaty with the Americans that would give them exclusive rights to sell firearms to Japan.

They shot some of the temple scenes in Japan, to the delight of the locals. But they were mainly done on the Warner back lot at Burbank and in New Zealand, where the Japanese army training sequence takes place on a cricket pitch!

The project became a mission of physical and mental dedication for the actor, who he gave over his life to it. 'I worked for eight months to get in shape for this picture. I learned Kendo – Japanese swordplay, Japanese martial arts, all manner of weapon handling. I not only had to ride a horse but I had to effectively fight while riding. I studied Japanese. I had wanted to do this since I was a child. I started feeling like Algren in the village. I got a sense of the emotional and physical transformation he was going through.'

Cruise altered his entire physique for the part – he had, for instance, a sabre fight against four assailants which consisted of more than thirty-five consecutive moves. 'Suddenly I was moving faster and more precisely than I ever thought possible. I changed the way I moved and the way that I carried myself. As time went on I felt the different levels of awareness and how the mind controls the body. Since the twelfth century the Samurai were artists, philosophers and warriors; their training made them more powerful than the average man. But with power comes responsibility. When you knew something was wrong you must be able to rise above the masses and fight for what is right.' For Tom Cruise it is rarely just another movie. Usually it is a life-altering experience – seldom more so than in this instance.

Zwick felt that Akira Kurosawa was more of an influence on Western cinema than Brando (certainly his films converted fluently into *The Magnificent Seven* and *A Fistful of Dollars*), so the Japanese actors found themselves at home in an American film. But Zwick is no David Lean. He is more a documentarist than a seasoned story-teller, so the page-turning element of 'What on earth is going to happen now?' proved lacking in the final film. Although he placed his figures poetically in the landscape and his battle scenes were convincingly frenetic, his pacing was patchy and the ending decidedly soft. The truth of the matter is that at the time of the story the Samurai had become dinosaurs, sadly out of kilter with the evolving world.

Tom – powerful in the part, using his intensity to its utmost to become the most credible Californian Samurai – was, for the fourth time, Horatio to Hamlet in the Oscar stakes. Ken Watanabe got a nomination as Best Supporting Actor, while Tom's own superb performance was ignored.

But not by the public. The film made $456 million worldwide, including an unprecedented $125 million in Japan alone, so presciently his decision to forego a pay cheque for a healthy percentage of the gross was prudent and – as ever – his choice of subject was pioneeringly in advance of studio caution, where the suits fear the shock of the new and relish a remake or a continuing series like Harry Potter.

20

A BRACE OF SPIELBERGS

Despite Cruise's unalloyed adherence to L. Ron Hubbard and Scientology, he was astute enough as a film producer not to turn to his master's voice when it came to his professional projects. John Travolta, a fellow Scientologist, had made that mistake. With dozens of stories to choose from ranging from *The Doomed Planet* to *Voyage of Vengeance*, Travolta settled on Hubbard's *Battlefield Earth*. The year was 3000. A race of aliens known as the Psychlos, led by Terl (Travolta), have taken over the earth from mankind by gobbling up all the natural resources. Fortunately Jonnie Goodboy Tyler emerges from his eyrie in the Rocky Mountains to save mankind.

It cost approximately $50 million but flopped at the cinema, and the reviews were more fun than the movie. 'Battlefield Earth should be shown only at maximum security prisons when a prisoner is tossed in solitary for bad behaviour,' was the advice of one critic, while another described the experience as 'like taking a bus trip with someone who has needed a bath for a long time'.

It is questionable whether it is wise to encounter some of the works of L. Ron even in print. Forrest Ackerman, his literary agent, recalled that Hubbard told him how he had a near-fatal experience on an operating table during World War II. According to Ackerman, Hubbard claimed to have wafted out of his body in spirit form and encountered a smorgasbord of information on everything that ever puzzled the mind of man. When did the world begin? Was there a God? He then re-entered his body, jumped off the operating table and wrote a work called *Excalibur* or *The Quiet Sword* (it contained many concepts and ideas that later informed Scientology). But the book was universally rejected by publishers in New York – wisely since, according to Ron, the people who read it either went insane or committed suicide. He was sitting in a publisher's office waiting for a reader to give an opinion but unfortunately never got one, as the reader walked into the room, tossed the manuscript on the desk and jumped out of a high window. Whether this was the effect of the contents or a comment on the prose the man didn't live to tell.

So Tom Cruise prudently turned to the less lethal works of Philip K. Dick for his own foray into sci-fi. Ridley Scott, his director on *Legend*, had made his name with *Blade Runner*, based on Dick's *Do Androids Dream of Electric Sheep?*, and Arnold Schwarzenegger had had a popular success with *Total Recall*, based on the same author's *We Can Remember It for You Wholesale*. Now Cruise could see himself as the protagonist in *Minority Report*, a police experiment set in Washington DC in 2050 in which 'pre-cogs' could foresee crime before it was committed and potential criminals were imprisoned for what they were about to do.

It was to an extent paradoxical that Cruise should be drawn to Dick, whose prodigal output was largely due to drug experimentation, something Scientologists abhorred. It led to the author's premature death at the age of fifty-three, but not before he had squeezed twenty-five books, nearly a hundred short stories and five wives into his abbreviated life. 'He was unconnected to this world,' says Jo Cohen, who did the screenplay for Tom. 'He never felt he was part of the same world as the rest of us. And he was paranoid about what was real and what was not real.' Dick's own explanation was: 'Reality is that which, when you stop believing in it, doesn't go away.'

At any given time Cruise has a number of story ideas and pitches being developed into script form, and this one came out of the oven mouth-wateringly cooked. The rights to the material reposed with Twentieth Century-Fox, who would distribute the film. Steven Spielberg had admired Cruise in *Risky Business* and watched his ascent through the ranks. When the two men were at the top of their respective professions they planned to work together. 'We had two abortive attempts,' Spielberg recalls, 'but I guess they were not his cup of tea. And he brought a couple of things to me but they didn't work out.' Tom's timing on *Minority Report* was more auspicious. Neither man needed to add to his accumulation of fame or fortune; both wanted to try something different. 'Right now in my life I'm at a period where I'm experimenting,' Spielberg avowed. 'I want to challenge myself and, in turn, challenge the audience. I'm trying to find myself in my mid-fifties.'

A.I. and *Minority Report* are both experimental, but it was a controlled experiment. They wanted to anchor the action in a world fifty years into the future which they would make as credible as foreseeably possible. So they assembled that high-powered think-tank at the Shutters Hotel before the film reached final draft and was designed. What they wanted from the experts was a predicted picture of 'future reality' as opposed to 'science fiction'. Sixteen high-powered experts from multiple disciplines were flown in, including Jaron Lanier, the man who invented Virtual Reality; Stewart Brand, who created the Whole Earth Catalog – a forerunner of the Internet; Shaun Jones, the biomedical genius who runs the US reconnaissance satellites; and Neil Gershenfeld, the expert on quantum computing and nanotechnology who runs MIT's Atoms Laboratory. But not all their suggestions, as Cruise recalls, were that helpful, especially the thought that Washington DC might be under water in 2054 due to global warming. The film-makers needed a city of skyscrapers with Mag-Lev cars on roller coasters so that Tom could make daring leaps from one to another.

The Mag-Lev, part roadster, part elevator, was actually designed by Lexus; and since it was concluded that advertising will play a far more intrusive part in the future, with the ability to scan your eye from billboards and then call out your name offering a product it is known you might like, the movie provided a field day for product placement, the leading beneficiaries being American Express, Pepsi, and Reebok.

Cruise was in awe of Spielberg. 'I saw *Jaws* when I was just thirteen and I leapt out of my seat when that head appeared in the hole in the bottom of the boat. I dragged my family to see *E.T.* He is an amazing artist and he has given so many moments of complete joy. He is also an amazing person. Everyone wants to work with him and I have relished and cherished every moment I have done so.'

Despite the eighteen-year age gap, the two men became very close friends – certainly up to the sofa-jumping moment on *Oprah* when Spielberg was reportedly not best pleased that the promotion of *War of the Worlds* was all but forgotten amidst the promotion of Katie. They had much in common: both were all-powerful emperors of Hollywood with vast fortunes and no imperative to work. But both lived for the moment when the camera turned. More than that, they were both possessors of a powerful Peter Pan gene, with a wide-eyed sense of wonderment and almost total absence of cynicism – all the more remarkable in Steven, then in his late of fifties. Spielberg could see in Tom the same intensity that had made Harrison Ford focal in *Star Wars* and *Indiana Jones*. And possibly a little more.

'Tom comes to the set word perfect and knowing precisely what he has to do,' said Spielberg. 'But then he will respond to any good ideas – say four or five – that you might have on the day. And, if you don't have any new ideas, he will challenge you to come up with some because you can be sure he has got about twenty of them himself.' Tom acknowledged: 'Film is a director's medium. Steven comes up with brilliant ideas, things I have never seen before. But it is important that we are both at the same stage.' Those on the set were greatly impressed by the series of weaving arm movements Tom evolved to follow the pictorial imagery presented to him by the Precogs. Spielberg likened it to John Williams conducting a huge orchestra.

Cruise delights in the danger of the new: 'I like going on a journey as an actor. I want to go to a place my character has never been before. I like challenging my-self.' Certainly no Cruise character had ever encountered the nightmare that faced John Anderton, Head of Pre-crime, in *Minority Report*. On the evidence of the Precog Cassandras, he is used to sentencing potential criminals to the Hall of Containment where they are kept in comatose condition in cylinders for the length of their sentence. But suddenly the gamekeeper becomes a poa-cher accused of a murder that is going to take place in thirty-six hours. He turns into a fugitive, on the run from the very people he has trained, with the near-impossible task of proving his innocence.

'I thought that was such a great idea,' says Tom. 'I was reading the other day on the Internet that there's this scientist who developed a programme that could predict human behaviour. I think they're going to test it in airports. Basically it's to spot terrorists. It's all done on computer. I'd like a system in place that would prevent crime, prevent terrorism, certainly, but when you look at the ramifications of that and the freedoms that you'll have to give up, that is something people should be aware of.'

Spielberg has a more misty-eyed view of the downside of too rapid an advance in technology. 'Technology can be our best friend and technology can be the biggest party pooper of our lives. It interrupts our own story. It interrupts our ability to have a thought or a daydream, to imagine something wonderful because we're too busy bridging the walk from the cafeteria back to the office on the cell phone.'

Unlike *A.I.*, *Minority Report* was an overwhelming success: 92 per cent of its American reviews were raves and it made more than $350 million worldwide at the box-office alone, before doubling that in ancillary sales. Not unsurprisingly, both men vowed to collaborate again. But it happened sooner than they expected. Spielberg, like Tom, keeps a number of scripts on the boil and goes ahead on gut instinct. 'If I were to think it through logically, I doubt if I would ever decide on my next film.' Something in his gut told him that the script for *Indiana Jones 4* was not there yet. At the same time Tom was not satisfied with the script for his next project – *Mission: Impossible III*. But Spielberg had been developing an updated version of H. G. Wells's 1897 novel *The War of the Worlds*, which told of a Martian invasion of Earth. David Koepp, co-writer of *Mission: Impossible* for Tom as well as *Jurassic Park* for Spielberg, had delivered a draft that was such a powerful read that it demanded to be shot. Tom was happy to postpone *Mission: Impossible III* and

War of the Worlds went into pre-production in August 2004.

Tom had not been born when Orson Welles made his famous radio broadcast of *The War of the Worlds* in October 1938, which caused people to rush into the streets in panic, but was only too well acquainted with it. 'The first thing I heard about *The War of the Worlds* was a repeat of the radio play. I actually much preferred radio to television and, as a child when my mother was asleep, I would sneak downstairs and turn on the radio and listen to plays. I read the book a couple of years ago, actually before we decided to make it. And I knew its history: basically how it was written because of British colonialism. And how Orson Welles in 1938 was concerned that America and the world were being pulled into this European war.'

When Wells wrote his novel a fifth of the globe comprised the British Empire, and the author was incandescent with rage about the wholesale extermination of the natives in Tasmania. He wanted to teach the British that no nation had the right to dominate the world, and that there were stronger forces in outer space. The Orson Welles broadcast had such impact because the Martian landings were presented as a series of location reports and most people missed the first ten minutes of the programme, where it was emphasised that this was a play, because they were listening to the end of the popular programme with the dummy Charlie McCarthy, operated by Edgar Bergen (father of Candice), on the other channel. Fear of war was already in the airwaves: German Jews were being deported and the pogrom known as *Kristallnacht* was only days away.

It would be more than three years before Germany declared war on the United States. But on 20 March 2003 the United States had invaded Iraq. Was Spielberg's film a statement about this? 'I didn't make this movie out of anger,' he says. 'I didn't make this movie to attack an administration. I have no issues about colonialism because it doesn't exist any more in that way. Although in America we do have imperialism [the policy of extending a country's power by military force], have had for five years. There is much more unilateralism happening under the Republican administration today than has ever happened in my experience before.'

Tom was less political in his outlook and, informed by his Scientology beliefs, more humanitarian. 'For ever it has been man killing man for territory, for beliefs, for not believing. Man trying to dominate man. But man's common enemy is drug addiction, illiteracy, immorality. These things are rotting our societies at the core. I have travelled around a lot and every culture has that. That is the real war of the worlds today.' On the subject of aliens he was decidedly diffident, considering his religion claims that Earth was originally populated by them. 'I think it's quite arrogant to think we're the only living species in all of the universes. As far as alien abduction is concerned, nothing like that has ever happened to me. I tend to believe what I've experienced, and I don't know for sure.'

Even Spielberg, creator of two of the greatest alien films ever – *E.T.* and *Close Encounters of the Third Kind* – was wavering in his beliefs. 'Do I believe in alien visitation? I certainly believe that out in the universe there are millions of intelligent civilisations thriving. But today I am less of a believer that we have been visited than I was twenty-five years ago. I don't know if Area 51 was a place that was used to dissect a spaceship and transfer the occupants to Wright Patterson Air Force Field in Dayton, Ohio as the story goes. I'd certainly like to believe it's true, but I know a couple of Presidents who have not been clued in as to the existence of any hard evidence that we've been visited.'

Millions of Americans believe they have been temporarily abducted by aliens who, they frequently say on their return to Earth, molested them sexually. The screenwriter David Koepp isn't so sure. 'If they're so intelligent, they're probably not going be interested in coming here to do anal probes. I just think that that's so overstated. It's such a human-centric point of view that intelligent life elsewhere would be interested in our asses.' Koepp had transported the story from nineteenth-century England to modern New Jersey, so that American – and international – audiences could better empathise with the plight of the protagonist, Ray Ferrier. Cruise came up with the crucial element that made the story more penetratingly poignant. 'I wanted to play a father in the film. This is a very intimate story about a family. There is this estranged, deadbeat dad but he has to become the friend of his weekend children. It's a film that represents what parents feel and talk about: how far you're going to go for your child.'

In a paradoxical way Spielberg wanted to have his cake

and eat it with regard to the casting of Cruise. He needed a star name to sell what was a very expensive movie; he also needed a good actor who would make the horror of a world gone mad credible and terrifying; and in both respects few came better than Tom. At the same time he wanted the audience to empathise with an everyman figure so that they, like him, would be caught up in the madness. 'I'm trying my best to de-Cruise Tom,' he told me. 'I want him to be a real blue collar worker, a real guy from Bayonne, New Jersey, who works a cargo container crane at the port. And I want him to blend in, to become like a lot of people so that he represents our own fears and our own resourcefulness to survive.'

That he achieved this aim was, in large part, due to a female. It was a fact, wholly unreported in the press, that Tom fell in love on *War of the Worlds*. When they were not shooting, he and she would hug and cuddle and laugh. When they walked on to the set it was, inevitably, hand-in-hand. He filled an iPod with a thousand songs and gave it to her. She, in turn, knitted him a scarf. Her name was Dakota Fanning, and she was ten years old. She played his daughter in the film.

Spielberg had spotted her talent when she was only eight. In his television series about alien abductions, *Taken*, she not only played the final product of the alien-human mélange but narrated the series as well. Her faith in Tom was touching. In the film, giant Tripods overturn the ferry in which they are trying to escape. Cruise had to jump fourteen feet down into the studio tank for the close-ups and he persuaded Dakota to do it with him. 'I had to take her to the bottom of the pool and then we had to come up with her holding on to my neck. I actually had weights that I had to hold on to keep me down. We had to hold our breath for a long time and after the first take I said to her, "If there's anything you don't feel comfortable about, tell me" and she said, "Maybe you could come up a little faster, Tom."' He roared with laughter at the thought of such a polite request.

Later, the couple are attacked not by aliens but by fellow human refugees, thugs with steel bars who want to hijack their truck. First the stunt arranger, Vic Armstrong, choreographed the incident, making it frighteningly real. Then Spielberg moved in and earmarked his shots. But Tom, sensing the fear the child might experience, made it his duty to see there was no risk that an accident might harm Dakota and insisted that the scene could be aborted at any moment.

The film was at its strongest in this long escape sequence, only losing its grip with an ending that just faded away, failing to mirror David Koepp's vision of Tom in the emotional position of John Wayne in John Ford's *The Searchers* after he has safely delivered Natalie Wood home. Nevertheless it proved to be Cruise's biggest box-office hit. Cruise, his sister and PR Lee Anne DeVette, his agent Kevin Huane and, finally, Steven Spielberg all had to appeal personally to the President of Universal Studios, Ron Mayer, to allow a Scientology tent peopled by ministers and assistants to be erected on the studio lot, where no solicitation is allowed. Permission was at last given, provided the tent was not used for recruitment purposes. This, combined with DeVette's insistence that United International Pictures executives involved in the international release of the film go on a four-hour tour of the Scientology Center in Los Angeles, and that journalists visiting for the junket be obliged to do the same, presaged a summer of bizarre behaviour by her brother.

21

NATURAL BORN KILLER

Between his two big Spielberg movies, Tom made another film for DreamWorks – *Collateral*. Steven had little or nothing to do with it. The production fell under the aegis of the married couple Walter Parkes and Laurie MacDonald, who had produced *Catch Me if You Can* and *The Terminal* and were Spielberg's two closest colleagues after Kathleen Kennedy.

Collateral was an ingenious idea by a young Australian, Stuart Beattie. In the short space of one night a hit man, Vincent, arrives in town with the mission to kill five witnesses in an impending drugs trial. He hires a cab for the night. The intended sixth victim is the attractive female Federal prosecutor whom the driver, Max, picked up earlier and with whom he has established a romantic rapport.

Michael Mann was hired to direct. He had not

done anything since his rather plodding biopic *Ali*, with Will Smith, but his curriculum vitae before that was infinitely more impressive. A writer on *Starsky and Hutch*, he had masterminded *Miami Vice* and directed what was easily the most outstanding Hannibal Lecter film, *Manhunter*, with Brian Cox as the Chianti, fava beans and human liver gourmet. Mann, an American, had trained at the London International Film School under the veteran Charles Crichton who, despite masterly Ealing comedies like *The Lavender Hill Mob*, suffered a twenty-five-year break from features following a dispute with Burt Lancaster on *The Birdman of Alacatraz* in 1961. John Cleese then resuscitated his career by inviting him to direct *A Fish Called Wanda*.

Crichton would recall how at Ealing they used to cast two stars in the leads, say Alec Guinness and Stanley Holloway, and then ask them to switch roles. Mann used Crichton's technique on *Collateral*. He hired the 'urbane, kinetic, impulsive stand-up comedian and singer' Jamie Foxx (né Eric Morlon Bishop) as the humble and inhibited taxi driver and the whiter-than-white, all American hero Tom Cruise as a hired killer, 'a stone hearted sociopath, a really bad guy'. Mann added: 'It puts actors on the frontier, at the end of a branch with no net. And that brings out the best in them because they have never been there before.'

Mann hardly had the Hollywood firepower to do an Ealing switch, being quite a long drop down the batting order from Tom Cruise. But the latter was undoubtedly in the mood for a change of character. 'Michael Mann sent me a script. It was not an intellectual decision. I read something and think about why I was interested in it later. Churchill once said of Hitler: "I'm glad I never met the man. I might have been charmed by the little devil". And that's a perfect line. A person like Vincent doesn't feel responsible for what he's doing, that he's got to go and kill these people. They deserve what they're going to get. There is this disconnection from life, from responsibility to your fellow man. What you find out about these people is that they think they are absolutely right in what they're doing.'

Mann helped him design Vincent, whom Tom calls 'the silver fox'. Greying hair and stubble, immaculate grey suit, white shirt, grey tie. 'As an actor,' Cruise observed, 'sometimes you work from the inside out and sometimes from the outside in.' Cruise, who by now had a compulsive need to become the character he was playing, rejoiced in Mann's desire to give Vincent a back story even though it is never mentioned in the film. Mann told him that Vince grew up in the steel mill town of Gary, Indiana. They studied pictures of the place and his likely home. His mother died in childbirth and he was brought up by foster parents. If every person who suffered these privations were to kill six people a night, the world would be a parlous place.

More relevantly, Mann was anxious that Cruise become a natural born killer. The star spent three months with a British SAS soldier, Mick Gould, learning the body language of a man who shoots with real bullets (as opposed to cowboy blanks). It shows in the movie, with Tom manipulating his gun as his best friend, especially in a moment when he is thrown on his back in a nightclub and releases a stream of fire between his knees. Cruise's religion, too, came in handy in creating the character. 'I've studied antisocial behaviour and personalities, and in Scientology there is a large body of knowledge about anti-socials. So I worked to create Vincent's moral code from that.'

The film was a huge commercial step for Mann but a lesser one for Cruise. The reviews were tepid and the American box-office just nudged above what was now Cruise's base figure for a movie: $100 million. As ever, his co-star took the Oscar glory. Jamie Foxx was nominated as Best Supporting Actor, something that undoubtedly paved his way to *Ray*, the biopic of the blind pianist Ray Charles. In 2005 Foxx won the Best Actor Oscar for his interpretation of the part.

In March 2004 Tom's elder sister, Lee Anne DeVette, told the world that her brother had ended his relationship with Penelope Cruz in January of that year. Lee Anne stated that it was 'an amicable break-up', a state of affairs underlined by Penelope's spokesman, Robert Garlock, who revealed that they remained 'good friends.' Penelope did not seem to be obsessed with Scientology and, since splitting with Tom, has not appeared to be an advocate of the religion.

Breaking up must have been hard to do since in January Penelope was in the middle of the Sahara desert making a movie of the same name while Tom was shooting both a film and a lot of people in *Collateral*. But the wonders of email possibly played their part.

Sẽnorita Cruz had been photographed several times at premieres with Tom, but spent most of their relationship seemingly taking part in a bad film competition ranging from *Masked and Anonymous* with Bob Dylan to *Fanfani la tulipe*, *Gothika*, *Non ti muovere*, *Noel* and *Head in the Clouds*. Little is to be gained by outlining the storylines of these works since virtually nobody went to see them. What is noteworthy is that they took her to France, Canada, Italy, Canada again, Paris and London. Tom, meanwhile, had repaired for a substantial time to the ends of the earth – New Zealand, which did duty for Japan in his Samurai movie and Australia for *Mission: Impossible II*.

It would take a diary secretary to compute how many days the couple spent together during the three years, but the story does have a semi-happy ending for Penny. *Sahara*, starring Matthew McConaughey, was something of a hit, enough at least to ensure her continuing presence in celebrity magazines even without being an appendage to Tom.

In the junkets and attendant interviews to promote *Collateral* in August 2004 Cruise chose to bang the drum for Scientology and, even before the Brooke Shields outburst, lectured reporters on the evils of anti-depressants. It is now almost exactly fifty years since moniamine oxidase inhibitors were successfully used in the treatment of depression, with the subsequent selective serotonin reuptake inhibitors effectively altering the level of mood-changing serotonin in the brain and lifting dark moods, to be followed by the Prozac family which did the same job more speedily and effectively. The chemical facts of these have been empirically verified internationally by the best brains in medical science, not least in an in-depth study by Rockefeller University. Cruise, however, lectured journalists that anti-depressants, in fact, were harmful according to Lafayette Ron Hubbard, the science fiction storyteller. We are free to decide which body of learning is correct.

Without doubt the *abuse* of Prozac is just as dangerous as the abuse of alcohol or aspirin but it was the very *presence* of Prozac that the star saw as evil, not to mention the whole history and practice of clinical psychiatry.

Tom is now thought to have audited his way to Scientology's highest grade and crossed the 'Bridge to Total Freedom'. He is very close to the head of the organisation, David Miscavige, and spends time at Golden Era Productions, an exclusive desert compound. Jessica Rodriguez, one of the staff there, was assigned to look after Katie Holmes when she became engaged to Tom and sat in on her *Batman Returns* interviews. Katie eagerly embraced the faith and, when she found she was pregnant, had her baby shower at the Scientology Celebrity Center in Los Angeles.

Tom's behaviour in 2005 turned several previously favourable publications against him. *Vanity Fair* carried the cover banner 'Has Tom Cruise Lost His Marbles?' on its August issue and in its edition of March 2006 *Rolling Stone* led with a thirteen thousand-word, minutely researched story that was deeply critical of Scientology.

This was the cruellest cut of all. Not only had *Rolling Stone* been a constant champion of Tom and his movies but the editor, Jann Wenner, had had a cameo role in *Jerry Maguire* and Cameron Crowe, the film's director and *Rolling Stone* reporter and, subsequently, devotee, had been a loyal friend to Tom. The magazine appeared to doubt what it described as Hubbard's claim that 75 million years ago an evil warlord named Xenu put 13.5 trillion beings from overpopulated planets on to Earth and took issue with the fact that people were having to spend hundreds of thousands of dollars to reach 'Total Freedom'.

So when it came to *Mission: Impossible III*, *Rolling Stone* got no set access or interviews. This episode of the series moved from Rome to Naples (where the Palazzo Reale at nearby Di Caserta doubled for the Vatican) to Chesapeake Bay Bridge, which was blown up in a manner reminiscent of the Florida Keys in Arnold Schwarzenegger's *True Lies*. In fact throughout the film one is reminded of similar scenes from other action movies. No crime in this: neither Mozart nor Shakespeare was averse to a bit of borrowing. The Mozart/Shakespeares in this instance were Alex Kurtzman and Roberto Orci, who had helped director J. J. Abrams create the 2001 television series *Alias* in which Jennifer Garner played a CIA double agent.

It had been rumoured that *Mission: Impossible III* was in trouble when directors David Fincher and Joe Carnaghan pulled out and Tom did *War of the Worlds* instead. But the loss was theirs – both men went on to make unsuccessful movies and, after seeing *Alias* DVDs, Tom was convinced that Abrams, creator of the wonderfully impenetrable *Lost*, could direct an action feature – and he was right. In this episode Ethan is obliged to prise a Hitchcockian MacGuffin called the Rabbit from the size-able hands of utterly evil Philip Seymour Hoffman. Sadly his part is woefully underwritten – they didn't know they were dealing with an Oscar-winner then. The film is all Ethan. He leaps from skyscraper rooftops in China, drops hundreds of feet by wire until his nose almost grazes the pavement, and gets married to Michelle Monaghan who thinks he studies traffic systems. In some respect he does as he dodges speeding vehicles in the streets of Shanghai. After the shoot Michelle confessed: 'I couldn't have asked to kiss a better guy. When we finished I went over to Katie Holmes and said I understood why she kept him around.'

The film remains true to the TV template with the Lalo Schifrin tune, the latex masks being pulled off when you least expect it, and – for the first time – being created, along with the voice computer that completes Cruise's transfor-mation into Hoffman. This scene has a very nervy count-down, but the imperative that drives the entire movie is about countdowns. From the pre-title sequence where Tom is given ten seconds by nasty Seymour Hoffman to reveal the whereabouts of the Rabbit before pulling the trigger on his bride to Ethan's five-seconds-to-destruct orders to the time-release capsules in the IMF victim's brain to the forty-eight hours Tom has to find the damned Rabbit's foot to Tom's own '1-2-3-4 execute!' and innumerable – well, exactly numerable, others – the movie has more count-downs than the late, and sadly lamented, Richard White-ley's television show.

EPILOGUE

I saw Tom for the last time outside the Odeon Leicester Square in May 2006 at the London premiere of the film. He was wearing his traditional black with shades and his sempiternal smile, signing autographs for fans. Inside the cinema cameras covered this performance for the audience waiting to see *Mission: Impossible III*, and some people must have wondered what other 43-year-old man would spend four hours posing for photographs with strangers or making calls on their cell phones to friends and relatives of further strangers.

Katie had duly given birth to a baby, Suri, six days before the movie's European premieres. With what some might see as dramatic irony, in the same hospital, St John's in Santa Monica, on the same day, the maligned Brooke Shields gave birth to Grier – a girl. 'Suri' means 'Wealthy' in Armenian, 'Mother of the Sun' in Sanskrit, and 'Go Away' in Hebrew.

Katie had remained solidly in the news in the spring of 2006 as she went out and about in Beverly Hills proudly displaying a spherical stomach. An intellectual debate raged in the press as to whether she would be allowed to cry out during childbirth (Ron Hubbard evidently recommended no words be spoken during birth), and Tom solved the problem by saying she could have an epidural injection.

Tom had intended to spend the next month changing nappies but his wife prevailed upon him to take off for the premieres of *Mission: Impossible III*. After Rome, London, Paris and Mexico City he traversed New York by motorcycle, speedboat, taxi, helicopter, sports car and subway, with pit stops in Tribeca and Harlem, to promote the film. Nicole was said to have sent congratulations to Katie on the baby but then, somewhat ungraciously, the Australian star's PR informed the media that she hadn't. Some things are better left uncorrected.

After their separation, Kidman's attitude to Cruise had started out as somewhat cutting. On the *David Letterman Show* the host said to her: 'I hear you're getting divorced. How's that going?' And the actress replied: 'Well, I can wear high heels now' – a barely concealed reference to her estranged husband's diminutive stature. But by May 2006 she had revised her estimate of him informing *Ladies' Home Journal* that he was 'big'.

Her choice of films after winning the Oscar was more consistent. *The Human Stain*, *The Stepford Wives* and

Bewitched were uniformly unwatchable. She did have a success, however, with a film in which she portrayed the most famous woman in the world, desperate to escape media attention. It ran for two minutes and extolled the virtues of Chanel No. 5. In real life, Nicole was less bashful: rarely a week went by when she was not on the cover of a glossy magazine and few red carpets went untrod by her newly acquired high heels. Was she haunting Tom with her continuing glamour? Probably due to the constraints of an onerous divorce agreement Nicole was unable to vent the fury of a woman scorned. But evidently she feels better now, telling *Ladies' Home Journal*: 'I still love him.'

Whether the American public still do is another matter. A USA Today/Gallup Poll of 1013 adults during *MI III*'s first weekend of release found that 35 per cent had a favourable opinion of the star, and 51 per cent an unfavourable opinion. In 2005, when *War of the Worlds* opened, the ratings were 58 per cent favourable and 31 per cent unfavourable. How much this matters seems of little consequence unless he was going to run for high office as opposed to jumping from high buildings. The reviews for *Mission: Impossible III* were the best yet, with 71 per cent of 175 critics polled by the web site Rotten Tomatoes saying it was good (as opposed to 58 per cent for *Mission: Impossible II* and 66 per cent for the first film), but the initial takings for the all-important opening US weekend were a mere $48 million whereas the second film had made $58 million – although that had had an added Memorial Day on which to attract cinemagoers. However, market research before the film's release did show that Tom had lost ground in that important part of his fan base – female moviegoers. This is hardly surprising. In 1992 the Queen had an 'annus horribilis'; in 2005 Cruise had an 'annus dementius'. This was compounded by the fact that he was constantly held up to ridicule by the press, on television and by internet bloggers.

The irony is that although Cruise says he would not be where he is today without Scientology, it may be Scientology and its philosophy that remove him from where he is today. This would be a shame. In my opinion he is one of the finest film actors the cinema has produced and a bold, inventive producer. But he is not like other men, not even like other film stars. His repeat pattern behaviour in casting women in his films and then marrying or entering relationships with them is indicative of the perilously thin line between his movies and his life. When he summoned Jessica Alba, Jennifer Garner and Scarlett Johansson to meetings in Los Angeles in the spring of 2005, was it for the purpose of being in a movie or a marriage?

When David Miscavige presented him with the Freedom Medal of Honour he told the assembled Scientologists that each of them had a responsibility to do everything possible to support and spread the Church's teachings. 'Bearing that in mind,' he said of Cruise, 'what happens when your zone of influence is the global stage?' Exactly.

That May night London's packed Leicester Square was Tom Cruise's stage. Leicester Square – and all the world.

PHOTOGRAPHIC
ACKNOWLEDGEMENTS

BFI: 2 (20th Century Fox), 9, 14 (Universal); Big Pictures: 20 (Cruise-Wagner/Paramount/Neal Preston); Corbis: 7, 10, 12 (Francois Duhamel/Sygma), 15 (EPA/Warner Bros Italy), 16 (Mitchell Gerber), 17 (B.D.V.), 18, 19 & 21 (Reuters), 23 (Marc Lecureuil), 24 (Paul Hanna/Reuters); Empics: 1, 25 (Paul White), 27; Kobal Collection: 5 (Warner Bros), 6 (Paramount Pictures), 8 (Touchstone/Ron Phillips), 11 (United Artists), 13 (Columbia/Tri-Star), 22 (Warner Bros, David James), 28 (Paramount Pictures/Stephen Vaughan); Rex Features: 4 (Everett Collection).

Every effort has been made to contact all copyright holders of material reproduced in this book. If any have been inadvertently overlooked, the publishers will be pleased to make the necessary arrangement at the first opportunity.

INDEX